HENRY IV
Part I

The RSC Shakespeare

Edited by Jonathan Bate and Eric Rasmussen
Chief Associate Editors: Héloïse Sénéchal and Jan Sewell
Associate Editors: Trey Jansen, Eleanor Lowe, Lucy Munro, Dee Anna Phares

HENRY IV PART I

Textual editing: Eric Rasmussen
Introduction and Shakespeare's Career in the Theatre: Jonathan Bate
Commentary: Jan Sewell and Héloïse Sénéchal
Scene-by-Scene Analysis: Esme Miskimmin
In Performance: Karin Brown (RSC stagings), Jan Sewell (overview)
The Actor's Voice and the Director's Cut
(interviews by Jonathan Bate and Kevin Wright): Michael Pennington, Adrian Noble, Michael Boyd

Editorial Advisory Board

Gregory Doran, Chief Associate Director,
Royal Shakespeare Company
Jim Davis, Professor of Theatre Studies, University of Warwick, UK
Charles Edelman, Senior Lecturer, Edith Cowan University,
Western Australia
Lukas Erne, Professor of Modern English Literature,
Université de Genève, Switzerland
Akiko Kusunoki, Tokyo Woman's Christian University, Japan
Jacqui O'Hanlon, Director of Education, Royal Shakespeare Company
Ron Rosenbaum, author and journalist, New York, USA
James Shapiro, Professor of English and Comparative Literature,
Columbia University, USA
Tiffany Stern, Professor of English, University of Oxford, UK

The RSC Shakespeare

WILLIAM SHAKESPEARE

HENRY IV
Part I

Edited by
Jonathan Bate and Eric Rasmussen

Introduced by Jonathan Bate

Macmillan

Published by arrangement with Modern Library, an imprint of The Random House Publishing Group, a division of Random House, Inc.

Published 2009 by
MACMILLAN PUBLISHERS LTD
registered in England, company number 785998, of Houndmills, Basingstoke, Hampshire RG21 6XS.
Companies and representatives throughout the world.

ISBN-13 978–0–230–23212–9 hardback
ISBN-10 0–230–23212–4 hardback

ISBN-13 978–0–230–23213–6 paperback
ISBN-10 0–230–23213–2 paperback

This book is printed on paper suitable for recycling and made from fully managed and sustained forest sources. Logging, pulping and manufacturing processes are expected to conform to the environmental regulations of the country of origin.

A catalogue record for this book is available from the British Library.

10   9   8   7   6   5   4   3   2   1
18   17   16   15   14   13   12   11   10   09

Printed in China

CONTENTS

INTRODUCTION

TRAGICAL-COMICAL-HISTORICAL-PASTORAL

Shakespeare's art of mingling comedy, history and tragedy reached its peak in the two parts of *Henry IV*. As history, the plays paint a panorama of England, embracing a wider social range than any previous historical drama as the action moves from court to tavern, council chamber to battlefield, city to country, Archbishop and Lord Chief Justice to whore and thief. As comedy, they tell the story of a prodigal son's journey from youth to maturity and an old rogue's art of surviving by means of jokes, tall tales and the art of being not only witty in himself, but the cause that wit is in other men. As tragedy, they reveal the slow decline of a king who cannot escape his past, the precipitate demise of an impetuous young warrior who embodies both the glory and the futility of military heroism, and the heartbreaking dismissal of a substitute father who has loved a prince with a warmth of which his true father is incapable.

The action begins some time after the events that ended Shakespeare's earlier play, *Richard II*. Henry Bullingbrook has usurped the throne of King Richard, who has been murdered. But now the rebels who helped Henry to the throne have turned against him. Whereas *Richard II* conformed to the traditional structure of tragedy – the story of the fall of a powerful man – the *Henry IV* plays adopt a wider perspective. *Richard II* had been written entirely in verse, the medium of royal and aristocratic characters, whereas long stretches of the *Henry IV* plays are in prose, the medium of the common people. The little scene with the Carriers at the tavern just before the highway robbery is a miniature of ordinary working-day life and common speech: 'This house is turned upside down since Robin the ostler died'.

The deep structure of the two parts of *Henry IV* is that not of tragedy but of pastoral comedy. They were written around the same time as *Much Ado about Nothing* and *As You Like It*, when Shakespeare's comic muse was at its zenith. They are his most enjoyable history plays because they are his funniest – and in the figure of Sir John Falstaff they introduce his greatest comic character – but they also share with the comedies a technique of counterpointing the intrigue of court and power politics against what has been called the 'green' or 'festive' world.

The traditional comic pattern turns on the successful effort of a young man to outwit an opponent and possess the girl of his choice. The girl's father, or some other authority figure of the older generation, resists the match, but is outflanked, often thanks to an ingenious scheme devised by a clever servant, perhaps involving disguise or flight (or both). The union of the lovers brings a renewed sense of social integration, expressed by some kind of festival at the climax of the play – a marriage, a dance or a feast. All right-thinking people come over to the side of the lovers, but in Shakespearean comedy there is usually a party-pooper, a figure who refuses to be assimilated into the harmony – Malvolio in *Twelfth Night*, Don John in *Much Ado about Nothing*, Jaques in *As You Like It*, Shylock in *The Merchant of Venice*. The key to the two parts of *Henry IV* is that they take the comic structure and apply it to Prince Harry – with the difference that, instead of his courtship (which ends up being tacked on very briefly at the end of *Henry V*), the action turns on his maturation from wild youth to exemplary warrior prince and statesman. And, in a brilliant reversal, the figure who is isolated at the end is not the party-pooper but the embodiment of the festive spirit: Falstaff. Comedy is thus placed in opposition to the march of history. The necessity to reject Falstaff in the name of historical destiny and social order is why the final resolution is tinged with the feeling of tragedy.

The distinctive feature of pastoral comedy is that the action develops by means of a shift of location from the everyday world of work, business, politics, patriarchy and power to a 'green' or 'festive' place of play, leisure, anarchy, feminine influence and love – the wood in *A Midsummer Night's Dream*, Belmont in *The Merchant of Venice*, the Forest of Arden in *As You Like It*, rural Bohemia in *The Winter's Tale*. After the comic resolution is achieved, there has to be a return to the normative world, but recreative change has been effected by the values of the festive world. In *Henry IV Part I*, a tavern in Eastcheap plays the part of the festive world. In *Part II*, there is a reprise of that setting, but also a rural green world. As in the comedies, the shuttle between contrasting worlds and contradictory value systems creates the dialectic of the drama. But because of the calling of the prince to power, there can be no reconciliation between the value systems. Prince Hal announces in his first soliloquy that his time of 'playing holidays' and 'loose behaviour' will be but an interlude before he takes upon himself the mantle of historical duty.

HARRY TO HARRY

Richard II had followed the tragic pattern of a mismatch between the character of a man of high estate and the demands of his position as a ruler. It juxtaposed the fall of King Richard to the rise of Henry Bullingbrook, comparing them to a pair of buckets on a pulley, one descending into a well as the other ascends. Once Bullingbrook has become King Henry IV, the pattern is reasserted and reversed in the next generation. Henry sees his son seeming to become another Richard, a time-waster surrounding himself with unsuitable companions and allowing the country to run to seed. He sees himself – a soldier, a man of decision and action – not in his son, but in Hotspur, child of the Percy family who had helped him to displace Richard from the throne.

Historically, Henry Percy, known as Hotspur, was more than twenty years older than Prince Henry (usually called Harry and, by Falstaff alone, Hal), the future King Henry V, victor of Agincourt. With his habitual dramatic licence, Shakespeare altered history and made them rival youths of the same generation. Henry IV's nightmare of history repeating itself is that Hotspur will play his own role to his son's Richard. He wishes that 'some night-tripping fairy' had exchanged the two Harries in their cradles 'And called mine Percy, his [i.e. Northumberland's] Plantagenet'. But this time it is the rebel who falls and the true heir who succeeds. *Henry IV*, a double-header of a play, is full of doubles. There are paired fathers and sons: the king and the prince, Northumberland and Hotspur in *Part I*. There are surrogate fathers to the young hero: Sir John Falstaff and, in *Part II*, his antithesis, the Lord Chief Justice. There are brothers in blood (in *Part I*, Northumberland and Worcester, Hotspur and his brother-in-law Mortimer; in *Part II*, Prince Harry and Prince John, the aged kinsmen Shallow and Silence) and brothers in jest (Hal's 'sworn brethren' among the tavern crowd, Ned Poins chief among them).

One of the questions that fascinates Shakespeare in these plays is, what is the appropriate education for a future king? The Tudor view was that the ideal king should combine the qualities of soldier, scholar and courtier. Fencing, jousting and hunting offered training in the chivalric arts of the medieval aristocracy, but a learned humanist tutor was also required to drill the prince in languages, literature, history, ethics, law and theology. And at the same time it was necessary to imbibe the elaborate codes of behaviour, the conventions of propriety and deference, upon which courtship depended.

Hotspur is the embodiment of an old-style chivalric warrior. He would rather be astride his horse than engaging in courtly parley with his wife. He lives by the code of honour and is deliciously scornful of the courtly manners embodied by the trimly-dressed clean-shaven lord who comes with 'pouncet-box' in hand to demand Hotspur's prisoners: the clash of styles between battlefield and court is enough to turn him into a rebel. Hotspur has boundless courage and energy, but his desire 'To pluck bright honour from the pale-faced moon' is susceptible to parody: his own wife teases him and Prince Hal mocks him as 'the Hotspur of the north, he that kills me some six or seven dozen of Scots at a breakfast, washes his hands, and says to his wife "Fie upon this quiet life! I want work."' His impulsiveness means that he cannot calculate, he is never the politician. '[A] plague upon it, / I have forgot the map!' he says during a council of war. A more politic customer would be most unlikely to have forgotten it – and would never admit as much if he had.

As Hotspur embodies the old chivalric code, his fellow-warrior, the Welshman Glendower, stands for an equally antiquated mode of being: magical thinking. He boasts of portents at his birth – fiery shapes in the air and goats running from the mountain – but this kind of talk is ridiculed. When he claims that he can call spirits from the vasty deep, Hotspur wryly asks, 'But will they come when you do call for them?' Talk of dragons and finless fish is 'skimble-skamble stuff' which does nothing to advance the cause of the rebellion. In the end, the consequence of Glendower's desire to listen to prophecies is that he fails to turn up for the battle.

HONOUR VERSUS INSTINCT

Part I shows Prince Harry playing 'truant' from 'chivalry', but returning to it when the time is ripe. Even as he proves himself on the battlefield, the critique of honour continues with Falstaff's mock 'catechism': 'Can honour set to a leg? No . . . Who hath it? He that died o'Wednesday.' Falstaff's philosophy is a simple 'give me life': never mind about ethical and political codes of behaviour. 'I am not a double man', he says to Hal, putting down the dead Hotspur, whom he has been carrying on his back. Yet he is double the size of anyone else in the play and he has a double life, rising from feigned death on the battlefield of Shrewsbury so that he can return in *Part II*. It will be altogether harder to get rid of cowardly Falstaff than to defeat brave Hotspur. 'Thou art not what thou seem'st', remarks Hal: in seeming to have killed Hotspur, Falstaff is not the coward he has appeared to be. But he has not slain Hotspur, merely stabbed him when he is already dead – a supremely dishonourable deed. And yet, what is honour? A mere word, an empty code. It is the trickster, the chancer, who survives, not the honourable man.

Falstaff is at once the great deceiver and the great truth-teller, who reduces war to its bottom line: common foot-soldiers are but 'food for powder'. One of the reasons why Shakespeare made him fat was to remind the audience of the solidity of the human body: Falstaff's girth is a way of saying that history is made not only of big speeches and dramatic events, but also of the daily lives of people who eat, drink, sleep and die: 'Rare words! Brave world! Hostess, my breakfast, come! / O, I could wish this tavern were my drum!'

A key word is 'instinct'. Hotspur has instinctive courage and Falstaff an instinctive sense of self-preservation. The king thinks that his son is instinctively idle and irresponsible. The aim of a sixteenth-century royal humanist education was to overcome such innate propensities by developing the ethical, linguistic and political faculties of the pupil prince. For Hal, the King's Tavern in Eastcheap serves as a parody of the schoolroom at court. Falstaff is explicitly identified as his 'tutor' and a central part of his education is to learn a new language – not, however, Latin, Greek or the rhetorical elaboration of courtly speech, but the language of the people. This is a Harry who develops the art of speaking with every 'Tom, Dick and Francis'. He learns their jargon – 'They call drinking deep, dyeing scarlet' – and he becomes 'so good a proficient in one quarter of an hour' that he will be able to 'drink with any tinker in his own language' for the rest of his life.

Henry IV believes that one of the failings of his predecessor Richard II had been to seek to make himself popular, thus eroding the necessary distance that creates awe and gives mystique to the monarchy. But King Henry's own distance from public life – he is nearly always seen surrounded by an inner circle of courtiers or closeted alone in his chamber – causes power to ebb from him. His son, by contrast, comes to know the common people, developing a rapport that will enable him to inspire and lead his army in *Henry V*. The point is made through the very linguistic medium of the drama: all Shakespeare's other English kings speak entirely in verse, whereas Prince Hal has command of a flexible prose voice, with which he reduces himself to the level of his people, an Eastcheap trick that he repeats when he goes in disguise among his men on the night before the battle of Agincourt.

The prince works according to the principle articulated by the cunning politician Ulysses in *Troilus and Cressida*: a man 'Cannot make boast to have that which he hath, / Nor feels not what he owes, but by reflection, / As when his virtues shining upon others / Heat them and they retort that heat again / To the first giver'. That is to say, we can only make value judgements through a process of comparison. 'Percy is but my factor, good my lord, / To engross up glorious deeds on my behalf': by temporarily ceding glory to Henry Hotspur, Henry Monmouth will seem all the more glorious when he eventually triumphs over him. His whole strategy is revealed in the imagery of his first soliloquy: the sun seems brighter after cloud and a jewel on a dull background will 'show more goodly and attract more eyes / Than that which hath no foil to set it off'. The offsetting of the prince against his various foils is the structural key to the drama.

THE PRINCE AS MACHIAVEL?

What is the basis of political rule? Orthodox Tudor theory propounded that kings and magistrates were God's representatives on earth, their authority sanctioned by divine law. But the Elizabethan stage had another possible answer. Christopher Marlowe's tragedy *The Jew of Malta*, written in about 1589 and well known to Shakespeare, has an extraordinary opening. The prologue is spoken by an actor pretending to be the Florentine political theorist Niccolò Machiavelli. He voices a series of deeply subversive suggestions about the nature of sovereignty. His riposte to political orthodoxy is that the only basis of effective government is raw power:

> I count religion but a childish toy,
> And hold there is no sin but ignorance . . .
> Many will talk of title to a crown:
> What right had Caesar to the empery?
> Might first made kings, and laws were then most sure
> When, like the Draco's, they were writ in blood.

Religion as an illusion; the idea that human knowledge does not require divine sanction; the notion that it is 'might' not 'right' that decides who rules; the proposition that the most effective laws are those based not on justice but on the severity exemplified by the ancient Greek lawgiver Draco (from whose name we get the word 'draconian'). French and English thinkers of Shakespeare's time demonized Machiavelli for holding these views, but for Christopher Marlowe the act of thinking the unthinkable made Machiavelli a model for his own over-reaching stage heroes.

Shakespeare's history plays are steeped in the influence of Marlowe, but politically he was much more cautious – he would never have risked suffering Marlowe's end, stabbed to death by a government spy while awaiting questioning in a heresy investigation. But that did not stop Shakespeare from recognizing the theatrical charisma of the Marlovian machiavel. He created a string of such characters himself – Aaron the Moor in *Titus Andronicus*, Richard III, Iago in *Othello*, Edmund in *King Lear*. What attracted him to the type was not so much the subversive politics as the stage panache of the unapologetic villain. Political orthodoxy is staid and solemn. The machiavel is nimble and witty. But is he necessarily brutal and irreligious?

Prince Harry is a man of the future; his father is haunted by the past. Both parts of *Henry IV* are suffused with the memory of the 'by-paths and indirect crooked ways' by which Bullingbrook 'met' (or rather took) the crown. The king is revealed at his most vulnerable half way through *Part II*, in a scene that may have troubled the censor: sick and sleepless, he meditates on the cares of state, the fragility of office and the weight of his past sin. A usurper himself, Henry IV has no ground on which to base his authority over the rebels who were once his allies. The only basis of his power is victory on the battlefield. In each part, this is achieved by means of a trick. At Shrewsbury in *Part I*, the device consists of dressing several different men as the king in order to confuse the enemy. Having slain one of the impersonators, Douglas assumes that he is addressing another of them: 'What art thou, / That counterfeit'st the person of a king?' This time, however, it is the king, not a counterfeit – which beautifully dramatizes the point that the king *is* a counterfeit because of his usurpation. In *Part II*, the king is too sick to fight his own battle, so at Gaultree Forest the machiavellian strategy of reneging upon the terms of a negotiated truce is carried out by his second son, Prince John of Lancaster. Does that make Prince Harry into the true follower of Machiavelli, who advised that the effective prince is one who gets someone else to do his dirty work for him?

At the beginning of *Part I*, the king says that he must postpone his Crusade to the Holy Land because of the new civil broils at home, the fresh wound upon the earth of England. His dream of expiating his sins by liberating Jerusalem from the heathen is never translated into action. The prophecy that he would end his life there is only realized ironically: he dies in the 'Jerusalem chamber' of his own palace. Henry IV's fear, apparently borne out by the bad company that Prince Harry keeps, is that the sin of the father will be visited upon the reign of his son:

> For the fifth Harry from curbèd licence plucks
> The muzzle of restraint, and the wild dog
> Shall flesh his tooth in every innocent.
> O my poor kingdom, sick with civil blows!
> When that my care could not withhold thy riots,
> What wilt thou do when riot is thy care?
> O, thou wilt be a wilderness again,
> Peopled with wolves, thy old inhabitants!

He imagines that the 'riot' of the wayward prince will be translated into civil disorder when he becomes king. That is also Falstaff's hope on hearing that his beloved Hal is now Henry V: 'the laws of England are at my commandment . . . and woe unto my Lord Chief Justice!' But he is in for a shock: Hal immediately adopts Falstaff's adversary, the Lord Chief Justice, as his new surrogate father. As in *Part I* he had startled the rebels by transforming himself from tavern idler to armed warrior on horseback, so in *Part II* he will prove that he has learned the civic virtues as well as the military ones.

The prince's self-revelatory soliloquy early in *Part I* began with the words 'I know you all'. The newly-crowned king's rejection of Falstaff late in *Part II* begins with the words 'I know thee not, old man'. The verbal echo is unmistakable: he has ceased to be Hal, he is now delivering on his promise that the time would come when he would throw off the companions and misleaders of his youth. As predicted in the soliloquy, Harry has succeeded in falsifying men's hopes. His reformation glitters over his fault. Falstaff and company suddenly seem to be no more than instruments in a princely conjuring trick, a theatrical act of self-transformation designed to impress a public audience.

Radically opposing interpretations thus become possible. By one account, the politic march of history stands in violent contrast to the humane virtues of friendship, loyalty, good humour, sociability, verbal inventiveness, self-mockery, loyalty and love. Humanity gives way to what the Bastard in *King John* called 'commodity'. History is a machiavellian nightmare of violence and self-interest. The alternative view is that Falstaff embodies the temptations of the flesh. He scores highly for at least three of the seven deadly sins – gluttony, lust and sloth. He is the Vice figure of the old tradition of morality plays and his rejection is accordingly Hal's final step on the path towards political and moral redemption. So it is that Hal can be played equally persuasively as a young man going on a journey towards maturity but still enjoying his departures from the straight and narrow path, or as one of Shakespeare's machiavellian manipulators – energetic and intellectually astute, a brilliant actor, but intensely self-conscious, emotionally reined in.

We may perhaps reconcile the opposing readings by supposing that, in the character of Prince Hal, Shakespeare – perhaps as his own riposte to Marlowe – set out to create a new and distinctive kind of 'good machiavel': a political realist who is prepared to take difficult, even brutal, decisions when it is necessary, but who, instead of being atheistic and self-interested, always tries to do what he takes to be God's will and so to serve the best interests of his nation and his people. Still, though, the dilemma remains: even as Falstaff uses Hal for his own advancement, he is always a truer father than the cold and politic King Henry IV can ever be. The point is made with beautiful clarity by the contrast between Falstaff's heated engagement in the scene in which he and Hal act out the prodigal prince's forthcoming interview with his father and the king's chilly detachment in the interview itself.

REFORMATION AND REJECTION

It is not known whether Shakespeare always intended *Henry IV* to be a two-part play or whether he discovered at some point in the writing or production of *Part I* that it would be dramatically unsatisfying to contain a double climax in a single play, to have Prince Harry prove himself a chivalric hero by defeating Hotspur on the battlefield and then immediately dissociate himself from Falstaff and the other thieves. Instead, the rejection of Falstaff is withheld until *Part II*, but anticipated in the play-within-the-play in *Part I*, where the prince's return to his father is pre-enacted in the tavern.

The scene is a glorious piece of improvised theatre, with the actors changing roles and parodying different linguistic registers. Thus, for instance, when Falstaff plays King Henry he apes the affected courtly prose style of the once fashionable writer John Lyly: 'for though the camomile, the more it is trodden the faster it grows, yet youth, the more it is wasted the sooner it wears'. It is a mark of Shakespeare's attention to detail that, when Falstaff is playing the king, he calls the prince 'Harry' instead of his pet-name, 'Hal'. Though the language of the mock-play is intricate and varied, the staging is simple: 'This chair shall be my state, this dagger my sceptre and this cushion my crown'. The meta-theatrical effect reminds the audience that they are in a theatre, and at the same time suggests that power is itself a form of theatre. There is no intrinsic reason why a golden crown is sacred and a stuffed cushion anarchic; whether in a theatre or a palace, a throne may represent a 'chair of state', but it is still a mere chair.

A chair is a chair and, as Gadshill puts it, '*Homo* is a common name to all men'. Falstaff may be 'that reverend Vice, that grey Iniquity, that father Ruffian, that Vanity in years', but he is also the embodiment of the shared frailty of all humanity: 'If sack and sugar be a fault, heaven help the wicked: if to be old and merry be a sin, then many an old host that I know is damned'. To banish plump Jack is to banish 'all the world'. 'I do', says Hal, playing the role of his father the king. 'I will', he adds, anticipating what he will do when he becomes king himself. As so often when Shakespeare's art is working in its most concentrated form, judgement is left suspended. Is Hal 'essentially made', with or without knowing it? And is it possible to be a true friend and a true prince? At the end of the 'play extempore', he is friend more than prince, lying to an authority figure, the sheriff, in order to protect Falstaff. So is he – as some editors emend – 'essentially mad', fundamentally as opposed to temporarily a 'madcap'? 'The true prince may, for recreation sake, prove a false thief', says Falstaff: is the play-time of 'recreation' a space for a brief interlude of misrule or a crucible in which the self is re-created?

There is little historical warrant for the story of Henry V's riotous youth. A 'prodigal son' narrative was attached to him in the chronicles and the anonymous play *The Famous Victories of Henry the Fifth* in order to highlight the change he undergoes when he becomes king, submits to the rule of law and so unifies and brings to order the nation that his father divided. The rejection of Falstaff and company is part and parcel of Harry's symbolically becoming a new person at the moment of his coronation. The notion of 'reformation' and the washing away of past iniquities clearly have strong religious connotations. Each time the prince returns to the court, he speaks a language of 'fall' and 'pardon'. When he fights well, his father tells him that 'Thou hast redeemed thy lost opinion'.

The rhythm of Prince Hal's life is that of providential history, leading to his 'reformation' and his assumption of the roles which attracted Queen Elizabeth to him: unifier of the body politic, victor over a rival kingdom, heroic leader of a great and independent nation. The rhythm of Falstaff's life is that of the body and the seasons. In *Part II* he will journey into the deep England of Justice Shallow's Gloucestershire orchard. We learn from Shallow that Falstaff began his career as page to Thomas Mowbray, Duke of Norfolk. This appears to be a Shakespearean fancy without source: it is true of neither the historical Sir John Falstaff, who flees the battlefield in *Henry VI Part I*, nor the historical Sir John Oldcastle, of whom the character of Falstaff was originally an irreverent portrait. Why did Shakespeare give his fictional Falstaff a past that began in the service of Mowbray? At one level, it links him with opposition to the Lancastrian ascendancy represented by King Henry IV and his son. Mowbray was Henry IV's opponent when the latter was still Bullingbrook, back at the beginning of *Richard II*. Like father, like son: as Bullingbrook's accusation of treachery was instrumental in the banishment of Mowbray from the land, so Hal will banish Falstaff from his presence. Mowbray departs with a moving farewell to his native land and language; the effect of his words is to suggest that love of the English earth and the English word goes deeper than dynastic difference. We do not hear similar patriotic sentiments in the mouth of the self-interested Bullingbrook; he does nothing to bring back the old England idealized in the death-bed speech of his father, John of Gaunt (whose name and whose England will also be remembered by Shallow).

In Shakespeare's own time, those who suffered banishment because of ideological difference, but who claimed that they were nevertheless loyal to England, were predominantly Catholics. And this suggests another level to the allusion that binds Falstaff to the Duke of Norfolk. To an Elizabethan audience, the name of Norfolk – the only surviving dukedom in the land – was synonymous with overt or suspected Catholic sympathy. The old Catholic ways persisted in the country long after the official change of religion inaugurated by Henry VIII's break from Rome. The Catholic liturgy's integral relationship with the agricultural calendar and the cycles of human biology could not be shattered overnight. There may, then, be a sense in which Falstaff's journey into deep England is also a journey into the old religion of Shakespeare's father and maternal grandfather. One wonders if it is a coincidence that, in fleshing out the skeletal character of the prince's riotous companion which he inherited from the old play of *The Famous Victories of Henry the Fifth*, Shakespeare retained and made much of his own father's name, John. It is ironic that Falstaff's original surname, Oldcastle, had to be changed because the character was regarded as an insult to the memory of the proto-Protestant Lollard of that name: 'for Oldcastle died martyr', says the epilogue to *Part II*, 'and this is not the man'.

Indeed, it is not the man, for Falstaff is if anything an embodiment of those ancient Catholic rhythms which were suppressed in the name of Reformation. Vestiges of Oldcastle litter the text: 'Falstaff sweats to death' suggests a martyr burning on a bonfire, and 'if I become not a cart as well as another man' could suggest a religious dissident on the way to the stake as well as a criminal being taken to the gallows. Protestants, especially in the extreme form of puritans, were traditionally lean; fat monks were symbolic of the corruptions of Catholicism. By making Sir John fat and not calling him Oldcastle, Shakespeare raises the spectre of Catholic as opposed to Protestant martyrdoms. Falstaff is Malvolio's opposite: he stands for cakes and ale, festival and holiday, all that was anathema to puritanism. At the beginning of *Henry V*, the Archbishop of Canterbury confirms that Prince Harry's transformation was completed with the rejection of Falstaff: 'Never came reformation in a flood, / With such a heady currance, scouring faults'. If there is a proto-Protestant or embryonic puritan in the plays, it is King Harry V, newly washed of his past, casting off his old companions, turning away England's former self.

ABOUT THE TEXT

Shakespeare endures through history. He illuminates later times as well as his own. He helps us to understand the human condition. But he cannot do this without a good text of the plays. Without editions there would be no Shakespeare. That is why every twenty years or so throughout the last three centuries there has been a major new edition of his complete works. One aspect of editing is the process of keeping the texts up to date – modernizing the spelling, punctuation and typography (though not, of course, the actual words), providing explanatory notes in the light of changing educational practices (a generation ago, most of Shakespeare's classical and biblical allusions could be assumed to be generally understood, but now they can't).

But because Shakespeare did not personally oversee the publication of his plays, editors also have to make decisions about the relative authority of the early printed editions. Half of the sum of his plays only appeared posthumously, in the elaborately produced First Folio text of 1623, the original 'Complete Works' prepared for the press by Shakespeare's fellow-actors, the people who knew the plays better than anyone else. The other half had appeared in print in his lifetime, in the more compact and cheaper form of 'Quarto' editions, some of which reproduced good quality texts, others of which were to a greater or lesser degree garbled and error-strewn. In the case of a few plays there are hundreds of differences between the Quarto and Folio editions, some of them far from trivial.

If you look at printers' handbooks from the age of Shakespeare, you quickly discover that one of the first rules was that, whenever possible, compositors were recommended to set their type from existing printed books rather than manuscripts. This was the age before mechanical typesetting, where each individual letter had to be picked out by hand from the compositor's case and placed on a stick (upside down and back to front) before being laid on the press. It was an age of murky rush-light and of manuscripts written in a secretary hand that had dozens of different, hard-to-decipher forms. Printers' lives were a lot easier when they were reprinting existing books rather than struggling with handwritten copy. Easily the quickest way to have created the First Folio would have been simply to reprint those eighteen plays that had already appeared in Quarto and only work from manuscript on the other eighteen.

But that is not what happened. Whenever Quartos were used, playhouse 'promptbooks' were also consulted and stage directions copied in from them. And in the case of several major plays where a reasonably well-printed Quarto was available, the Folio printers were instructed to work from an alternative, playhouse-derived manuscript. This meant that the whole process of producing the first complete Shakespeare took months, even years, longer than it might have done. But for the men overseeing the project, John Hemings and Henry Condell, friends and fellow-actors who had been remembered in Shakespeare's will, the additional labour and cost were worth the effort for the sake of producing an edition that was close to the practice of the theatre. They wanted all the plays in print so that people could, as they wrote in their prefatory address to the reader, 'read him and again and again', but they also wanted 'the great variety of readers' to work from texts that were close to the theatre-life for which Shakespeare originally intended them. For this reason, the *RSC Shakespeare*, in both *Complete Works* and individual volumes, uses the Folio as base text wherever possible. Significant Quarto variants are, however, noted in the Textual Notes.

Henry IV Part I is one of the plays where the Folio text was printed from a Quarto, though with reference to a playhouse manuscript, in which a large number of oaths had been removed in accordance with the 1606 Parliamentary 'Act to Restrain the Abuses of Players', whereby theatre companies were prohibited from taking God's name in vain. Most modern editors use the First Quarto of 1598 as their copy-text but import stage directions, act divisions and some corrections from Folio. Our Folio-led editorial practice follows the reverse procedure, using Folio as copy-text, but deploying the First Quarto as a 'control text' that offers assistance in the correction and identification of compositors' errors in the Folio, of which there are many. The traditional notion of fidelity to Shakespeare's first Quartos, on the grounds that they represent the texts closest to 'what the author wrote', is sometimes more an ideal than a reality. Early Quartos have errors too. And later Quartos made good corrections as well as introducing new errors. The lesson of textual transmission is the same as that of the theatre: the Shakespearean text was mobile in its own time and remains ever mobile. Each time one of the plays is performed, whatever the 'copy-text', the words will be slightly different, thanks to the tricks of actors' memories. So, too, each time the play is edited, there will be dozens of differences of punctuation, emendation and interpretation. Textual mobility is an essential part of Shakespeare's evolving creative afterlife. Our text is a modernized version of one moment in that life – the moment of the Folio, when all Shakespeare's history plays were gathered and put in sequence for the first time.

In order to respect the integrity of the Folio text, we have not reinserted the Quarto oaths that were removed from it. They are, however, listed at the end of the text and we recommend classroom discussion of the effect of their removal and rehearsal room reinsertion of them for the purposes of contemporary performance.

The following notes highlight various aspects of the editorial process and indicate conventions used in the text of this edition:

Lists of Parts are supplied in the First Folio for only six plays, not including *Henry IV Part I*, so the list here is editorially supplied. Capitals indicate that part of the name which is used for speech headings in the script (thus 'Sir Richard VERNON').

Locations are provided by the Folio for only two plays. Eighteenth-century editors, working in an age of elaborately realistic stage sets, were the first to provide detailed locations. Given that Shakespeare wrote for a bare stage and often an imprecise sense of place, we have relegated locations to the explanatory notes at the foot of the page, where they are given at the beginning of each scene where the imaginary location is different from the one before.

Act and Scene Divisions were provided in the Folio in a much more thoroughgoing way than in the Quartos. Sometimes, however, they were erroneous or omitted; corrections and additions supplied by editorial tradition are indicated by square brackets. Five-act division is based on a classical model, and act breaks provided the opportunity to replace the candles in the indoor Blackfriars playhouse which the King's Men used after 1608, but Shakespeare did not necessarily think in terms of a five-part structure of dramatic composition. The Folio convention is that a scene ends when the stage is empty. Nowadays, partly under the influence of film, we tend to consider a scene to be a dramatic unit that ends with either a change of imaginary location or a significant passage of time within the narrative. Shakespeare's fluidity of composition accords well with this convention, so in addition to act and scene numbers we provide a *running scene* count in the right margin at the beginning of each new scene, in the typeface used for editorial directions. Where there is a scene break caused by a momentary bare stage, but the location does not change and extra time does not pass, we use the convention *running scene continues*. There is inevitably a degree of editorial judgement in making such calls, but the system is very valuable in suggesting the pace of the plays.

Speakers' Names are often inconsistent in Folio. We have regularized speech headings, but retained an element of deliberate inconsistency in entry directions, in order to give the flavour of Folio.

Verse is indicated by lines that do not run to the right margin and by capitalization of each line. The Folio printers sometimes set verse as prose, and vice versa (either out of misunderstanding or for reasons of space). We have silently corrected in such cases, although in some instances there is ambiguity, in which case we have leaned towards the preservation of Folio layout. Folio sometimes uses contraction ('turnd' rather than 'turned') to indicate whether or not the final '-ed' of a past participle is sounded, an area where there is variation for the sake of the five-beat iambic pentameter rhythm. We use the convention of a grave accent to indicate sounding (thus 'turnèd' would be two syllables), but would urge actors not to overstress. In cases where one speaker ends with a verse half-line and the next begins with the other half of the pentameter, editors since the late eighteenth century have indented the second line. We have abandoned this convention, since the Folio does not use it, and nor did actors' cues in the Shakespearean theatre. An exception is made when the second speaker actively interrupts or completes the first speaker's sentence.

Spelling is modernized, but older forms are occasionally maintained where necessary for rhythm or aural effect.

Punctuation in Shakespeare's time was as much rhetorical as grammatical. 'Colon' was originally a term for a unit of thought in an argument. The semi-colon was a new unit of punctuation (some of the Quartos lack them altogether). We have modernized punctuation throughout, but have given more weight to Folio punctuation than many editors, since, though not Shakespearean, it reflects the usage of his period. In particular, we have used the colon far more than many editors: it is exceptionally useful as a way of indicating how many Shakespearean speeches unfold clause by clause in a developing argument that gives the illusion of enacting the process of thinking in the moment. We have also kept in mind the origin of punctuation in classical times as a way of assisting the actor and orator: the comma suggests the briefest of pauses for breath, the colon a middling one and a full stop or period a longer pause. Semi colons, by contrast, belong to an era of punctuation that was only just coming in during Shakespeare's time and that is coming to an end now: we have accordingly only used them where they occur in our copy-texts (and not always then). Dashes are sometimes used for parenthetical interjections where the Folio has brackets. They are also used for interruptions and changes in train of thought. Where a change of addressee occurs within a speech, we have used a dash preceded by a full stop (or occasionally another form of punctuation). Often the identity of the respective addressees is obvious from the context. When it is not, this has been indicated in a marginal stage direction.

Entrances and Exits are fairly thorough in Folio, which has accordingly been followed as faithfully as possible. Where characters are omitted or corrections are necessary, this is indicated by square brackets (e.g. '[*and Attendants*]'). *Exit* is sometimes silently normalized to *Exeunt* and *Manet* anglicized to 'remains'. We trust Folio positioning of entrances and exits to a greater degree than most editors.

Editorial Stage Directions such as stage business, asides, indications of addressee and of characters' position on the gallery stage are only used sparingly in Folio. Other editions mingle directions of this kind with original Folio and Quarto directions, sometimes marking them by means of square brackets. We have sought to distinguish what could be described as *directorial* interventions of this kind from Folio-style directions (either original or supplied) by placing them in the right margin in a different typeface. There is a degree of subjectivity about which directions are of which kind, but the procedure is intended as a reminder to the reader and the actor that Shakespearean stage directions are often dependent upon editorial inference alone and are not set in stone. We also depart from editorial tradition in sometimes admitting uncertainty and thus printing permissive stage directions, such as an Aside? (often a line may be equally effective as an aside or a direct address – it is for each production or reading to make its own decision) or a *may exit* or a piece of business placed between arrows to indicate that it may occur at various different moments within a scene.

Line Numbers in the left margin are editorial, for reference and to key the explanatory and textual notes.

Explanatory Notes at the foot of each page explain allusions and gloss obsolete and difficult words, confusing phraseology, occasional major textual cruces, and so on. Particular attention is given to non-standard usage, bawdy innuendo and technical terms (e.g. legal and military language). Where more than one sense is given, commas indicate shades of related meaning, slashes alternative or double meanings.

Textual Notes at the end of the play indicate major departures from the Folio. They take the following form: the reading of our text is given in bold and its source given after an equals sign, with 'Q' indicating that it derives from the First Quarto of 1598, Q5 that it derives from the Fifth Quarto of 1613, Q7 from the Seventh Quarto of 1632, 'F' from the First Folio of 1623, 'F2' a correction introduced in the Second Folio of 1632, F3 a correction introduced in the Third Folio of 1663–64 and 'Ed' one that derives from the subsequent editorial tradition. The rejected Folio ('F') reading is then given. Selected Quarto variants and plausible unadopted editorial readings are also included. Thus, for example, '**1.2.89 for**... **it** = F. Q = for wisedome cries out in the streets and no man regards it' indicates that we have retained the Folio reading 'for no man regards it', but that 'for wisedome cries out in the streets and no man regards it,' is an interestingly different reading in the First Quarto of 1598.

KEY FACTS

MAJOR PARTS: (with percentage of lines/number of speeches/ scenes on stage) Falstaff (20%/151/8), Prince Henry (18%/170/10), Hotspur (18%/102/8), King Henry (11%/30/6), Worcester (6%/35/ 7), Poins (3%/36/3), Glendower (3%/23/1). Several characters speak between 15 and 30 of the play's 3,000 lines: Douglas, Hostess Quickly, Gadshill, Vernon, Mortimer, Lady Percy, Bardolph, Blunt, Northumberland, Westmorland, Francis.

LINGUISTIC MEDIUM: 55% verse, 45% prose.

DATE: Probably written and first performed 1596–97; registered for publication February 1598. Falstaff's name was originally Oldcastle; it was probably changed to Falstaff either during the months when William Brooke, Lord Cobham (an indirect descendant of the historical Sir John Oldcastle), was Lord Chamberlain (August 1596 to March 1597) or following the suppression of playing (July– October 1597) caused by a politically inflammatory play called *The Isle of Dogs*.

SOURCES: Based on the account of the reign of Henry IV in the 1587 edition of Holinshed's *Chronicles*, with some use of Samuel Daniel's epic poem *The First Four Books of the Civil Wars* (1595). Thus, for instance, the historical Hotspur was twenty years older than Hal, but Daniel made them contemporaries for dramatic effect. The intermingling of historical materials and comedy, in the context of the prince's riotous youth, is developed from the anonymous Queen's Men play, *The Famous Victories of Henry the Fifth* (performed late 1580s), which includes characters who may be regarded as crude prototypes of Falstaff and Poins.

TEXT: Quarto 1598 (text probably based on a scribal transcript of Shakespeare's manuscript; two printings, one of them lost save for a few sheets), reprinted 1599, 1604, 1608, 1613, 1622 (indicating that this was one of Shakespeare's most popular plays). The Folio text was set from the Fifth Quarto, correcting some but nowhere near all of its mistakes. Oaths were systematically removed in accordance with the 1606 Parliamentary 'Act to Restrain the Abuses of Players': since the Act applied to stage performances, not printed books, this suggests that a theatrical manuscript also lay behind the Folio text. There is therefore good reason to regard Folio as an autonomous text, with its own authority. Our text is based on Folio, but where there are manifest errors, either derived from the Quarto tradition or introduced by the Folio compositors, we restore readings from the First Quarto.

THE FIRST PART OF HENRY THE FOURTH, with the Life and Death of Henry surnamed Hotspur

KING HENRY IV, formerly Henry Bullingbrook, Duke of Lancaster

PRINCE HENRY, Prince of Wales, Hal or Harry Monmouth

PRINCE JOHN, his younger brother, Lord of Lancaster

Earl of WESTMORLAND

Sir Walter BLUNT

Sir John FALSTAFF

Edward or Ned POINS

PETO

BARDOLPH

Earl of NORTHUMBERLAND, Henry Percy

Earl of WORCESTER, Thomas Percy, his younger brother

HOTSPUR, Sir Henry (or Harry) Percy, Northumberland's son

Lord Edmund MORTIMER, Earl of March, Hotspur's brother-in-law,

Owen GLENDOWER, Welsh lord, Mortimer's father-in-law

Earl of DOUGLAS, a Scots Lord

Sir Richard VERNON

ARCHBISHOP of York, Richard Scroop

SIR MICHAEL, member of Archbishop's household

LADY PERCY (Kate), Hotspur's wife, Mortimer's sister

LADY MORTIMER, Mortimer's wife, Glendower's daughter

FIRST CARRIER (Mugs)

OSTLER

SECOND CARRIER (Tom)

GADSHILL

CHAMBERLAIN

FIRST TRAVELLER

SECOND TRAVELLER

FRANCIS, an apprentice drawer or tapster

VINTNER

HOSTESS QUICKLY, landlady of a tavern

SHERIFF

SERVANT

MESSENGER

Lords, Soldiers, other Travellers, and Attendants

Act 1 Scene 1

running scene 1

*Enter the King, Lord John of Lancaster, [the] Earl of
Westmorland, with others*

KING HENRY IV So shaken as we are, so wan with care,
Find we a time for frighted peace to pant,
And breathe short-winded accents of new broils
To be commenced in strands afar remote.
5   No more the thirsty entrance of this soil
Shall daub her lips with her own children's blood.
No more shall trenching war channel her fields,
Nor bruise her flow'rets with the armèd hoofs
Of hostile paces. Those opposèd eyes,
10   Which, like the meteors of a troubled heaven,
All of one nature, of one substance bred,
Did lately meet in the intestine shock
And furious close of civil butchery
Shall now, in mutual well-beseeming ranks,
15   March all one way and be no more opposed
Against acquaintance, kindred and allies.
The edge of war, like an ill-sheathèd knife,
No more shall cut his master. Therefore, friends,
As far as to the sepulchre of Christ —
20   Whose soldier now, under whose blessèd cross
We are impressèd and engaged to fight —
Forthwith a power of English shall we levy,
Whose arms were moulded in their mother's womb
To chase these pagans in those holy fields
25   Over whose acres walked those blessèd feet
Which fourteen hundred years ago were nailed
For our advantage on the bitter cross.
But this our purpose is a twelvemonth old,

1.1 *Location: the royal court. Henry Bullingbrook had usurped the English crown in 1399 when he
forced his cousin, Richard II, to abdicate. Richard died shortly afterwards in mysterious circumstances.
The early years of Henry's reign were dominated by a determination to justify and consolidate his claim
to the throne and by a number of insurrections. As the play opens, Henry voices his anxiety about civil
unrest* **1 we** i.e. the king/the nation as a whole **wan** pale, sickly **2 Find we** let us find **frighted**
frightened **3 breathe short-winded accents** speak while out of breath **broils** quarrels, fighting
4 strands afar remote distant shores **5 entrance** mouth **6 daub** smear, plaster **7 trenching**
ploughing **8 flow'rets** small flowers **armèd** iron-shod/armoured **9 paces** (horse's) tread/gallop
opposèd hostile, malevolent **10 meteors** regarded as bad omens **12 intestine shock** internal, domestic
military encounter **13 close** hand-to-hand fighting **14 mutual well-beseeming** united and ordered
19 sepulchre of Christ Christ's tomb (at Jerusalem; Henry is planning a crusade to the Holy Land)
21 impressèd conscripted **engaged** pledged, committed **22 power** army **levy** raise, muster
23 arms upper limbs/weapons **mother's** natural mother's/England's **24 fields** lands/battlefields
25 blessèd feet i.e. Christ's **27 bitter** painful/pitiable

And bootless 'tis to tell you we will go:
30 Therefore we meet not now.— Then let me hear
Of you, my gentle cousin Westmorland,
What yesternight our council did decree
In forwarding this dear expedience.

WESTMORLAND My liege, this haste was hot in question,
35 And many limits of the charge set down
But yesternight, when all athwart there came
A post from Wales loaden with heavy news;
Whose worst was that the noble Mortimer,
Leading the men of Herefordshire to fight
40 Against the irregular and wild Glendower,
Was by the rude hands of that Welshman taken,
And a thousand of his people butcherèd,
Upon whose dead corpse there was such misuse,
Such beastly shameless transformation,
45 By those Welshwomen done as may not be
Without much shame retold or spoken of.

KING HENRY IV It seems then that the tidings of this broil
Brake off our business for the Holy Land.

WESTMORLAND This matched with other like, my
gracious lord.
50 Far more uneven and unwelcome news
Came from the north and thus it did report:
On Holy Rood day, the gallant Hotspur there,
Young Harry Percy, and brave Archibald,
That ever-valiant and approvèd Scot,
55 At Holmedon met, where they did spend
A sad and bloody hour,
As by discharge of their artillery,
And shape of likelihood, the news was told,
For he that brought them, in the very heat
60 And pride of their contention did take horse,
Uncertain of the issue any way.

---

29 **bootless** pointless   31 **gentle** kindly/noble   **cousin** kinsman   32 **yesternight** last night   33 **dear** important/urgent/noble/costly   **expedience** expedition   34 **liege** lord, superior to whom feudal service was due   **hot in question** hotly debated   35 **limits...charge** responsibilities relating to the undertaking   36 **But** only, as recently as   **athwart** adversely, at odds with our business   37 **post** messenger   **loaden** weighed down   **heavy** sad/weighty   40 **irregular...Glendower** uncivilized guerrilla fighter (**Glendower** was leader of the Welsh rebels)   41 **rude** rough   43 **corpse** corpses   44 **transformation** mutilation   47 **tidings** news   48 **Brake** archaic past tense of 'break'   49 **matched with** together with, accompanied by   50 **uneven** rough, unsettling   52 **Holy Rood day** 14 September, dedicated to the cross (**rood**) of Christ   **Hotspur** Henry Percy's nickname suggests that he is vigorous, hasty and hot-headed   54 **approvèd** tried and tested (in battle)   55 **Holmedon** the Northumberland site of the battle   56 **sad** serious/leading to sorrow   58 **shape of likelihood** likely conjecture   59 **heat...contention** middle of the fiercest fighting   61 **issue** outcome   **any** either

KING HENRY IV Here is a dear and true industrious friend,
Sir Walter Blunt, new lighted from his horse,
Stained with the variation of each soil
65   Betwixt that Holmedon and this seat of ours,
And he hath brought us smooth and welcome news.
The Earl of Douglas is discomfited,
Ten thousand bold Scots, two and twenty knights,
Balked in their own blood did Sir Walter see
70   On Holmedon's plains. Of prisoners, Hotspur took
Mordake, Earl of Fife, and eldest son
To beaten Douglas, and the Earl of Athol,
Of Murray, Angus, and Menteith.
And is not this an honourable spoil?
75   A gallant prize? Ha, cousin, is it not?
WESTMORLAND In faith, it is a conquest for a prince to
           boast of.
KING HENRY IV Yea, there thou mak'st me sad and mak'st
           me sin
In envy that my Lord Northumberland
Should be the father of so blest a son:
80   A son who is the theme of honour's tongue;
Amongst a grove, the very straightest plant,
Who is sweet Fortune's minion and her pride,
Whilst I, by looking on the praise of him,
See riot and dishonour stain the brow
85   Of my young Harry. O, that it could be proved
That some night-tripping fairy had exchanged
In cradle-clothes our children where they lay,
And called mine Percy, his Plantagenet:
Then would I have his Harry, and he mine.
90   But let him from my thoughts. What think you, coz,
Of this young Percy's pride? The prisoners,
Which he in this adventure hath surprised,
To his own use he keeps, and sends me word
I shall have none but Mordake Earl of Fife.

---

62 Here either 'here at court' or a line indicating Blunt's presence among the 'other' lords in attendance on stage   **63 new lighted** only just dismounted   **64 variation of each** different types of   **65 Betwixt** between   **seat** residence/throne   **66 smooth** pleasant, welcome   **67 discomfited** defeated   **69 Balked** heaped up (in 'balks', i.e. ridges)   **71 Mordake . . . Douglas** Mordake was Earl of Fife but not Douglas' son – Shakespeare misread Holinshed's *Chronicles*, his main source   **73 Menteith** not in fact another earl, but one of Mordake's titles   **74 honourable spoil** noble gains of war   **75 gallant** fine, splendid   **80 theme** subject, chief topic   **81 straightest plant** most upright tree   **82 minion** favourite   **84 riot** debauchery, corruption   **86 night-tripping** moving nimbly through the night   **fairy** popular belief held that fairies sometimes stole human infants, substituting (troublesome) fairy children for them   **88 Plantagenet** the surname of this royal dynasty   **90 from** go from   **coz** short for 'cousin' (i.e. kinsman)   **92 adventure** enterprise, venture   **surprised** captured, ambushed

95 WESTMORLAND This is his uncle's teaching. This is
      Worcester,
      Malevolent to you in all aspects,
      Which makes him prune himself, and bristle up
      The crest of youth against your dignity.
    KING HENRY IV But I have sent for him to answer this.
100   And for this cause awhile we must neglect
      Our holy purpose to Jerusalem.
      Cousin, on Wednesday next our council we
      Will hold at Windsor, and so inform the lords.
      But come yourself with speed to us again,
105   For more is to be said and to be done
      Than out of anger can be utterèd.
    WESTMORLAND I will, my liege.   *Exeunt*

Act 1 Scene 2   *running scene 2*

Enter Henry, Prince of Wales [and] Sir John Falstaff

FALSTAFF Now, Hal, what time of day is it, lad?
PRINCE HENRY Thou art so fat-witted with drinking of old
    sack and unbuttoning thee after supper and sleeping
    upon benches in the afternoon, that thou hast
5   forgotten to demand that truly which thou wouldst
    truly know. What a devil hast thou to do with the
    time of the day? Unless hours were cups of sack and
    minutes capons and clocks the tongues of bawds
    and dials the signs of leaping-houses and the blessed
10   sun himself a fair hot wench in flame-coloured
    taffeta, I see no reason why thou shouldst be so
    superfluous to demand the time of the day.
    FALSTAFF Indeed, you come near me now, Hal, for we
    that take purses go by the moon and seven stars, and
15   not by Phoebus, he, 'that wand'ring knight so fair'.
    And, I prithee, sweet wag, when thou art king, as

---

97 prune preen (like a bird) **bristle** raise, ruffle angrily **98 dignity** worthiness/kingship **100 cause**
reason **106 out**…**utterèd** can be spoken openly in anger **1.2** *Location: in London, but unspecified;*
perhaps the prince's apartments **2 fat-witted** dull-witted (plays on Falstaff's physical size) **3 sack**
Spanish white wine **5 forgotten** neglected/forgotten how **demand that truly** ask accurately,
rightly **6 truly** genuinely/accurately **8 capons** castrated cockerels, a common dish **bawds** pimps,
procurers of sex **9 dials** sundials/clock faces **leaping-houses** brothels **10 hot** lustful **11 taffeta**
silky material associated with prostitutes **12 superfluous** unnecessarily curious, irrelevant **13 come**
near me touch the point, begin to understand me **14 go by** travel by the light of/tell the time according
to **seven stars** the Pleiades (a group of stars in the constellation Taurus) **15 Phoebus** the sun god
'wand'ring…**fair'** probably a phrase from a ballad or popular romance, referring to the sun as a knight in a
tale of romance **16 wag** mischievous boy

God save thy grace — majesty I should say, for grace
thou wilt have none—
PRINCE HENRY What, none?

20   FALSTAFF No, not so much as will serve to be prologue to
an egg and butter.
PRINCE HENRY Well, how then? Come, roundly, roundly.
FALSTAFF Marry, then, sweet wag, when thou art king,
let not us that are squires of the night's body be

25   called thieves of the day's beauty. Let us be Diana's
foresters, gentlemen of the shade, minions of the
moon; and let men say we be men of good
government, being governed, as the sea is, by our
noble and chaste mistress the moon, under whose

30   countenance we steal.
PRINCE HENRY Thou say'st well, and it holds well too, for
the fortune of us that are the moon's men doth ebb
and flow like the sea, being governed, as the sea is, by
the moon. As, for proof, now: a purse of gold most

35   resolutely snatched on Monday night and most
dissolutely spent on Tuesday morning; got with
swearing 'Lay by' and spent with crying 'Bring in',
now in as low an ebb as the foot of the ladder and by
and by in as high a flow as the ridge of the gallows.

40   FALSTAFF Thou say'st true, lad. And is not my hostess of
the tavern a most sweet wench?
PRINCE HENRY As is the honey of Hybla, my old lad of
the castle. And is not a buff jerkin a most sweet robe
of durance?

---

17 grace term of address for royalty (but sense then shifts to 'spiritual grace' and then to 'prayer before a
meal')   **21 egg and butter** i.e. a very light meal (barely requiring **grace** to be said as a blessing)
22 roundly plainly, straightforwardly (may play on Falstaff's shape)   **23 Marry** by the Virgin Mary
24 squires ... body the night's personal attendants (**night's** puns on 'knight's')   **25 thieves ... beauty** i.e.
by sleepily wasting the day (**beauty** puns on 'booty')   **Diana** Roman goddess of the moon, patron of hunting
and virginity   **26 foresters** forest dwellers, servants   **minions** favourites   **27 of good government** of
good conduct/who live under a good ruler   **30 countenance** face, appearance/support, authority   **steal**
rob/move furtively   **31 holds** applies, is apt   **37 'Lay by'** highwayman's command that his victims lay
aside their weapons   **'Bring in'** an order for drinks   **38 now ... gallows** one moment one's fortune is as
low as the bottom of the ladder leading to the gallows, the next as high as the crossbar at the top of the
gallows – i.e. whatever a thief's course, the result (hanging) is the same   **40 hostess** landlady   **42 Hybla**
Sicilian town famous for its **honey**   **old ... castle** carouser (plays on 'Oldcastle', Shakespeare's original
name for Falstaff; **castle** may play on the sense of 'stocks', instruments of public punishment in which a thief
might be confined; a London brothel called The Castle may also be alluded to, appropriately named given that
castle was slang for 'vagina')   **43 buff jerkin** tight leather jacket worn by sheriff's officers (plays on the sense
of 'naked vagina')   **robe of durance** long-lasting garment (with sexual connotations; **durance** plays on the
sense of 'imprisonment')

45 FALSTAFF How now, how now, mad wag? What, in thy
quips and thy quiddities? What a plague have I to do
with a buff jerkin?

PRINCE HENRY Why, what a pox have I to do with my
hostess of the tavern?

50 FALSTAFF Well, thou hast called her to a reck'ning many
a time and oft.

PRINCE HENRY Did I ever call for thee to pay thy part?

FALSTAFF No, I'll give thee thy due, thou hast paid all
there.

55 PRINCE HENRY Yea, and elsewhere, so far as my coin
would stretch, and where it would not, I have used
my credit.

FALSTAFF Yea, and so used it that were it here apparent
that thou art heir apparent — but, I prithee, sweet

60 wag, shall there be gallows standing in England when
thou art king? And resolution thus fobbed as it is with
the rusty curb of old father antic the law? Do not thou,
when thou art a king, hang a thief.

PRINCE HENRY No, thou shalt.

65 FALSTAFF Shall I? O rare! I'll be a brave judge.

PRINCE HENRY Thou judgest false already: I mean, thou
shalt have the hanging of the thieves and so become
a rare hangman.

FALSTAFF Well, Hal, well, and in some sort it jumps with

70 my humour as well as waiting in the court, I can tell
you.

PRINCE HENRY For obtaining of suits?

FALSTAFF Yea, for obtaining of suits, whereof the
hangman hath no lean wardrobe. I am as

75 melancholy as a gib cat or a lugged bear.

PRINCE HENRY Or an old lion, or a lover's lute.

FALSTAFF Yea, or the drone of a Lincolnshire bagpipe.

---

46 quiddities quibbles   **What a plague** emphatic form of 'what'   **48 pox** venereal disease
50 called . . . reck'ning asked her for the bill/asked her to explain herself/had sex with her   **52 pay thy part**
pay for your share/have sex   **55 coin would stretch** money would go/penis would grow; **coin** puns on
'quoin' – i.e. carpenter's wedge (a euphemism for 'penis')   **59 heir** puns on **here** (which was pronounced in
a similar manner)   **61 resolution** determination   **fobbed** cheated   **62 curb** restraint (literally, chain
passed under a horse's jaw)   **old father antic** the elderly buffoon (that is)   **65 rare** splendid   **brave** fine,
excellent   **69 jumps . . . humour** fits my disposition   **70 waiting** waiting around/being in attendance
72 suits requests, legal petitions (Falstaff plays on the sense of 'suits of clothes'; the hangman had the right to
keep his victims' garments)   **74 no lean wardrobe** i.e. no small amount (because hangings were common;
wardrobe may pun on 'wardrope', a type of thick rope)   **75 gib cat** tom cat   **lugged bear** baited bear,
pulled by the ears and tugged on a chain   **76 lute** the stringed instrument was associated with lovers
77 bagpipe musical instrument/tedious, moaning speaker

PRINCE HENRY What say'st thou to a hare, or the melancholy of Moorditch?

80 **FALSTAFF** Thou hast the most unsavoury similes and art indeed the most comparative, rascalli'st, sweet young prince. But, Hal, I prithee trouble me no more with vanity. I would thou and I knew where a commodity of good names were to be bought. An old lord of the

85 council rated me the other day in the street about you, sir, but I marked him not. And yet he talked very wisely, but I regarded him not; and yet he talked wisely, and in the street too.

PRINCE HENRY Thou didst well, for no man regards it.

90 **FALSTAFF** O, thou hast damnable iteration and art indeed able to corrupt a saint. Thou hast done much harm unto me, Hal, God forgive thee for it! Before I knew thee, Hal, I knew nothing. And now I am, if a man should speak truly, little better than

95 one of the wicked. I must give over this life, and I will give it over. An I do not, I am a villain. I'll be damned for never a king's son in Christendom.

PRINCE HENRY Where shall we take a purse tomorrow, Jack?

100 **FALSTAFF** Where thou wilt, lad, I'll make one. An I do not, call me villain and baffle me.

PRINCE HENRY I see a good amendment of life in thee, from praying to purse-taking.

FALSTAFF Why, Hal, 'tis my vocation, Hal: 'tis no sin for

105 a man to labour in his vocation. Poins! Now shall we know if Gadshill have set a watch. O, if men were to be saved by merit, what hole in hell were hot enough for him? This is the most omnipotent villain that ever cried 'Stand' to a true man.

---

78 **hare** a proverbially melancholy animal   79 **Moorditch** notoriously filthy drainage ditch outside the northern walls of the City of London   81 **comparative** prone to making comparisons   **rascalli'st** most rascal-like   83 **vanity** foolishness, trifles   **commodity** supply   84 **names** reputations   85 **rated** scolded   86 **marked him not** took no notice of him   89 **no . . . it** biblical allusion, 'Wisdom crieth without . . . and no man regarded' (Proverbs 1:20–4), truncated in Folio because of the 1606 Parliamentary 'Act to restrain the Abuses of Players'   90 **damnable iteration** a way of constantly quoting Scripture that will lead to damnation   91 **saint** puritan term for a person chosen by God to be saved   96 **An** if   97 **never a** no   99 **Jack** affectionate form of 'John'   100 **make one** make up one of the party   101 **baffle** publicly disgrace (a knight)   102 **amendment** reformation   104 **vocation** calling (from God)   106 **Gadshill** named after Gad's Hill in Kent, a notorious place for highway robberies   **set a watch** surveyed the targeted area, conducted a recce (as part of planning a robbery; some editors emend to 'set a match' – slang for 'plan a robbery')   107 **saved by merit** had their souls saved through good works and personal desert (as opposed to divine grace)   108 **omnipotent** unparalleled, almighty   109 **'Stand'** stand and deliver – highwayman's command   **true** honest

[*Enter Poins*]

110 **PRINCE HENRY** Good morrow, Ned.

POINS Good morrow, sweet Hal. What says Monsieur Remorse? What says Sir John Sack and Sugar, Jack? How agrees the devil and thee about thy soul, that thou soldest him on Good Friday last for a cup of
115 Madeira and a cold capon's leg?

PRINCE HENRY Sir John stands to his word, the devil shall have his bargain, for he was never yet a breaker of proverbs: he will give the devil his due.

POINS Then art thou damned for keeping thy word with
120 the devil.

PRINCE HENRY Else he had been damned for cozening the devil.

POINS But, my lads, my lads, tomorrow morning, by four o'clock, early at Gad's Hill, there are pilgrims going to
125 Canterbury with rich offerings, and traders riding to London with fat purses. I have vizards for you all; you have horses for yourselves. Gadshill lies tonight in Rochester. I have bespoke supper tomorrow in Eastcheap; we may do it as secure as sleep. If you will
130 go, I will stuff your purses full of crowns: if you will not, tarry at home and be hanged.

FALSTAFF Hear ye, Yedward, if I tarry at home and go not, I'll hang you for going.

POINS You will, chops?

135 **FALSTAFF** Hal, wilt thou make one?

PRINCE HENRY Who, I rob? I a thief? Not I.

FALSTAFF There's neither honesty, manhood, nor good fellowship in thee, nor thou cam'st not of the blood royal, if thou dar'st not stand for ten shillings.

140 **PRINCE HENRY** Well then, once in my days I'll be a madcap.

FALSTAFF Why, that's well said.

PRINCE HENRY Well, come what will, I'll tarry at home.

---

111 Monsieur Remorse teasing reference to Falstaff   **112 Sir...Jack** i.e. Falstaff; another mocking reference, apparently alluding to Falstaff's taste for sweetened wine   **114 Good Friday** the Friday before Easter Sunday, a strict fast day   **115 Madeira** a strong white wine   **118 give...due** proverbial   **121 Else he had** Otherwise he had been   **cozening** cheating   **124 Gad's Hill** the notorious spot for robberies was situated on the Dover road near **Rochester** in Kent; pilgrims travelling to **Canterbury** were often targets   **126 vizards** masks   **127 lies** lodges   **128 bespoke** ordered   **129 Eastcheap** London street running from the junction of Cannon and Gracechurch Streets to Great Tower Street   **secure** safely   **130 crowns** gold coins   **131 tarry** stay   **132 Yedward** dialect form of 'Edward'   **133 hang you** i.e. report it and get you hanged   **134 chops** fat cheeks   **138 blood royal** regal descent (Falstaff goes on to play on the sense of 'gold coin worth **ten shillings**')   **139 stand for** stand and fight for/be worth

FALSTAFF I'll be a traitor then, when thou art king.

145 **PRINCE HENRY** I care not.

POINS Sir John, I prithee leave the prince and me alone: I will lay him down such reasons for this adventure that he shall go.

FALSTAFF Well, mayst thou have the spirit of persuasion
150 and he the ears of profiting, that what thou speakest may move and what he hears may be believed, that the true prince may, for recreation sake, prove a false thief; for the poor abuses of the time want countenance. Farewell. You shall find me in
155 Eastcheap.

PRINCE HENRY Farewell, the latter spring! Farewell, All-hallown summer!

[Exit Falstaff]

POINS Now, my good sweet honey lord, ride with us tomorrow. I have a jest to execute that I cannot
160 manage alone. Falstaff, Peto, Bardolph and Gadshill shall rob those men that we have already waylaid: yourself and I will not be there. And when they have the booty, if you and I do not rob them, cut this head from my shoulders.

165 **PRINCE HENRY** But how shall we part with them in setting forth?

POINS Why, we will set forth before or after them, and appoint them a place of meeting, wherein it is at our pleasure to fail; and then will they adventure upon
170 the exploit themselves, which they shall have no sooner achieved, but we'll set upon them.

PRINCE HENRY Ay, but 'tis like that they will know us by our horses, by our habits and by every other appointment, to be ourselves.

175 **POINS** Tut! Our horses they shall not see: I'll tie them in the wood. Our vizards we will change after we leave them. And, sirrah, I have cases of buckram for the nonce, to immask our noted outward garments.

PRINCE HENRY But I doubt they will be too hard for us.

---

149 **Well . . . believed** Falstaff parodies the language of a Protestant sermon on the power of God's word to move the congregation   153 **abuses** wrongdoings, sins   **want countenance** lack recognition and support   156 **latter . . . summer** late spring and summer lasting until All Hallows' Eve (31 October); the suggestion is that Falstaff's youthful behaviour is not in keeping with his age   161 **waylaid** set an ambush for   169 **pleasure** preference, decision   **fail** i.e. to turn up   172 **like** likely   173 **habits** clothes 174 **appointment** piece of gear   177 **sirrah** sir (familiar form often used to inferiors, jocular here)   **cases of buckram** suits of coarse cloth   178 **nonce** purpose, occasion   **immask** disguise   **noted** well-known 179 **doubt** fear   **hard** tough, powerful

180 POINS Well, for two of them, I know them to be as true-
bred cowards as ever turned back. And for the third,
if he fight longer than he sees reason, I'll forswear
arms. The virtue of this jest will be the
incomprehensible lies that this fat rogue will tell us
185 when we meet at supper: how thirty at least he
fought with, what wards, what blows, what
extremities he endured; and in the reproof of this
lies the jest.
PRINCE HENRY Well, I'll go with thee. Provide us all
190 things necessary and meet me tomorrow night in
Eastcheap. There I'll sup. Farewell.
POINS Farewell, my lord.   *Exit Poins*
PRINCE HENRY I know you all, and will awhile uphold
The unyoked humour of your idleness.
195 Yet herein will I imitate the sun,
Who doth permit the base contagious clouds
To smother up his beauty from the world,
That when he please again to be himself,
Being wanted, he may be more wondered at,
200 By breaking through the foul and ugly mists
Of vapours that did seem to strangle him.
If all the year were playing holidays,
To sport would be as tedious as to work;
But when they seldom come, they wished-for come,
205 And nothing pleaseth but rare accidents.
So, when this loose behaviour I throw off
And pay the debt I never promisèd,
By how much better than my word I am,
By so much shall I falsify men's hopes,
210 And like bright metal on a sullen ground,
My reformation, glittering o'er my fault,
Shall show more goodly and attract more eyes
Than that which hath no foil to set it off.
I'll so offend to make offence a skill,
215 Redeeming time when men think least I will. [*Exit*]

---

181 turned back turned their backs to flee **182 forswear** swear to give up **184 incomprehensible**
boundless, unlimited **186 wards** defensive manoeuvres (fencing term) **187 reproof** disproving,
refutation/shame, reprimand **191 sup** have supper (the last meal of the day) **193 uphold** carry on with/
support **194 unyoked humour** unrestrained behaviour, wild whim **195 sun** common symbol of
royalty **196 contagious** noxious, infectious; **clouds** were thought to harbour disease **199 wanted**
missed, lacked **203 sport** play, entertain oneself **205 rare accidents** unusual events **209 falsify men's
hopes** prove expectations of me false **210 sullen ground** dark background **213 foil** contrast,
background (technically, setting for a jewel) **214 so offend** misbehave in such a way **skill** art/cunning
tactic **215 Redeeming time** making up for lost time (**Redeeming** has religious connotations)

Act 1 Scene 3 *running scene 3*

Enter the King, Northumberland, Worcester, Hotspur, Sir Walter Blunt and others

KING HENRY IV My blood hath been too cold and
  temperate,
 Unapt to stir at these indignities,
 And you have found me; for accordingly
 You tread upon my patience. But be sure
5 I will from henceforth rather be myself,
 Mighty and to be feared, than my condition,
 Which hath been smooth as oil, soft as young down,
 And therefore lost that title of respect
 Which the proud soul ne'er pays but to the proud.
10 **WORCESTER** Our house, my sovereign liege, little
  deserves
 The scourge of greatness to be used on it.
 And that same greatness too which our own hands
 Have holp to make so portly.
 NORTHUMBERLAND My lord—   *To the King*
15 **KING HENRY IV** Worcester, get thee gone, for I do see
 Danger and disobedience in thine eye.
 O, sir, your presence is too bold and peremptory,
 And majesty might never yet endure
 The moody frontier of a servant brow.
20 You have good leave to leave us. When we need
 Your use and counsel, we shall send for you.—
         [Exit Worcester]
 You were about to speak. *To Northumberland*
 NORTHUMBERLAND Yea, my good lord.
 Those prisoners in your highness' name demanded,
25 Which Harry Percy here at Holmedon took,
 Were, as he says, not with such strength denied
 As was delivered to your majesty,
 Who either through envy or misprision
 Was guilty of this fault and not my son.

1.3 *Location: the royal court* **1 temperate** calm, restrained **2 Unapt** not inclined or ready to
3 found me found me to be so **4 tread upon** try, take advantage of **5 myself** my royal self **6 condition**
natural disposition **8 title of** claim **9 proud** fine, splendid, possessed of self-respect **10 house** family
11 scourge punishing whip **13 holp** helped **portly** prosperous, majestic/overweight, too comfortable
17 peremptory determined/imperious **19 moody frontier** threatening look **frontier** literally, military
fortification **20 good leave** full permission **21 use** services **26 with…denied** refused so emphatically
27 delivered reported **28 envy or misprision** malice or misunderstanding

30 HOTSPUR My liege, I did deny no prisoners.   *To the King*
But I remember, when the fight was done,
When I was dry with rage and extreme toil,
Breathless and faint, leaning upon my sword,
Came there a certain lord, neat and trimly dressed,
35 Fresh as a bridegroom, and his chin new reaped
Showed like a stubble-land at harvest-home.
He was perfumèd like a milliner,
And 'twixt his finger and his thumb he held
A pouncet-box, which ever and anon
40 He gave his nose and took't away again,
Who therewith angry, when it next came there,
Took it in snuff. And still he smiled and talked,
And as the soldiers bore dead bodies by,
He called them untaught knaves, unmannerly,
45 To bring a slovenly unhandsome corpse
Betwixt the wind and his nobility.
With many holiday and lady terms
He questioned me, among the rest demanded
My prisoners in your majesty's behalf.
50 I then, all smarting with my wounds being cold,
To be so pestered with a popinjay,
Out of my grief and my impatience,
Answered neglectingly I know not what,
He should or should not. For he made me mad
55 To see him shine so brisk and smell so sweet
And talk so like a waiting-gentlewoman
Of guns and drums and wounds — God save the
   mark! —
And telling me the sovereign'st thing on earth
Was parmaceti for an inward bruise,
60 And that it was great pity, so it was,
That villainous saltpetre should be digged

---

32 dry with rage thirsty after the fury of battle   **34 neat** elegant   **trimly** finely, immaculately   **35 new reaped** freshly shaven   **36 stubble-land at harvest-home** shorn stalks of crops at the end of the harvest   **37 milliner** seller of fancy goods (originally those from Milan)   **39 pouncet-box** small box with a perforated lid, used for holding perfume or snuff   **ever and anon** time and again   **40 gave** held up to   **41 Who therewith angry** at which (removal of the box) his nose became angry   **42 Took...snuff** inhaled/took offence   **still** continually   **44 untaught** ignorant, ill-mannered   **45 slovenly** dirty, untidy   **unhandsome** unattractive, unbecoming   **46 nobility** elegant, aristocratic personage   **47 holiday... terms** refined, genteel expressions   **48 questioned** conversed with/asked questions of   **50 cold** untended/congealing   **51 popinjay** parrot (i.e. gaudy prattler)   **52 grief** pain   **53 neglectingly** unthinkingly, carelessly   **55 brisk** sprucely, smartly   **56 waiting-gentlewoman** woman of good family attending on a great lady   **57 God...mark!** conventional expression of apology   **58 sovereign'st** best, most healing   **59 parmaceti** corruption of 'spermaceti' – fat from the head of a sperm whale, used for treating bruises   **61 saltpetre** potassium nitrate, the chief ingredient of gunpowder, also used medicinally

Out of the bowels of the harmless earth,
Which many a good tall fellow had destroyed
So cowardly, and but for these vile guns,
65   He would himself have been a soldier.
This bald unjointed chat of his, my lord,
Made me to answer indirectly, as I said,
And I beseech you let not this report
Come current for an accusation
70   Betwixt my love and your high majesty.

BLUNT The circumstance considered, good my lord,   *To the king*
Whatever Harry Percy then had said
To such a person and in such a place,
At such a time, with all the rest retold,
75   May reasonably die and never rise
To do him wrong or any way impeach
What then he said, so he unsay it now.

KING HENRY IV Why, yet he doth deny his prisoners,
But with proviso and exception,
80   That we at our own charge shall ransom straight
His brother-in-law, the foolish Mortimer,
Who, in my soul, hath wilfully betrayed
The lives of those that he did lead to fight
Against the great magician, damned Glendower,
85   Whose daughter, as we hear, the Earl of March
Hath lately married. Shall our coffers, then,
Be emptied to redeem a traitor home?
Shall we buy treason, and indent with fears
When they have lost and forfeited themselves?
90   No, on the barren mountain let him starve,
For I shall never hold that man my friend
Whose tongue shall ask me for one penny cost
To ransom home revolted Mortimer.

HOTSPUR Revolted Mortimer?
95   He never did fall off, my sovereign liege,
But by the chance of war. To prove that true
Needs no more but one tongue for all those wounds,

---

63 tall fine, valiant   **66 bald unjointed chat** empty, incoherent chatter   **67 indirectly** inattentively
68 beseech beg   **69 Come current** be accepted at face value   **74 retold** related, explained   **75 die** i.e. be
forgotten   **76 impeach** discredit, accuse   **77 so** provided that   **78 yet he** still Hotspur (the king does not
reply to him directly)   **deny** refuse (to hand over)   **79 proviso and exception** terms and conditions
80 charge expense   **straight** straight away   **85 Earl of March** i.e. Mortimer; in fact, Shakespeare confuses
two Edmund Mortimers: one was indeed the Earl of March, but it was his uncle of the same name who
married Glendower's daughter   **86 coffers** money chests, treasury   **88 indent** make a contract   **fears**
those traitors who give us cause for fear/cowards   **93 revolted** rebellious   **95 fall off** abandon loyalty

Those mouthèd wounds, which valiantly he took
When on the gentle Severn's sedgy bank,
100 In single opposition, hand to hand,
He did confound the best part of an hour
In changing hardiment with great Glendower.
Three times they breathed and three times did they
    drink,
Upon agreement, of swift Severn's flood;
105 Who then, affrighted with their bloody looks,
Ran fearfully among the trembling reeds,
And hid his crisp head in the hollow bank,
Bloodstainèd with these valiant combatants.
Never did base and rotten policy
110 Colour her working with such deadly wounds;
Nor never could the noble Mortimer
Receive so many, and all willingly.
Then let him not be slandered with revolt.
KING HENRY IV Thou dost belie him, Percy, thou dost
    belie him;
115 He never did encounter with Glendower.
I tell thee, he durst as well have met the devil alone
As Owen Glendower for an enemy.
Art thou not ashamed? But, sirrah, henceforth
Let me not hear you speak of Mortimer.
120 Send me your prisoners with the speediest means,
Or you shall hear in such a kind from me
As will displease ye.— My lord Northumberland,
We license your departure with your son.—
Send us your prisoners, or you'll hear of it.   *To Hotspur*
            Exeunt King [Henry, Blunt and train]
125 **HOTSPUR** An if the devil come and roar for them
I will not send them. I will after straight
And tell him so, for I will ease my heart,
Although it be with hazard of my head.

---

98 **mouthèd** open, gaping/famous, spoken of   99 **Severn's sedgy bank** reed-covered banks of the River Severn, which divided England and south Wales   101 **confound** spend, consume   102 **changing hardiment** exchanging valiant blows   103 **breathed** broke off to catch their breath   104 **Upon agreement** by mutual consent   **flood** water, torrent   105 **affrighted** frightened   107 **crisp** wavy, rippled (personifies the river as curly-haired)   **hollow** empty, sunken   109 **base ... policy** lowly and corrupt plotting   110 **Colour** disguise/dye   113 **slandered** 'sland'red' in Folio   **revolt** i.e. the accusation of being a rebel   114 **belie** misrepresent, lie about   115 **encounter** fight   116 **durst** (would have) dared   121 **kind** manner   123 **license** formally authorize   125 **An if** if   126 **after** follow   128 **with hazard of** at the risk (of losing)

NORTHUMBERLAND What? Drunk with choler? Stay and
    pause awhile.
130   Here comes your uncle.
    Enter Worcester
HOTSPUR Speak of Mortimer?
    Yes, I will speak of him, and let my soul
    Want mercy, if I do not join with him.
    In his behalf I'll empty all these veins,
135   And shed my dear blood drop by drop i'th'dust,
    But I will lift the downfall Mortimer
    As high i'th'air as this unthankful king,
    As this ingrate and cankered Bullingbrook.
NORTHUMBERLAND Brother, the king hath made your
    nephew mad.
140 WORCESTER Who struck this heat up after I was gone?
HOTSPUR He will, forsooth, have all my prisoners.
    And when I urged the ransom once again
    Of my wife's brother, then his cheek looked pale,
    And on my face he turned an eye of death,
145   Trembling even at the name of Mortimer.
WORCESTER I cannot blame him: was he not proclaimed
    By Richard, that dead is, the next of blood?
NORTHUMBERLAND He was. I heard the proclamation.
    And then it was when the unhappy king —
150   Whose wrongs in us God pardon! — did set forth
    Upon his Irish expedition,
    From whence he intercepted did return
    To be deposed and shortly murderèd.
WORCESTER And for whose death we in the world's wide
    mouth
155   Live scandalized and foully spoken of.
HOTSPUR But soft, I pray you; did King Richard then
    Proclaim my brother Mortimer
    Heir to the crown?
NORTHUMBERLAND He did. Myself did hear it.

---

129 choler anger   **133 Want mercy** lack God's mercy, i.e. be damned   **136 downfall** downfallen
138 ingrate ungrateful   **cankered** diseased, corrupted   **Bullingbrook** Henry's surname before he was
king (taken from the castle in which he was born – Hotspur refuses to acknowledge Henry's royal status)
140 heat anger   **141 forsooth** in truth   **142 urged** pressed, brought forward   **144 eye of death** fearful
look, perhaps also threatening   **146 he** i.e. Mortimer   **147 Richard** Richard II, deposed by Henry   **next of
blood** nearest blood relation, i.e. heir to the throne; confusion between the two Mortimers continues – it was
in fact the younger man who was proclaimed heir, rather than his uncle (husband of Glendower's daughter
and the man who is meant here)   **149 unhappy** unfortunate   **150 in us** i.e. at our hands – the Percy
family had supported Henry against Richard   **152 intercepted** interrupted (in the middle of his Irish
campaign)   **156 soft** wait a moment   **157 brother** brother-in-law

160 **HOTSPUR** Nay, then I cannot blame his cousin king,
That wished him on the barren mountains starved.
But shall it be that you that set the crown
Upon the head of this forgetful man
And for his sake wore the detested blot
165 Of murderous subornation, shall it be,
That you a world of curses undergo,
Being the agents, or base second means,
The cords, the ladder, or the hangman rather?
O, pardon if that I descend so low,
170 To show the line and the predicament
Wherein you range under this subtle king.
Shall it for shame be spoken in these days,
Or fill up chronicles in time to come,
That men of your nobility and power
175 Did gage them both in an unjust behalf,
As both of you — God pardon it! — have done,
To put down Richard, that sweet lovely rose,
And plant this thorn, this canker, Bullingbrook?
And shall it in more shame be further spoken,
180 That you are fooled, discarded and shook off
By him for whom these shames ye underwent?
No. Yet time serves wherein you may redeem
Your banished honours and restore yourselves
Into the good thoughts of the world again,
185 Revenge the jeering and disdained contempt
Of this proud king, who studies day and night
To answer all the debt he owes unto you
Even with the bloody payment of your deaths:
Therefore, I say—
190 **WORCESTER** Peace, cousin, say no more.
And now I will unclasp a secret book,
And to your quick-conceiving discontents
I'll read you matter deep and dangerous,
As full of peril and adventurous spirit
195 As to o'er-walk a current roaring loud
On the unsteadfast footing of a spear.

---

160 cousin may pun on 'cozen' (i.e. 'cheat')   **164 blot** (moral) stain   **165 subornation** incitement (to Richard's murder)   **167 second means** agents, instruments   **170 line** status (plays on the sense of 'rope')   **predicament** category/dangerous situation   **171 range** move/are ranked   **subtle** crafty   **175 gage** pledge   **178 canker** wild rose/worm that destroys plants/ulcer   **180 fooled** made fools of/duped, frustrated   **186 studies** reflects, plans, endeavours   **187 answer** repay   **191 unclasp** i.e. open   **192 quick-conceiving** ready, quick to understand   **193 deep** deep-rooted/grave/cunning   **195 o'er-walk** cross   **196 unsteadfast** unsteady   **spear** i.e. used as a bridge

HOTSPUR If he fall in, goodnight, or sink or swim.
    Send danger from the east unto the west,
    So honour cross it from the north to south,
200   And let them grapple. The blood more stirs
    To rouse a lion than to start a hare!
NORTHUMBERLAND Imagination of some great exploit   *To Worcester*
    Drives him beyond the bounds of patience.
HOTSPUR By heaven, methinks it were an easy leap,
205   To pluck bright honour from the pale-faced moon,
    Or dive into the bottom of the deep,
    Where fathom-line could never touch the ground,   *meaning*
    And pluck up drownèd honour by the locks,
    So he that doth redeem her thence might wear
210   Without corrival, all her dignities:
    But out upon this half-faced fellowship!
WORCESTER He apprehends a world of figures here,   *To Northumberland*
    But not the form of what he should attend.—
    Good cousin, give me audience for a while and list
      to me.
215 HOTSPUR I cry you mercy.
WORCESTER Those same noble Scots
    That are your prisoners —
HOTSPUR I'll keep them all.
    By heaven, he shall not have a Scot of them.
220   No, if a Scot would save his soul, he shall not.
    I'll keep them, by this hand.
WORCESTER You start away
    And lend no ear unto my purposes.
    Those prisoners you shall keep.
225 HOTSPUR Nay, I will; that's flat.
    He said he would not ransom Mortimer,
    Forbade my tongue to speak of Mortimer,
    But I will find him when he lies asleep,
    And in his ear I'll holla 'Mortimer!'
230   Nay, I'll have a starling shall be taught to speak
    Nothing but 'Mortimer', and give it him
    To keep his anger still in motion.
WORCESTER Hear you, cousin, a word.

---

197 goodnight i.e. he's dead **or . . . swim** whether he sinks or swims/he'll either sink or swim **199 So** provided **cross** meet/thwart, oppose **207 fathom-line** weighted line used for measuring the depth of water **209 redeem** rescue, restore **thence** from there **210 corrival** rival, competitor **211 out upon** away with **half-faced fellowship** partial, unsatisfactory partnership **212 apprehends** conceives of, perceives **figures** images/forms/figures of speech **213 form** essential principle **attend** consider **214 list** listen **215 cry you mercy** beg your pardon **219 Scot** puns on the sense of 'small payment' **229 holla** shout **232 still** constantly

HOTSPUR All studies here I solemnly defy,
235   Save how to gall and pinch this Bullingbrook.
And that same sword-and-buckler Prince of Wales,
But that I think his father loves him not
And would be glad he met with some mischance,
I would have poisoned him with a pot of ale.
240 **WORCESTER** Farewell, kinsman. I'll talk to you
When you are better tempered to attend.
NORTHUMBERLAND Why, what a wasp-tongued and   *To Hotspur*
impatient fool
Art thou to break into this woman's mood,
Tying thine ear to no tongue but thine own!
245 **HOTSPUR** Why, look you, I am whipped and scourged
with rods,
Nettled and stung with pismires, when I hear
Of this vile politician, Bullingbrook.
In Richard's time — what d'ye call the place? —
A plague upon't, it is in Gloucestershire,
250   'Twas where the madcap duke his uncle kept,
His uncle York, where I first bowed my knee
Unto this king of smiles, this Bullingbrook,
When you and he came back from Ravenspurgh.
NORTHUMBERLAND At Berkeley Castle.
255 **HOTSPUR** You say true.
Why, what a candy deal of courtesy
This fawning greyhound then did proffer me.
'Look when his infant fortune came to age',
And 'gentle Harry Percy' and 'kind cousin'.—
260   O, the devil take such cozeners! — God forgive me,   *To Worcester*
Good uncle, tell your tale, for I have done.
WORCESTER Nay, if you have not, to't again,
We'll stay your leisure.
HOTSPUR I have done, in sooth.
265 **WORCESTER** Then once more to your Scottish prisoners.
Deliver them up without their ransom straight,
And make the Douglas' son your only mean

---

234 defy renounce **235 gall and pinch** irritate and torment **236 sword-and-buckler** weapons
associated with servants; a gentleman carried rapier and dagger **buckler** small shield **237 But that** were
it not for the fact that **238 mischance** accident **241 better…attend** in the right frame of mind to
listen **244 Tying…own** listening to no one but yourself **246 pismires** ants **247 politician** crafty
plotter **250 duke his uncle** i.e. Edmund of Langley, Duke of York **kept** lived **253 Ravenspurgh** Spurn
Head on the Yorkshire coast **254 Berkeley Castle** a castle in Gloucestershire, near Bristol **256 candy
deal** sickly sweet (flattering) quantity **258 Look when** wait for the time when, as soon as **infant…age**
i.e. I come into my inheritance **260 cozeners** deceivers (puns on 'cousin') **263 stay** await **264 sooth**
truth **267 the Douglas' son** i.e. Mordake **mean For powers** agent or means of raising an army

For powers in Scotland, which, for divers reasons
Which I shall send you written, be assured
270 Will easily be granted.— You, my lord,   *To Northumberland*
Your son in Scotland being thus employed,
Shall secretly into the bosom creep
Of that same noble prelate well beloved,
The archbishop.
275 **HOTSPUR** Of York, is't not?
WORCESTER True, who bears hard
His brother's death at Bristol, the lord Scroop.
I speak not this in estimation,
As what I think might be, but what I know
280 Is ruminated, plotted and set down,
And only stays but to behold the face
Of that occasion that shall bring it on.
HOTSPUR I smell it:
Upon my life, it will do wondrous well.
285 **NORTHUMBERLAND** Before the game's afoot, thou still
let'st slip.
HOTSPUR Why, it cannot choose but be a noble plot.
And then the power of Scotland and of York,
To join with Mortimer, ha?
WORCESTER And so they shall.
290 **HOTSPUR** In faith, it is exceedingly well aimed.
WORCESTER And 'tis no little reason bids us speed,
To save our heads by raising of a head.
For, bear ourselves as even as we can,
The king will always think him in our debt,
295 And think we think ourselves unsatisfied,
Till he hath found a time to pay us home.
And see already how he doth begin
To make us strangers to his looks of love.
HOTSPUR He does, he does. We'll be revenged on him.
300 **WORCESTER** Cousin, farewell. No further go in this
Than I by letters shall direct your course.
When time is ripe, which will be suddenly,
I'll steal to Glendower and Lord Mortimer,
Where you and Douglas and our powers at once,

---

268 divers various   **272 bosom** i.e. confidence, trust   **273 prelate** church dignitary   **276 bears hard**
takes badly   **277 Lord Scroop** William Scroop, Earl of Wiltshire, executed by Bullingbrook in 1399; in fact
the archbishop's cousin   **278 estimation** guessing   **281 stays** waits   **face . . . occasion** i.e. opportunity
283 smell it catch the scent, as in hunting   **285 Before . . . slip** you always release the dogs before the
prey has been sighted   **287 power** army   **290 aimed** devised, directed   **292 head** army   **293 even**
steadily, patiently   **296 pay us home** repay us in full/administer a fatal blow   **302 suddenly** soon
303 steal go secretly   **304 at once** all at the same time

305 As I will fashion it, shall happily meet,
To bear our fortunes in our own strong arms,
Which now we hold at much uncertainty.

NORTHUMBERLAND Farewell, good brother. We shall
thrive, I trust.

HOTSPUR Uncle, adieu. O, let the hours be short
310 Till fields and blows and groans applaud our sport!

Exeunt

Act 2 Scene 1   *running scene 4*

Enter a Carrier with a lantern in his hand

FIRST CARRIER Heigh-ho! An't be not four by the day, I'll
be hanged. Charles' wain is over the new chimney,
and yet our horse not packed. What, ostler!

OSTLER Anon, anon.   *Within*

5 **FIRST CARRIER** I prithee, Tom, beat Cut's saddle, put a
few flocks in the point. The poor jade is wrung in the
withers out of all cess.

Enter another Carrier

SECOND CARRIER Peas and beans are as dank here as a
dog, and this is the next way to give poor jades the
10 bots. This house is turned upside down since Robin
the ostler died.

FIRST CARRIER Poor fellow, never joyed since the price of
oats rose. It was the death of him.

SECOND CARRIER I think this is the most villainous
15 house in all London Road for fleas: I am stung like a
tench.

FIRST CARRIER Like a tench? There is ne'er a king in
Christendom could be better bit than I have been
since the first cock.

20 **SECOND CARRIER** Why, you will allow us ne'er a jordan,
and then we leak in your chimney, and your
chamber-lye breeds fleas like a loach.

---

305 happily fortunately   **310 fields** battlefields   **2.1** *Location: an inn-yard on the road between London and Canterbury* **Carrier** delivery-man   **1 by the day** in the morning   **2 Charles' wain** Charlemagne's wagon, old name for the constellation of the Plough   **3 packed** loaded   **ostler** groom at an inn   **4 Anon** soon, in a moment   **5 Tom** presumably the Second Carrier, though possibly the Ostler   **beat Cut's saddle** beating a saddle would soften it; Cut is the horse's name   **6 flocks** tufts of wool (for padding)   **point** pommel of saddle   **jade** worn-out old horse   **wrung...withers** rubbed sore between the shoulders   **7 out...cess** beyond measure   **8 Peas and beans** i.e. horses' food   **dank...dog** damp   **10 bots** intestinal worms   **house** inn   **12 joyed** was happy   **16 tench** freshwater fish with spots said to resemble flea bites   **19 first cock** first cockcrow, midnight   **20 jordan** chamber-pot   **21 leak** urinate   **chimney** fireplace   **22 chamber-lye** urine   **loach** small freshwater fish, thought to harbour fleas

FIRST CARRIER What, ostler! Come away and be hanged! Come away!

25   SECOND CARRIER I have a gammon of bacon and two razes of ginger, to be delivered as far as Charing Cross.

FIRST CARRIER The turkeys in my pannier are quite starved. What, ostler! A plague on thee! Hast thou never an eye in thy head? Canst not hear? An 'twere

30   not as good a deed as drink to break the pate of thee, I am a very villain. Come, and be hanged! Hast no faith in thee?

Enter Gadshill

GADSHILL Good morrow, carriers. What's o'clock?

FIRST CARRIER I think it be two o'clock.

35   GADSHILL I prithee lend me thy lantern to see my gelding in the stable.

FIRST CARRIER Nay, soft, I pray ye; I know a trick worth two of that.

GADSHILL I prithee lend me thine.   *To the Second Carrier*

40   SECOND CARRIER Ay, when? Can'st tell? Lend me thy lantern, quoth a? Marry, I'll see thee hanged first.

GADSHILL Sirrah carrier, what time do you mean to come to London?

SECOND CARRIER Time enough to go to bed with a

45   candle, I warrant thee.— Come, neighbour Mugs, we'll call up the gentlemen. They will along with company, for they have great charge.

Exeunt [Carriers]

Enter Chamberlain

GADSHILL What, ho, Chamberlain?

CHAMBERLAIN At hand, quoth pick-purse.

50   GADSHILL That's even as fair as — at hand, quoth the chamberlain, for thou variest no more from picking

---

23 Come away come along   25 gammon of bacon ham   26 razes either 'races' (roots) or 'rasers' (a measure amounting to four bushels)   Charing Cross village between London and Westminster, site of a market   27 pannier one of a pair of baskets   29 An ... thee if cracking your skull were not as good a thing as drinking   31 Hast have you   faith honesty, trustworthiness   34 two o'clock either an error, since the First Carrier earlier said that he thought it was four o'clock, or a lie to mislead Gadshill (who may have aroused suspicion)   35 gelding castrated horse   37 I know ... that i.e. I'm not so stupid as to fall for such an old trick   40 Ay ... tell? What time is it? Do you know? (repeating Gadshill's earlier request); or proverbial phrase meaning 'you must be joking'   41 quoth a did you say   44 Time ... candle i.e. sometime tonight   45 warrant assure   neighbour Mugs i.e. the First Carrier; neighbour is a friendly form of address   46 call wake   along ... charge want to travel in a group because they're carrying valuable goods   Chamberlain inn attendant in charge of the bedrooms   49 At ... pick-purse I'm ready, as the pickpocket says   50 That's ... as i.e. you might as well have said

of purses than giving direction doth from labouring.
Thou lay'st the plot how.

CHAMBERLAIN Good morrow, Master Gadshill. It holds
55   current that I told you yesternight: there's a franklin
in the wild of Kent hath brought three hundred
marks with him in gold. I heard him tell it to one of
his company last night at supper, a kind of auditor,
one that hath abundance of charge too, God knows
60   what. They are up already, and call for eggs and
butter. They will away presently.

GADSHILL Sirrah, if they meet not with Saint Nicholas'
clerks, I'll give thee this neck.

CHAMBERLAIN No, I'll none of it: I prithee keep that for
65   the hangman, for I know thou worship'st Saint
Nicholas as truly as a man of falsehood may.

GADSHILL What talkest thou to me of the hangman? If
I hang, I'll make a fat pair of gallows, for if I hang, old
Sir John hangs with me, and thou know'st he's no
70   starveling. Tut, there are other Trojans that thou
dream'st not of, the which for sport sake are content
to do the profession some grace; that would, if
matters should be looked into, for their own credit
sake, make all whole. I am joined with no foot-land
75   rakers, no long-staff sixpenny strikers, none of these
mad mustachio purple-hued malt-worms, but with
nobility and tranquillity, burgomasters and great
oneyers, such as can hold in, such as will strike
sooner than speak, and speak sooner than drink, and
80   drink sooner than pray. And yet, I lie, for they pray
continually unto their saint, the commonwealth; or
rather not to pray to her, but prey on her, for they

---

52 **giving ... labouring** giving orders does from working   53 **lay'st ... how** devise the plan, direct the
thief   54 **holds current that** remains true what   55 **franklin** small landowner   56 **wild of Kent** Kentish
weald, wooded country between the North and South Downs of southern England   **three ... gold** i.e. £200,
a mark was an accounting unit (rather than a coin) worth two thirds of a pound   58 **auditor** treasury
official   59 **abundance of charge** a lot of baggage   60 **eggs and butter** i.e. breakfast   61 **presently**
immediately   62 **Saint Nicholas' clerks** thieves, highwaymen; **Saint Nicholas** was supposedly their patron
saint   63 **I'll ... neck** i.e. you can hang me   70 **starveling** skinny, starving person   **Trojans** fine fellows
(slang)   71 **the which** who   72 **profession** i.e. of robbery   74 **make all whole** put everything right, sort
things out   **foot-land rakers** thieves who operate on foot (as opposed to on a horse)   75 **long-staff
sixpenny strikers** thieves who, merely to steal sixpence, strike their victims with a long stick
76 **mustachio purple-hued malt-worms** purple-faced drunkards with large moustaches   77 **tranquillity**
those living a peaceful life   **burgomasters** town officials   78 **oneyers** exact meaning uncertain, perhaps
'ones', i.e. **great** personages   **hold in** hold firm/keep silent   81 **commonwealth** nation

ride up and down on her and make her their boots.
CHAMBERLAIN What, the commonwealth their boots?
85 Will she hold out water in foul way?
GADSHILL She will, she will; justice hath liquored her.
We steal as in a castle, cocksure. We have the receipt
of fern-seed, we walk invisible.
CHAMBERLAIN Nay, I think rather you are more
90 beholding to the night than to fern-seed for your
walking invisible.
GADSHILL Give me thy hand. Thou shalt have a share in
our purpose, as I am a true man.
CHAMBERLAIN Nay, rather let me have it, as you are a
95 false thief.
GADSHILL Go to. *Homo* is a common name to all men.
Bid the ostler bring the gelding out of the stable.
Farewell, ye muddy knave.   *Exeunt*

Act 2 Scene 2   *running scene 5*

Enter Prince, Poins and Peto [and Bardolph]

POINS Come, shelter, shelter. I have removed Falstaff's
horse, and he frets like a gummed velvet.
PRINCE HENRY Stand close.   *Poins, Peto and Bardolph stand aside*
Enter Falstaff
FALSTAFF Poins! Poins, and be hanged! Poins!
5 PRINCE HENRY Peace, ye fat-kidneyed rascal. What a
brawling dost thou keep!
FALSTAFF What, Poins? Hal?
PRINCE HENRY He is walked up to the top of the hill. I'll   *Stands aside*
go seek him.   *with the others*
10 FALSTAFF I am accursed to rob in that thief's company.
That rascal hath removed my horse, and tied him
I know not where. If I travel but four foot by the square
further afoot, I shall break my wind. Well, I doubt not

---

83 **ride** i.e. like a horse, but also with sexual connotations   **boots** booty, plunder (the Chamberlain plays on the sense of 'footwear'; there is also a quibble on the sense of 'vagina')   85 **hold...way** keep you dry on a muddy road/piss herself   86 **liquored** oiled (to make waterproof)/plied with alcohol   87 **as...castle** i.e. in complete safety   **cocksure** completely secure   **receipt of fern-seed** recipe for fern-seed (supposed to confer invisibility)   93 **true** honest   96 *Homo* Latin for 'man'   **common name to** general name for   98 **muddy** muddled, dull-witted (plays on the sense of 'dirty')   **2.2** *Location: the highway near Gad's Hill*   2 **frets...velvet** fusses or, literally, frays like cheap velvet stiffened with gum   3 **close** concealed   5 **fat-kidneyed** i.e. fat-bellied (**rascal** may play on the sense of 'young or inferior deer', a creature Falstaff is frequently compared to)   6 **keep** make, keep up   12 **by the square** exactly   **square** a measuring instrument   13 **break my wind** lose my breath (plays on the sense of 'fart')   **Well...rogue** I expect to die well despite everything, as long as I'm not hanged for killing Poins

but to die a fair death for all this, if I scape hanging for
15   killing that rogue. I have forsworn his company hourly
any time this two-and-twenty year, and yet I am
bewitched with the rogue's company. If the rascal have
not given me medicines to make me love him, I'll be
hanged; it could not be else: I have drunk medicines.
20   Poins, Hal, a plague upon you both! Bardolph! Peto! I'll
starve ere I rob a foot further. An 'twere not as good a
deed as to drink, to turn true man and to leave these
rogues, I am the veriest varlet that ever chewed with a
tooth. Eight yards of uneven ground is threescore and
25   ten miles afoot with me, and the stony-hearted villains
know it well enough. A plague upon't when thieves
cannot be true one to another!   *They whistle*   *The Prince,*
Whew! A plague light upon you all! Give me my horse,   *Poins, Peto and*
you rogues. Give me my horse, and be hanged!   *Bardolph come*
30   **PRINCE HENRY** Peace, ye fat-guts! Lie down, lay thine ear   *forward*
close to the ground and list if thou can hear the tread
of travellers.

FALSTAFF Have you any levers to lift me up again, being
down? I'll not bear mine own flesh so far afoot again
35   for all the coin in thy father's exchequer. What a
plague mean ye to colt me thus?

PRINCE HENRY Thou liest. Thou art not colted, thou art
uncolted.

FALSTAFF I prithee, good Prince Hal, help me to my
40   horse, good king's son.

PRINCE HENRY Out, you rogue! Shall I be your ostler?

FALSTAFF Go, hang thyself in thine own heir-apparent
garters! If I be ta'en, I'll peach for this. An I have not
ballads made on all and sung to filthy tunes, let a cup
45   of sack be my poison. When a jest is so forward, and
afoot too! I hate it.

Enter Gadshill

GADSHILL Stand.

FALSTAFF So I do, against my will.

POINS O, 'tis our setter. I know his voice.

---

18 medicines potions   **21 ere** before   **An** if   **22 turn true man** reform, become honest/become an
informer   **23 veriest varlet** most complete rogue   **28 Whew!** Expression of alarm or perhaps Falstaff trying
to whistle   **35 exchequer** treasury   **36 colt** cheat   **38 uncolted** without a horse   **39 to** i.e. to find, but
the prince takes him to mean 'to mount'   **42 heir-apparent garters** jokes on the fact that as heir apparent,
the prince belonged to the knightly Order of the Garter   **43 peach** turn informer, betray (my
accomplices)   **44 ballads…all** songs made up about you   **filthy** disgraceful, obscene   **45 forward** far
advanced/presumptuous, immodest   **46 afoot** when the robbery plot is underway/when I am on foot
49 setter one who plans robberies

50 **BARDOLPH** What news?

GADSHILL Case ye, case ye; on with your vizards. There's
money of the king's coming down the hill, 'tis going
to the king's exchequer.

FALSTAFF You lie, you rogue, 'tis going to the King's
55 Tavern.

GADSHILL There's enough to make us all.

FALSTAFF To be hanged.

PRINCE HENRY You four shall front them in the narrow
lane. Ned and I will walk lower; if they scape from
60 your encounter, then they light on us.

PETO But how many be of them?

GADSHILL Some eight or ten.

FALSTAFF Will they not rob us?

PRINCE HENRY What, a coward, Sir John Paunch?

65 **FALSTAFF** Indeed, I am not John of Gaunt, your
grandfather; but yet no coward, Hal.

PRINCE HENRY We'll leave that to the proof.

POINS Sirrah Jack, thy horse stands behind the hedge.
When thou need'st him, there thou shalt find him.
70 Farewell, and stand fast.

FALSTAFF Now cannot I strike him, if I should be hanged.

PRINCE HENRY Ned, where are our disguises?   *To Poins*

POINS Here, hard by. Stand close.   *To Prince Henry*

[*Exeunt Prince Henry and Poins*]

FALSTAFF Now, my masters, happy man be his dole, say I.
75 Every man to his business.

Enter Travellers

FIRST TRAVELLER Come, neighbour. The boy shall lead
our horses down the hill. We'll walk afoot awhile,
and ease our legs.

THIEVES Stay!

80 **TRAVELLERS** Jesu bless us!

FALSTAFF Strike, down with them! Cut the villains'
throats. Ah, whoreson caterpillars, bacon-fed knaves!
They hate us youth, down with them, fleece them.

TRAVELLERS O, we are undone, both we and ours for ever!

---

51 **Case ye** mask yourselves   56 **make us all** make our fortunes   58 **front** confront   59 **lower** further
down   60 **light on** come upon   61 **be** are there   65 **Gaunt** plays on the literal sense of 'thin' (though
actually the name was a form of 'Ghent')   67 **proof** test   73 **hard** near   74 **happy…dole** may good
fortune be every man's lot   82 **whoreson caterpillars** bastard parasites   **whoreson** son of a whore
bacon-fed fat, well-fed   83 **youth** youngsters   84 **undone** ruined

85 **FALSTAFF** Hang ye, gorbellied knaves, are you undone?
No, ye fat chuffs, I would your store were here! On,
bacons, on! What, ye knaves? Young men must live.
You are grand-jurors, are ye? We'll jure ye, i'faith.
Here they rob them and bind them   [*Exeunt*]
Enter the Prince and Poins
PRINCE HENRY The thieves have bound the true men.
90 Now could thou and I rob the thieves and go merrily
to London, it would be argument for a week, laughter
for a month and a good jest for ever.
POINS Stand close. I hear them coming.
Enter Thieves again
FALSTAFF Come, my masters, let us share, and then to
95 horse before day. An the prince and Poins be not two
arrant cowards, there's no equity stirring. There's no
more valour in that Poins than in a wild duck.
PRINCE HENRY Your money!
POINS Villains!
As they are sharing, the Prince and Poins set upon them.
They all run away, leaving the booty behind them
100 **PRINCE HENRY** Got with much ease. Now merrily to
horse.
The thieves are scattered and possessed with fear
So strongly that they dare not meet each other:
Each takes his fellow for an officer.
Away, good Ned. Falstaff sweats to death,
105 And lards the lean earth as he walks along.
Were't not for laughing, I should pity him.
POINS How the rogue roared!   *Exeunt*

Act 2 Scene 3   *running scene 6*

Enter Hotspur, solus, reading a letter

HOTSPUR 'But for mine own part, my lord, I could be
well contented to be there, in respect of the love
I bear your house.' He could be contented: why is he
not, then? In respect of the love he bears our house.
5 He shows in this, he loves his own barn better than

---

85 gorbellied big-bellied   **86 chuffs** clowns/misers   **store** savings, full possessions   **87 bacons** pigs
88 grand-jurors wealthy men, eligible to sit on a jury   **jure** judge, see to/make a juror of   **91 argument** a
topic of conversation   **94 my masters** sirs   **96 arrant** absolute   **equity stirring** judgement in the
world   **97 wild duck** i.e. easily frightened   **105 lards** drips fat on   **2.3** *Location: Hotspur's estate*
(historically, Warkworth Castle in Northumberland)   *solus* alone   **3 house** family (Hotspur goes on to
play on the literal meaning, contrasting it with **barn**)

he loves our house. Let me see some more. 'The
purpose you undertake is dangerous' — why, that's
certain: 'tis dangerous to take a cold, to sleep, to
drink. But I tell you, my lord fool, out of this nettle,
10   danger, we pluck this flower, safety. 'The purpose
you undertake is dangerous, the friends you have
named uncertain, the time itself unsorted and your
whole plot too light for the counterpoise of so great
an opposition.' Say you so, say you so? I say unto you
15   again, you are a shallow cowardly hind, and you lie.
What a lack-brain is this? I protest, our plot is as good
a plot as ever was laid; our friends true and constant:
a good plot, good friends, and full of expectation.
An excellent plot, very good friends. What a frosty-
20   spirited rogue is this? Why, my lord of York
commends the plot and the general course of the
action. By this hand if I were now by this rascal,
I could brain him with his lady's fan. Is there not my
father, my uncle and myself, Lord Edmund Mortimer,
25   my lord of York and Owen Glendower? Is there not
besides the Douglas? Have I not all their letters to
meet me in arms by the ninth of the next month?
And are they not some of them set forward already?
What a pagan rascal is this? An infidel! Ha, you shall
30   see now in very sincerity of fear and cold heart, will
he to the king and lay open all our proceedings. O,
I could divide myself and go to buffets, for moving
such a dish of skimmed milk with so honourable an
action! Hang him. Let him tell the king we are
35   prepared. I will set forwards tonight.

Enter his Lady

How now, Kate? I must leave you within these two
hours.

LADY PERCY O, my good lord, why are you thus alone?
For what offence have I this fortnight been
40   A banished woman from my Harry's bed?
Tell me, sweet lord, what is't that takes from thee

---

12 uncertain unreliable   **unsorted** unsuitable   **13 counterpoise** counterbalance   **15 hind** peasant/
menial/nervous female deer   **16 lack-brain** idiot   **protest** declare, affirm   **18 expectation** promise
20 lord of York the Archbishop of York, Richard Scroop   **23 brain ... fan** knock his brains out with a lady's
fan – light and suitable for one with little brain   **26 the Douglas** Archibald, Earl of Douglas; **the** signifies the
head of a Scottish clan   **30 in ... of** i.e. really motivated by   **32 go to buffets** come to blows (with
myself)   **moving** trying to persuade   **33 dish ... milk** i.e. weak, cowardly one   **34 action** course of action/
military enterprise/rhetorical gesture/division in a logical argument   **35 prepared** drawn up for military
action

Thy stomach, pleasure and thy golden sleep?
Why dost thou bend thine eyes upon the earth,
And start so often when thou sit'st alone?
45 Why hast thou lost the fresh blood in thy cheeks,
And given my treasures and my rights of thee
To thick-eyed musing and cursed melancholy?
In my faint slumbers I by thee have watched,
And heard thee murmur tales of iron wars,
50 Speak terms of manage to thy bounding steed,
Cry 'Courage! To the field!' And thou hast talked
Of sallies and retires, trenches, tents,
Of palisadoes, frontiers, parapets,
Of basilisks, of cannon, culverin,
55 Of prisoners' ransom and of soldiers slain,
And all the current of a heady fight.
Thy spirit within thee hath been so at war
And thus hath so bestirred thee in thy sleep,
That beads of sweat hath stood upon thy brow
60 Like bubbles in a late-disturbèd stream;
And in thy face strange motions have appeared,
Such as we see when men restrain their breath
On some great sudden haste. O, what portents are
    these?
Some heavy business hath my lord in hand,
65   And I must know it, else he loves me not.
HOTSPUR What, ho!
[*Enter a Servant*]
    Is Gilliams with the packet gone?
SERVANT He is, my lord, an hour agone.
HOTSPUR Hath Butler brought those horses from the
    sheriff?
70 **SERVANT** One horse, my lord, he brought even now.
HOTSPUR What horse? A roan, a crop-ear, is it not?
SERVANT It is, my lord.

---

42 stomach appetite **46 treasures…rights** treasured intimacy and wifely rights **47 thick-eyed** dull-sighted, preoccupied/heavy-lidded (from lack of sleep) **48 faint** light, restless **watched** remained awake **50 terms of manage** words of control **52 sallies and retires** advances and retreats **53 palisadoes** defensive fortifications **54 basilisks** large cannon (named after a mythical reptile) **culverin** another type of large cannon **56 current** movement, onward flow **heady** violent, swiftly moving **61 motions** movements, expressions/emotions **62 restrain** hold/catch **64 heavy** important, weighty **66 What, ho!** summons to servant **67 Gilliams** name of another servant **packet** packet of letters, dispatch **69 Butler** another servant **70 even** just **71 roan** with a coat of mixed colour **crop-ear** with the top of the ears cropped

HOTSPUR That roan shall be my throne.
Well, I will back him straight. *Esperance*!
75   Bid Butler lead him forth into the park. [*Exit Servant*]
LADY PERCY But hear you, my lord.
HOTSPUR What say'st thou, my lady?
LADY PERCY What is it carries you away?
HOTSPUR Why, my horse, my love, my horse.
80 LADY PERCY Out, you mad-headed ape!
A weasel hath not such a deal of spleen
As you are tossed with. In sooth,
I'll know your business, Harry, that I will.
I fear my brother Mortimer doth stir
85   About his title, and hath sent for you
To line his enterprise. But if you go—
HOTSPUR So far afoot, I shall be weary, love.
LADY PERCY Come, come, you paraquito, answer me
Directly unto this question that I shall ask:
90   Indeed, I'll break thy little finger, Harry,
If thou wilt not tell me true.
HOTSPUR Away,
Away, you trifler! Love? I love thee not.
I care not for thee, Kate. This is no world
95   To play with mammets and to tilt with lips.
We must have bloody noses and cracked crowns,
And pass them current too.— God's me, my horse!
What say'st thou, Kate? What wouldst thou have
with me?
LADY PERCY Do ye not love me? Do ye not, indeed?
100   Well, do not then, for since you love me not,
I will not love myself. Do you not love me?
Nay, tell me if thou speak'st in jest or no.
HOTSPUR Come, wilt thou see me ride?
And when I am a-horseback, I will swear
105   I love thee infinitely. But hark you, Kate,
I must not have you henceforth question me
Whither I go, nor reason whereabout.
Whither I must, I must. And to conclude,

---

74 back mount   **straight** straight away   ***Esperance*!** Hope! (the Percy family motto was '*Esperance ma comforte*', French for 'In hope is my strength/consolation')   **78 carries you away** transports you with emotion   **81 weasel** a notoriously aggressive animal (Hotspur responds literally)   **spleen** anger, impulsiveness   **84 stir** become roused, rebellious   **85 title** claim to the throne   **86 line** support   **88 paraquito** little parrot   **90 little finger** phallic connotations   **93 trifler** frivolous time-waster   **95 mammets** dolls, perhaps with play on Latin *mamma* ('breasts')   **tilt** joust   **96 crowns** heads (plays on the sense of 'coins' as well as having royal connotations)   **97 pass them current** pass them off as good currency   **God's me** God save me   **107 whereabout** speculate why

This evening must I leave thee, gentle Kate.
110   I know you wise, but yet no further wise
Than Harry Percy's wife. Constant you are,
But yet a woman: and for secrecy,
No lady closer, for I well believe
Thou wilt not utter what thou dost not know,
115   And so far will I trust thee, gentle Kate.

LADY PERCY How? So far?

HOTSPUR Not an inch further. But hark you, Kate:
Whither I go, thither shall you go too.
Today will I set forth, tomorrow you.
120   Will this content you, Kate?

LADY PERCY It must of force.   *Exeunt*

Act 2 Scene 4   *running scene 7*

Enter Prince and Poins

PRINCE HENRY Ned, prithee come out of that fat room,
and lend me thy hand to laugh a little.

POINS Where hast been, Hal?

PRINCE HENRY With three or four loggerheads amongst
5   three or fourscore hogsheads. I have sounded the
very base-string of humility. Sirrah, I am sworn
brother to a leash of drawers, and can call them by
their names, as Tom, Dick and Francis. They take it
already upon their confidence that though I be but
10   Prince of Wales, yet I am the king of courtesy, telling
me flatly I am no proud Jack like Falstaff, but a
Corinthian, a lad of mettle, a good boy, and when
I am king of England, I shall command all the good
lads in Eastcheap. They call drinking deep, dyeing
15   scarlet; and when you breathe in your watering, then
they cry 'Hem!' and bid you play it off. To conclude, I
am so good a proficient in one quarter of an hour that

---

111 **Constant** faithful, trustworthy   113 **closer** more tight-lipped   121 **force** necessity   2.4 *Location: a tavern in Eastcheap, London*   1 **fat** stuffy (possibly 'vat')   2 **lend...hand** help me   4 **loggerheads** blockheads, idiots   5 **three or fourscore** sixty or eighty (a score is twenty)   **hogsheads** large wine casks   **sounded...humility** played the lowest note of baseness/humbleness   6 **sworn brother** avowed intimate friend   7 **leash** set of three (usually animals tied together)   **drawers** bartenders, waiters   8 **Francis** name of the bartender Hal subsequently teases   11 **proud** pompous   **Jack** fellow, knave/Jack   **Falstaff** (diminutive version of John)   12 **Corinthian** fine fellow – Corinth in ancient Greece was notorious for riotous living   **mettle** spirit, worth   14 **dyeing scarlet** probably because heavy drinking reddens the complexion; perhaps because urine, a product of drinking, was used to fix dye   15 **breathe...watering** pause for breath while drinking (possibly 'fart while urinating')   16 **'Hem!'** sound of disapproval/a clearing of the throat   **play it off** finish it up

I can drink with any tinker in his own language
during my life. I tell thee, Ned, thou hast lost much
20   honour that thou wert not with me in this action. But,
sweet Ned — to sweeten which name of Ned, I give
thee this pennyworth of sugar, clapped even now into
my hand by an under-skinker, one that never spake
other English in his life than 'Eight shillings and
25   sixpence' and 'You are welcome', with this shrill
addition, 'Anon, anon, sir!— Score a pint of bastard in
the Half-Moon', or so. But, Ned, to drive away time till
Falstaff come, I prithee do thou stand in some by-room
while I question my puny drawer to what end he gave
30   me the sugar and do never leave calling 'Francis', that
his tale to me may be nothing but 'Anon'. Step aside,
and I'll show thee a precedent.

POINS Francis!

PRINCE HENRY Thou art perfect.

35   POINS Francis!   [*Exit Poins*]

Enter Drawer [Francis]

FRANCIS Anon, anon, sir.— Look down into the
Pomgarnet, Ralph.

PRINCE HENRY Come hither, Francis.

FRANCIS My lord?

40   PRINCE HENRY How long hast thou to serve, Francis?

FRANCIS Forsooth, five years, and as much as to—

POINS Francis!   *Within*

FRANCIS Anon, anon, sir.

PRINCE HENRY Five years. By'r lady, a long lease for the
45   clinking of pewter. But Francis, darest thou be so
valiant as to play the coward with thy indenture and
show it a fair pair of heels and run from it?

FRANCIS O lord, sir, I'll be sworn upon all the books in
England, I could find in my heart—

50   POINS Francis!   *Within*

FRANCIS Anon, anon, sir.

---

18 drink . . . language i.e. consort comfortably with a drinker of any social class/drink heavily (tinkers were reputedly heavy drinkers)   **20 action** encounter (usually military)   **22 pennyworth of sugar** small quantity of sugar used to sweeten wine   **23 under-skinker** low-ranking waiter (to 'skink' is to pour out liquor)   **26 Anon** (I'm) coming, just a moment   **Score** put on the bill   **bastard** sweet Spanish wine   **27 Half-Moon** one of the rooms in the tavern   **drive** pass   **28 by-room** side room   **29 puny** inexperienced/young/weedy   **to what end** why   **30 leave** stop   **32 precedent** example   **34 perfect** word-perfect   **37 Pomgarnet** Pomegranate, the name of another room in the tavern   **40 to serve** left of your apprenticeship (the usual length was seven years; Francis is probably fourteen or sixteen)   **44 By'r lady** by Our Lady (the Virgin Mary)   **long . . . pewter** long apprenticeship to learn to be a barman (drinking vessels were made of **pewter**)   **46 indenture** contract by which an apprentice was bound   **48 books** i.e. Bibles

PRINCE HENRY How old art thou, Francis?

FRANCIS Let me see — about Michaelmas next I shall be—

POINS Francis! *Within*

55 **FRANCIS** Anon, sir.— Pray you stay a little, my lord.

PRINCE HENRY Nay, but hark you, Francis, for the sugar
thou gavest me, 'twas a pennyworth, was't not?

FRANCIS O lord, sir, I would it had been two!

PRINCE HENRY I will give thee for it a thousand pound.

60 Ask me when thou wilt, and thou shalt have it.

POINS Francis! *Within*

FRANCIS Anon, anon.

PRINCE HENRY Anon, Francis? No, Francis. But tomorrow,
Francis, or, Francis, on Thursday, or indeed, Francis,

65 when thou wilt. But, Francis!

FRANCIS My lord?

PRINCE HENRY Wilt thou rob this leathern jerkin, crystal-
button, not-pated, agate-ring, puke-stocking, caddis-
garter, smooth-tongue, Spanish-pouch—

70 **FRANCIS** O lord, sir, who do you mean?

PRINCE HENRY Why, then, your brown bastard is your
only drink, for look you, Francis, your white canvas
doublet will sully. In Barbary, sir, it cannot come to
so much.

75 **FRANCIS** What, sir?

POINS Francis! *Within*

PRINCE HENRY Away, you rogue! Dost thou hear them
call?

*Here they both call him. The Drawer stands amazed, not
knowing which way to go*
Enter Vintner

VINTNER What, stand'st thou still, and hear'st such a

80 calling? Look to the guests within.   *[Exit Francis]*
My lord, old Sir John, with half-a-dozen more, are at
the door: shall I let them in?

PRINCE HENRY Let them alone awhile, and then open the
door.   *[Exit Vintner]*

85 Poins!

---

53 Michaelmas the feast of Saint Michael, 29 September   **55 stay** wait   **56 for** as for, about   **67 rob** i.e.
rob your master of service by running away   **leathern jerkin** (the master who wears a) tight-fitting leather
jacket   **crystal-button** fashionable shiny buttons   **68 not-pated** short-haired   **agate-ring** ring set with a
carved agate stone   **puke-stocking** dark-coloured heavy woollen stockings   **caddis-garter** garter made of
woollen tape   **69 smooth-tongue** smooth-talker, flatterer   **Spanish-pouch** wallet of Spanish leather
71 brown bastard Spanish wine, sweeter than the white variety   **your only drink** the best of drinks
73 doublet tight-fitting jacket   **sully** get dirty   **Barbary** region in northern Africa (from which sugar was
imported)   **it** i.e. sugar   *amazed* dumbfounded   *Vintner* innkeeper selling wine

Enter Poins

POINS Anon, anon, sir.

PRINCE HENRY Sirrah, Falstaff and the rest of the thieves
are at the door. Shall we be merry?

POINS As merry as crickets, my lad. But hark ye: what
90   cunning match have you made with this jest of the
drawer? Come, what's the issue?

PRINCE HENRY I am now of all humours that have
showed themselves humours since the old days of
goodman Adam to the pupil age of this present
95   twelve o'clock at midnight.

[*Enter Francis*]

What's o'clock, Francis?

FRANCIS Anon, anon, sir.   [*Exit*]

PRINCE HENRY That ever this fellow should have fewer
words than a parrot, and yet the son of a woman! His
100   industry is upstairs and downstairs, his eloquence the
parcel of a reckoning. I am not yet of Percy's mind,
the Hotspur of the north, he that kills me some six or
seven dozen of Scots at a breakfast, washes his hands,
and says to his wife 'Fie upon this quiet life! I want
105   work.' 'O my sweet Harry', says she, 'how many hast
thou killed today?' 'Give my roan horse a drench',
says he, and answers 'Some fourteen', an hour
after, 'a trifle, a trifle'. I prithee call in Falstaff. I'll
play Percy, and that damned brawn shall play
110   Dame Mortimer his wife. 'Rivo!' says the drunkard.
Call in ribs, call in tallow.   *Poins calls*

*Enter Falstaff, [Gadshill, Bardolph and Peto. Francis follows
with wine]*

POINS Welcome, Jack. Where hast thou been?

FALSTAFF A plague of all cowards, I say, and a
vengeance too, marry and amen!— Give me a cup
115   of sack, boy.— Ere I lead this life long, I'll sew nether
stocks and mend them and foot them too. A plague of   *To Francis*

---

89 merry as crickets proverbial presumably because they jump about 'singing'   **90 cunning match** clever
game, contest of wits   **91 issue** outcome, point   **92 I...midnight** I now understand all the moods that
have ever existed from the beginning of time until now (i.e. I'm in the mood for anything/I have seen
everything)   **94 goodman** title for those below the rank of gentleman (the biblical **Adam** was a gardener)
pupil age youthful time (i.e. the present)   **97 Anon** puns on 'one' (pronounced similarly)   **99 yet**
nevertheless (be)   **100 industry** business, labour, diligence   **is** is to run   **the...reckoning** consists of the
items on a bill   **101 mind** opinion, way of thinking   **102 kills me** kills (**me** is colloquial/emphatic)
106 drench drink/draught of medicine   **109 brawn** lump of flesh/fattened boar or pig   **110 'Rivo!'**
presumably a drinking cry; of uncertain origin   **111 ribs** fatty meat on bones (i.e. Falstaff)   **tallow** animal
fat   **113 of** on   **115 nether stocks** stockings for the lower leg   **116 foot** darn the sole, repair the foot

all cowards!— Give me a cup of sack, rogue. Is there
no virtue extant?   *Drinks*

PRINCE HENRY Didst thou never see Titan kiss a dish of
120 butter — pitiful-hearted Titan — that melted at
the sweet tale of the sun? If thou didst, then behold
that compound.

FALSTAFF You rogue, here's lime in this sack too.—
There is nothing but roguery to be found in villainous   *To Francis*
125 man; yet a coward is worse than a cup of sack with
lime in't.   [*Francis may exit*]
A villainous coward! Go thy ways, old Jack, die when
thou wilt, if manhood, good manhood, be not forgot
upon the face of the earth, then am I a shotten
130 herring. There lives not three good men unhanged
in England, and one of them is fat and grows old.
God help the while! A bad world, I say. I would I were
a weaver. I could sing all manner of songs. A plague
of all cowards, I say still.

135 **PRINCE HENRY** How now, wool-sack, what mutter you?

FALSTAFF A king's son? If I do not beat thee out of thy
kingdom with a dagger of lath, and drive all thy
subjects afore thee like a flock of wild geese, I'll never
wear hair on my face more. You Prince of Wales?

140 **PRINCE HENRY** Why, you whoreson round man, what's
the matter?

FALSTAFF Are you not a coward? Answer me to that.
And Poins there?

POINS Ye fat paunch, an ye call me coward, I'll stab thee.

145 **FALSTAFF** I call thee coward? I'll see thee damned ere I call
thee coward, but I would give a thousand pound
I could run as fast as thou canst. You are straight
enough in the shoulders, you care not who sees your
back. Call you that backing of your friends? A plague
150 upon such backing! Give me them that will face me.
Give me a cup of sack. I am a rogue, if I drunk today.

---

118 virtue extant courage still alive   **119 Titan** Roman sun god (large and red-faced like Falstaff as he
'kisses' the cup of sack); there may be sexual innuendo in **butter** (a whore was a 'dish of butter'), **melted**
(ejaculated) and **tale** (puns on 'tail', i.e. genitals)   **120 pitiful-hearted** compassionate, tender
122 compound mixture (melted butter), i.e. either Falstaff and sack or Falstaff and sweat   **123 lime**
calcium oxide, used to preserve wine   **127 Go thy ways** off you go   **129 shotten herring** a herring that
has spawned its eggs (i.e. thin and weak)   **132 while** present age   **133 weaver** many were Protestant
immigrants, known for psalm-singing   **135 wool-sack** large bale of wool; judges traditionally sat on
them   **137 dagger of lath** stage dagger made of soft wood, traditionally used by the comic Vice in morality
plays   **138 I'll...more** i.e. I'm not a real man   **139 hair** a beard   **140 round** fat/plain speaking
149 backing supporting/turning one's back, running away   **150 face** stand face to face/defy,
contradict   **151 drunk** have had anything to drink

PRINCE HENRY O, villain, thy lips are scarce wiped since
   thou drunk'st last.

FALSTAFF All's one for that.   *He drinks*
155   A plague of all cowards, still say I.

PRINCE HENRY What's the matter?

FALSTAFF What's the matter? Here be four of us have
   ta'en a thousand pound this morning.

PRINCE HENRY Where is it, Jack? Where is it?

160 **FALSTAFF** Where is it? Taken from us it is: a hundred
   upon poor four of us.

PRINCE HENRY What, a hundred, man?

FALSTAFF I am a rogue, if I were not at half-sword with a
   dozen of them two hours together. I have scaped by
165   miracle. I am eight times thrust through the doublet,
   four through the hose, my buckler cut through and
   through, my sword hacked like a hand-saw — *ecce
   signum*! I never dealt better since I was a man: all
   would not do. A plague of all cowards! Let them
170   speak; if they speak more or less than truth, they are
   villains and the sons of darkness.

PRINCE HENRY Speak, sirs, how was it?

GADSHILL We four set upon some dozen—

FALSTAFF Sixteen at least, my lord.

175 **GADSHILL** And bound them.

PETO No, no, they were not bound.

FALSTAFF You rogue, they were bound, every man of
   them, or I am a Jew else, an Ebrew Jew.

GADSHILL As we were sharing, some six or seven fresh
180   men set upon us—

FALSTAFF And unbound the rest, and then come in the
   other.

PRINCE HENRY What, fought ye with them all?

FALSTAFF All? I know not what ye call all, but if I fought
185   not with fifty of them, I am a bunch of radish: if there
   were not two or three and fifty upon poor old Jack,
   then am I no two-legged creature.

POINS Pray heaven you have not murdered some of them.

---

154 **All's . . . that** so what, it doesn't matter   158 **ta'en** taken   161 **poor** only   163 **at half-sword** at close
quarters/fighting with short swords   166 **hose** breeches   **buckler** small shield – sword and buckler were
considered old-fashioned or lower-class weapons   167 **like a hand-saw** with the edge so notched from
blows it appears serrated like the blade of a saw   *ecce signum* 'behold the sign or proof' (Latin; echoes
words from the Catholic Mass)   168 **dealt** fought   **all . . . do** all this was not enough though   171 **sons of
darkness** biblical phrase (1 Thessalonians 5:5)   178 **Ebrew Jew** a real (Hebrew) Jew, i.e. a knave
181 **come . . . other** the others came in

FALSTAFF Nay, that's past praying for, I have peppered
190   two of them: two I am sure I have paid, two rogues
in buckram suits. I tell thee what, Hal, if I tell thee a
lie, spit in my face, call me horse. Thou knowest my
old ward. Here I lay and thus I bore my point. Four
rogues in buckram let drive at me—

195 **PRINCE HENRY** What, four? Thou saidst but two even now.

FALSTAFF Four, Hal, I told thee four.

POINS Ay, ay, he said four.

FALSTAFF These four came all a-front, and mainly
thrust at me. I made no more ado but took all their
200   seven points in my target, thus.

PRINCE HENRY Seven? Why, there were but four even
now.

FALSTAFF In buckram?

POINS Ay, four, in buckram suits.

205 **FALSTAFF** Seven, by these hilts, or I am a villain else.

PRINCE HENRY Prithee let him alone. We shall have   *Aside to Poins*
more anon.

FALSTAFF Dost thou hear me, Hal?

PRINCE HENRY Ay, and mark thee too, Jack.

210 **FALSTAFF** Do so, for it is worth the listening to. These
nine in buckram that I told thee of—

PRINCE HENRY So, two more already.

FALSTAFF Their points being broken—

POINS Down fell his hose.

215 **FALSTAFF** Began to give me ground. But I followed me
close, came in foot and hand; and with a thought
seven of the eleven I paid.

PRINCE HENRY O, monstrous! Eleven buckram men
grown out of two?

220 **FALSTAFF** But, as the devil would have it, three
misbegotten knaves in Kendal green came at my
back and let drive at me; for it was so dark, Hal, that
thou couldst not see thy hand.

---

189 peppered made it hot for, stabbed repeatedly   **190 paid** settled with, killed   **191 buckram** coarse
linen cloth   **193 ward** defensive posture (fencing term)   **lay** positioned myself   **bore my point** pointed my
sword   **194 let drive at** bore down on, attacked   **198 a-front** abreast   **mainly** violently
199 made...ado didn't wait any longer   **200 points** sword points   **target** shield   **205 these hilts** this
sword handle   **209 mark** observe, take note of/keep count   **213 points** sword points, but Poins takes it to
mean the laces attaching the **hose** to the doublet   **215 give me ground** back away (**me** is emphatic)
216 foot and hand at close range   **with a thought** as quick as thought   **221 misbegotten** wretched,
bastard   **Kendal green** coarse, green woollen cloth from Kendal in Cumbria (associated with forest outlaws)

PRINCE HENRY These lies are like the father that begets
225   them, gross as a mountain, open, palpable. Why,
         thou clay-brained guts, thou knotty-pated fool, thou
         whoreson, obscene, greasy tallow-catch—
FALSTAFF What, art thou mad? Art thou mad? Is not the
         truth the truth?
230 PRINCE HENRY Why, how couldst thou know these men
         in Kendal green when it was so dark thou couldst not
         see thy hand? Come, tell us your reason: what say'st
         thou to this?
POINS Come, your reason, Jack, your reason.
235 FALSTAFF What, upon compulsion? No. Were I at the
         strappado, or all the racks in the world, I would not
         tell you on compulsion. Give you a reason on
         compulsion? If reasons were as plentiful as
         blackberries, I would give no man a reason upon
240   compulsion, I.
PRINCE HENRY I'll be no longer guilty of this sin. This
         sanguine coward, this bed-presser, this horseback-
         breaker, this huge hill of flesh—
FALSTAFF Away, you starveling, you elf-skin, you dried
245   neat's tongue, bull's pizzle, you stock-fish! O, for
         breath to utter what is like thee! You tailor's-yard,
         you sheath, you bowcase, you vile standing-tuck—
PRINCE HENRY Well, breathe awhile, and then to't again:
         and when thou hast tired thyself in base
250   comparisons, hear me speak but thus.
POINS Mark, Jack.
PRINCE HENRY We two saw you four set on four and
         bound them, and were masters of their wealth. Mark
         now, how a plain tale shall put you down. Then did

---

224 father i.e. Falstaff, here compared to the devil – the proverbial 'father of lies'   **begets** conceives,
creates **226 clay-brained** dull-witted   **knotty-pated** thick-headed   **227 tallow-catch** accumulation of
animal fat   **235 upon compulsion** under force   **236 strappado** means of torture: the victim was raised by
ropes that tied his arms behind his back, then dropped suddenly, which usually dislocated the joints   **racks**
instruments of torture: the victim was tied to a frame which was then extended, stretching the arms and legs
in opposite directions   **238 reasons** puns on 'raisins' (i.e. grapes, less readily available than **blackberries**)
242 sanguine red-faced (with **coward**, this creates an oxymoron, as a sanguine temperament was equated
with courage)   **bed-presser** heavyweight who will strain beds; perhaps also lazy, one who stays in
bed   **horseback-breaker** one so fat he breaks horse's backs (pun on 'horse'/'whore's')   **244 elf-skin** man
of shrunken, fragile form (often emended to 'eel-skin')   **245 neat's** ox's   **pizzle** penis; a dried bull's penis
was sometimes used as a whip   **stock-fish** dried cod (suggestive of physical weakness and an impotent
penis)   **246 tailor's-yard** measuring yardstick/penis (tailors were sometimes imaged as thin or effeminate
men)   **247 sheath** cover for knife or sword, i.e. empty case/vagina   **bowcase** long, thin case for an
archer's bow, hence starveling/vagina   **standing-tuck** slender sword that is either rigid (i.e. useless because
insufficiently resilient) or upright (not engaged in action) or idle, delaying; with phallic connotations

255   we two set on you four, and with a word, out-faced
    you from your prize, and have it, yea, and can show
    it you in the house. And, Falstaff, you carried your
    guts away as nimbly, with as quick dexterity, and
    roared for mercy and still ran and roared, as ever
260   I heard bull-calf. What a slave art thou, to hack
    thy sword as thou hast done, and then say it was in
    fight! What trick, what device, what starting-hole
    canst thou now find out to hide thee from this
    open and apparent shame?

265 **POINS** Come, let's hear, Jack: what trick hast thou now?
    FALSTAFF I knew ye as well as he that made ye. Why,
    hear ye, my masters, was it for me to kill the heir-
    apparent? Should I turn upon the true prince?
    Why, thou knowest I am as valiant as Hercules,
270   but beware instinct. The lion will not touch the true
    prince. Instinct is a great matter. I was a coward on
    instinct. I shall think the better of myself and thee
    during my life: I for a valiant lion, and thou for a true
    prince. But, lads, I am glad you have the money.—
275   Hostess, clap to the doors. Watch tonight, pray
    tomorrow. Gallants, lads, boys, hearts of gold, all the
    good titles of fellowship come to you! What, shall we
    be merry? Shall we have a play extempore?

    PRINCE HENRY Content, and the argument shall be thy
280   running away.

    FALSTAFF Ah, no more of that, Hal, an thou lovest me!
    Enter Hostess [Quickly]

    HOSTESS QUICKLY My lord the prince?

    PRINCE HENRY How now, my lady the hostess? What
    say'st thou to me?

285   **HOSTESS QUICKLY** Marry, my lord, there is a nobleman
    of the court at door would speak with you: he says he
    comes from your father.

    PRINCE HENRY Give him as much as will make him a
    royal man, and send him back again to my mother.

290   **FALSTAFF** What manner of man is he?

---

255 with a word in a word/with merely a single word   **out-faced** confronted and intimidated   **260 slave** base-minded villain   **262 starting-hole** bolt-hole, hiding place   **264 apparent** evident   **266 knew** recognized   **269 Hercules** Greek hero renowned for strength   **270 instinct** impulse/innate tendency/ intuition   **lion...prince** lions were popularly thought to recognize and refuse to harm royalty   **275 clap to** shut   **Watch** remain awake (for revelry)/be on guard   **276 Gallants** fine, fashionable young men **hearts** fine companions   **278 extempore** immediately, improvised without rehearsal   **279 argument** plot, theme   **281 an** if   **289 royal** plays on the sense of 'coin of greater value than the "noble" [another type of coin]'

HOSTESS QUICKLY An old man.

FALSTAFF What doth gravity out of his bed at midnight?
Shall I give him his answer?

PRINCE HENRY Prithee do, Jack.

295 **FALSTAFF** 'Faith, and I'll send him packing.   *Exit*

PRINCE HENRY Now, sirs: you fought fair; so did you,
Peto, so did you, Bardolph. You are lions too, you ran
away upon instinct. You will not touch the true
prince; no, fie!

300 **BARDOLPH** 'Faith, I ran when I saw others run.

PRINCE HENRY Tell me now in earnest, how came
Falstaff's sword so hacked?

PETO Why, he hacked it with his dagger, and said he
would swear truth out of England but he would make

305 you believe it was done in fight, and persuaded us to
do the like.

BARDOLPH Yea, and to tickle our noses with spear-grass
to make them bleed, and then to beslubber our
garments with it and swear it was the blood of true

310 men. I did that I did not this seven years before,
I blushed to hear his monstrous devices.

PRINCE HENRY O, villain, thou stolest a cup of sack
eighteen years ago, and wert taken with the manner,
and ever since thou hast blushed extempore. Thou

315 hadst fire and sword on thy side, and yet thou ran'st
away; what instinct hadst thou for it?

BARDOLPH My lord, do you see these meteors? Do you
behold these exhalations?

PRINCE HENRY I do.

320 **BARDOLPH** What think you they portend?

PRINCE HENRY Hot livers and cold purses.

BARDOLPH Choler, my lord, if rightly taken.

PRINCE HENRY No, if rightly taken, halter.

Enter Falstaff

Here comes lean Jack, here comes bare-bone.— How

---

292 **gravity** aged respectability   299 **fie** expression of reproach or disgust   304 **swear**...**England** swear
(falsely) with such conviction that truth fled the country   307 **spear-grass** tough, coarse grass
308 **beslubber** daub, smear   309 **true** valiant/honest   310 **that** something   311 **monstrous devices**
outrageous tricks   313 **taken**...**manner** caught red-handed with the evidence/got into the habit
314 **extempore** spontaneously (i.e. Bardolph has a permanently red face from drinking)   315 **fire** i.e. a fiery
face   317 **meteors**...**exhalations** i.e. red blotches on Bardolph's face; meteors were considered bad omens
and thought to result from the sun sucking up poisonous vapours from the earth   320 **portend** foretell
321 **Hot**...**purses** drunkenness and poverty   322 **Choler** anger (choler was one of the four bodily
'humours' governing the disposition)   **rightly taken** correctly understood (the prince shifts the sense to
'justly arrested')   323 **halter** a noose (Hal puns on **choler**/collar)

325   now, my sweet creature of bombast? How long is't
    ago, Jack, since thou saw'st thine own knee?

FALSTAFF My own knee? When I was about thy years,
    Hal, I was not an eagle's talon in the waist. I could
    have crept into any alderman's thumb-ring. A plague
330   of sighing and grief! It blows a man up like a bladder.
    There's villainous news abroad: here was Sir John
    Braby from your father; you must go to the court in
    the morning. That same mad fellow of the north,
    Percy, and he of Wales that gave Amamon the
335   bastinado and made Lucifer cuckold and swore the
    devil his true liegeman upon the cross of a Welsh
    hook — what a plague call you him?

POINS O, Glendower.

FALSTAFF Owen, Owen the same, and his son-in-law
340   Mortimer, and old Northumberland, and that
    sprightly Scot of Scots, Douglas, that runs
    o'horseback up a hill perpendicular—

PRINCE HENRY He that rides at high speed and with a
    pistol kills a sparrow flying.

345 **FALSTAFF** You have hit it.

PRINCE HENRY So did he never the sparrow.

FALSTAFF Well, that rascal hath good mettle in him. He
    will not run.

PRINCE HENRY Why, what a rascal art thou then, to
350   praise him so for running?

FALSTAFF A-horseback, ye cuckoo, but afoot he will not
    budge a foot.

PRINCE HENRY Yes, Jack, upon instinct.

FALSTAFF I grant ye, upon instinct. Well, he is there too,
355   and one Mordake, and a thousand blue-caps more.
    Worcester is stolen away by night. Thy father's beard
    is turned white with the news; you may buy land
    now as cheap as stinking mackerel.

---

325 bombast padding/high-flown language   **328 an . . . in** the width of an eagle's claw around
329 alderman's thumb-ring seal ring often worn by wealthy citizens on the thumb   **334 Percy** i.e.
Hotspur   **he of Wales** i.e. Glendower   **Amamon** name of a demon   **335 bastinado** beating with a
stick   **Lucifer** the devil   **cuckold** man with an unfaithful wife   **swore . . . liegeman** made the devil swear
to be his true servant   **336 Welsh hook** hooked staff used as a weapon and lacking the cross shape of a
sword (on which oaths were customarily sworn)   **337 what a plague** intensified form of 'what'   **345 hit it**
got it right (the prince plays on the literal sense)   **347 mettle** spirit (plays on the sense of 'metal', i.e. not
fluid and liable to **run**)   **348 run** flee (plays on sense of 'melt')   **350 running** i.e. speeding o' **horseback**
351 cuckoo i.e. mindless repeater of words   **355 blue-caps** Scottish soldiers, who wore blue hats
357 you . . . mackerel i.e. for very little indeed – mackerel was a cheap fish even when fresh; perhaps land
was being sold off to raise money for war or because of general economic anxiety about conflict (**mackerel**
plays on the sense of 'pimp/whore')

PRINCE HENRY Then 'tis like, if there come a hot sun and
360   this civil buffeting hold, we shall buy maidenheads as
they buy hob-nails, by the hundreds.

FALSTAFF By the mass, lad, thou say'st true. It is like we
shall have good trading that way. But tell me, Hal,
art not thou horrible afeard? Thou being heir
365   apparent, could the world pick thee out three such
enemies again as that fiend Douglas, that spirit
Percy, and that devil Glendower? Art not thou
horrible afraid? Doth not thy blood thrill at it?

PRINCE HENRY Not a whit, I lack some of thy instinct.

370   FALSTAFF Well, thou wilt be horrible chid tomorrow
when thou comest to thy father: if thou do love me,
practise an answer.

PRINCE HENRY Do thou stand for my father, and
examine me upon the particulars of my life.

375   FALSTAFF Shall I? Content. This chair shall be my
state, this dagger my sceptre and this cushion my
crown.

PRINCE HENRY Thy state is taken for a joint-stool, thy
golden sceptre for a leaden dagger, and thy precious
380   rich crown for a pitiful bald crown.

FALSTAFF Well, an the fire of grace be not quite out of
thee, now shalt thou be moved. Give me a cup of sack
to make mine eyes look red, that it may be thought
I have wept, for I must speak in passion, and I will do
385   it in King Cambyses' vein.

PRINCE HENRY Well, here is my leg.   *He bows or kneels*

FALSTAFF And here is my speech. Stand aside, nobility.

HOSTESS QUICKLY This is excellent sport, i'faith!

FALSTAFF Weep not, sweet queen, for trickling tears are
390   vain.

---

359 like likely   hot plays on angry/lecherous   360 buffeting hold strife continues   maidenheads
virginities   as . . . hundreds i.e. as cheaply as nails for boots, suggesting that in troubled times women will
be raped or forced to sell themselves   363 trading commerce/prostitution/sex   366 spirit devil (though the
word also has connotations of 'courage')   368 thrill tremble/go cold   370 chid scolded   373 stand for
stand in for, play the part of   374 particulars details   375 Content I'm content, very well   376 state
throne   378 joint-stool low stool made by a joiner ('I took you for a joint stool' was a way of mockingly
apologising for ignoring someone)   380 crown head   381 fire of grace effects of divine grace
382 moved affected emotionally, stirred   385 King Cambyses' vein ranting style; Cambyses was the
tyrant in Thomas Preston's *Life of Cambyses, King of Persia* (1569)   387 Stand aside, nobility presumably
those in the tavern are being asked to clear a space   389 Weep . . . vain Falstaff addresses Mistress Quickly,
who is presumably weeping from merriment (puns on 'quean', i.e. harlot, whore)

HOSTESS QUICKLY O, the father, how he holds his countenance!

FALSTAFF For God's sake, lords, convey my tristful queen, For tears do stop the flood-gates of her eyes.

395 **HOSTESS QUICKLY** O, rare, he doth it as like one of these harlotry players as ever I see!

FALSTAFF Peace, good pint-pot, peace, good ticklebrain.— Harry, I do not only marvel where thou spendest thy time, but also how thou art accompanied,

400 for though the camomile, the more it is trodden the faster it grows, yet youth, the more it is wasted the sooner it wears. Thou art my son, I have partly thy mother's word, partly my opinion, but chiefly a villainous trick of thine eye and a foolish hanging of

405 thy nether lip that doth warrant me. If then thou be son to me, here lieth the point: why, being son to me, art thou so pointed at? Shall the blessed sun of heaven prove a micher and eat blackberries? A question not to be asked. Shall the son of England

410 prove a thief and take purses? A question to be asked. There is a thing, Harry, which thou hast often heard of and it is known to many in our land by the name of pitch: this pitch, as ancient writers do report, doth defile; so doth the company thou keepest. For,

415 Harry, now I do not speak to thee in drink but in tears: not in pleasure but in passion: not in words only, but in woes also. And yet there is a virtuous man whom I have often noted in thy company, but I know not his name.

420 **PRINCE HENRY** What manner of man, an it like your majesty?

FALSTAFF A goodly portly man, i'faith, and a corpulent: of a cheerful look, a pleasing eye and a most noble

↓Quickly may exit, perhaps escorted by Bardolph↓

---

391 **O, the father** i.e. in God's name; or refers to Falstaff acting the part of the prince's father   **holds his countenance** keeps a straight face, remains in character   **393 convey** take away/escort (to a seat) **tristful** sorrowful   **394 stop** fill up   **395 rare** marvellous   **396 harlotry players** knavish actors **397 pint-pot** Falstaff addresses Mistress Quickly with a nickname for one who sells beer   **tickle-brain** potent liquor (here, one who sells it)   **400 camomile** daisy-like plant with medicinal qualities; it grows rapidly, proverbially more so when trodden on   **404 trick** habit, feature   **foolish...lip** way of hanging your lower lip, regarded as a sign of loose living   **foolish** affected/idiotic/lecherous   **405 warrant** assure   **407 pointed at** i.e. gossiped about/mocked   **sun** puns on 'son'   **408 micher** truant/loiterer/petty thief   **413 pitch** black tar-like substance   **414 defile** stain, corrupt; Falstaff paraphrases Ecclesiastes 13:1: 'Whoso toucheth pitch shall be defiled'   **416 passion** sincere emotion, distress   **420 an it like** if it please   **422 portly** dignified/fat   **corpulent** solid, well-built/fat   **423 noble carriage** dignified bearing

carriage, and as I think, his age some fifty, or, by'r
425   lady, inclining to threescore; and now I remember
me, his name is Falstaff. If that man should be lewdly
given, he deceives me; for, Harry, I see virtue in his
looks. If then the tree may be known by the fruit, as
the fruit by the tree, then peremptorily I speak it,
430   there is virtue in that Falstaff: him keep with, the rest
banish. And tell me now, thou naughty varlet, tell
me, where hast thou been this month?
PRINCE HENRY Dost thou speak like a king? Do thou
stand for me, and I'll play my father.
435   **FALSTAFF** Depose me? If thou dost it half so gravely,
so majestically, both in word and matter, hang me
up by the heels for a rabbit-sucker or a poulter's
hare.
PRINCE HENRY Well, here I am set.
440   **FALSTAFF** And here I stand. Judge, my masters.
PRINCE HENRY Now, Harry, whence come you?
FALSTAFF My noble lord, from Eastcheap.
PRINCE HENRY The complaints I hear of thee are
grievous.
445   **FALSTAFF** I'faith, my lord, they are false. — Nay, I'll
tickle ye for a young prince.
PRINCE HENRY Swearest   thou,   ungracious   boy?
Henceforth ne'er look on me. Thou art violently
carried away from grace: there is a devil haunts thee
450   in the likeness of a fat old man; a tun of man is thy
companion. Why dost thou converse with that trunk
of humours, that bolting-hutch of beastliness, that
swollen parcel of dropsies, that huge bombard of
sack, that stuffed cloak-bag of guts, that roasted
455   Manningtree ox with the pudding in his belly, that
reverend Vice, that grey Iniquity, that father Ruffian,

---

425 **three score** sixty   426 **lewdly given** wickedly, lasciviously inclined   429 **peremptorily**
determinedly   431 **naughty** wicked   437 **rabbit-sucker** unweaned baby rabbit   **poulter's hare** hare
hanging up in a poulterer's shop (which sold fowl and game)   439 **set** seated (on the mock throne)
440 **Judge, my masters** the tavern audience must decide who is the more kingly   446 **tickle ye** amuse
you in the role of   447 **ungracious** without grace, blasphemous   450 **tun** large barrel especially for wine
or beer/ton weight   451 **converse** associate   **trunk** container/body   452 **humours** diseases/fluids that
determine the disposition: blood, bile, choler, phlegm   **bolting-hutch** large bin used for sifting grain
453 **dropsies** diseases which made the body swell with an accumulation of fluid   **bombard** a leather wine
jug   454 **cloak-bag** large bag for carrying clothes   455 **Manningtree** Essex town with a well-known fair
and cattle market   **pudding** stuffing/sausage   456 **reverend** worthy of respect   **Vice** comic character in
medieval morality plays who tempted the youthful hero   **grey** grey-haired   **Iniquity** sinfulness/allegorical
name for morality play character   **father** i.e. elderly

that Vanity in years? Wherein is he good, but to taste
sack and drink it? Wherein neat and cleanly, but to
carve a capon and eat it? Wherein cunning, but in
460   craft? Wherein crafty, but in villainy? Wherein
villainous, but in all things? Wherein worthy, but
in nothing?

FALSTAFF I would your grace would take me with you:
whom means your grace?

465   PRINCE HENRY That villainous abominable misleader of
youth, Falstaff, that old white-bearded Satan.

FALSTAFF My lord, the man I know.

PRINCE HENRY I know thou dost.

FALSTAFF But to say I know more harm in him than in
470   myself, were to say more than I know. That he is old,
the more the pity, his white hairs do witness it. But
that he is, saving your reverence, a whoremaster,
that I utterly deny. If sack and sugar be a fault,
heaven help the wicked: if to be old and merry be a
475   sin, then many an old host that I know is damned: if
to be fat be to be hated, then Pharaoh's lean kine are
to be loved. No, my good lord, banish Peto, banish
Bardolph, banish Poins, but for sweet Jack Falstaff,
kind Jack Falstaff, true Jack Falstaff, valiant Jack
480   Falstaff, and therefore more valiant, being, as he is
old Jack Falstaff, banish not him thy Harry's
company, banish not him thy Harry's company:
banish plump Jack, and banish all the world.

PRINCE HENRY I do, I will.   *Knocking*

Enter Bardolph, running

485   BARDOLPH O, my lord, my lord! The sheriff with a most
monstrous watch is at the door.

FALSTAFF Out, you rogue!— Play out the play: I have
much to say in the behalf of that Falstaff.

Enter the Hostess [Quickly]

HOSTESS QUICKLY O, my lord, my lord!

---

457 **Vanity** vain, proud, foolish, worthless character   **in years** i.e. advanced in years, aged   **Where-in ... good** what is he good for   458 **neat and cleanly** refined and skilful   459 **cunning** knowledgeable, skilful   460 **craft** deceit   **crafty** skilful   463 **take ... you** enable me to follow you, help me to understand   467 **the ... know** i.e. I recognize the man but not the description   472 **saving your reverence** begging your pardon/if you will excuse my language   **whoremaster** user of whores, i.e. a wicked man   475 **host** innkeeper, pub landlord   476 **Pharaoh's lean kine** biblical reference to Pharaoh's dream in which the seven lean **kine** (cattle) devour the seven fat kine, foretelling famine to come (Genesis 41:1–31)   486 **monstrous** unnaturally large   **watch** group of citizens responsible for keeping order in the streets at night

490 PRINCE HENRY Heigh, heigh! The devil rides upon a
fiddlestick. What's the matter?

HOSTESS QUICKLY The sheriff and all the watch are at
the door: they are come to search the house. Shall
I let them in?

495 FALSTAFF Dost thou hear, Hal? Never call a true piece of
gold a counterfeit: thou art essentially made, without
seeming so.

PRINCE HENRY And thou a natural coward, without
instinct.

500 FALSTAFF I deny your major. If you will deny the
sheriff, so: if not, let him enter: if I become not a cart
as well as another man, a plague on my bringing
up! I hope I shall as soon be strangled with a halter
as another.

505 PRINCE HENRY Go, hide thee behind the arras. The rest
walk up above. Now, my masters, for a true face and
good conscience.

FALSTAFF Both which I have had: but their date is out,   *Falstaff hides*
and therefore I'll hide me.   *behind*

510 PRINCE HENRY Call in the sheriff.   *the arras*

               Exeunt [all except Prince Henry and Peto]
Enter Sheriff and the Carrier

    Now, master sheriff, what is your will with me?

SHERIFF First, pardon me, my lord. A hue and cry
Hath followed certain men unto this house.

PRINCE HENRY What men?

515 SHERIFF One of them is well known, my gracious lord,
A gross fat man.

CARRIER As fat as butter.

PRINCE HENRY The man, I do assure you, is not here,
For I myself at this time have employed him.

520   And, sheriff, I will engage my word to thee

---

490 The . . . fiddlestick i.e. here's a fine commotion (proverbial)   495 Never . . . counterfeit a much
debated line; Falstaff seems to be referring to himself as genuine gold (i.e. loyal, worthy), despite the prince's
earlier accusations of cowardice and hypocrisy   496 thou . . . so another obscure line; probably either 'you
are basically true (**essentially made**) to your friends, even if some of your recent declarations seem to
contradict this' or 'you are fundamentally a deceptive play-actor (**made**), despite seeming to be loyal'; some
editors adopt a later reading, and substitute 'mad' for 'made'   500 deny your major reject your main
premise   deny the refuse entrance to the   501 so so be it   become suit, befit   cart wagon used to
transport the condemned man to the gallows   502 bringing up upbringing, breeding (which entitled him,
as a knight, to death by beheading)/being brought before the authorities/being hanged   503 soon willingly/
quickly   505 arras large tapestry wall-hanging (hung so that there was space behind it to hide)   506 walk
up above go upstairs   true honest   508 date is out lease has expired, i.e. it's too late for that   512 hue
and cry the noise and shouting of citizens in pursuit of a felon   520 engage pledge

That I will, by tomorrow dinnertime,
Send him to answer thee, or any man,
For anything he shall be charged withal:
And so let me entreat you leave the house.

525 **SHERIFF** I will, my lord. There are two gentlemen
Have in this robbery lost three hundred marks.

PRINCE HENRY It may be so: if he have robbed these men,
He shall be answerable, and so farewell.

SHERIFF Goodnight, my noble lord.

530 **PRINCE HENRY** I think it is good morrow, is it not?

SHERIFF Indeed, my lord, I think it be two o'clock.

Exeunt [Sheriff and Carrier]

PRINCE HENRY This oily rascal is known as well as   *To Peto*
Paul's. Go, call him forth.

PETO Falstaff! Fast asleep behind the arras, and snorting
535 like a horse.

PRINCE HENRY Hark, how hard he fetches breath. Search
his pockets.

He searcheth his pockets, and findeth certain papers
What hast thou found?

PETO Nothing but papers, my lord.

540 **PRINCE HENRY** Let's see, what be they? Read them.

PETO 'Item, A capon, 2s 2d. Item, Sauce, 4d. Item, Sack,   *Reads*
two gallons, 5s 8d. Item, Anchovies and sack after
supper, 2s 6d. Item, Bread, ob.'

PRINCE HENRY O, monstrous! But one halfpenny-worth of
545 bread to this intolerable deal of sack? What there is
else, keep close, we'll read it at more advantage. There
let him sleep till day. I'll to the court in the morning.
We must all to the wars, and thy place shall be
honourable. I'll procure this fat rogue a charge of foot,
550 and I know his death will be a march of twelvescore.
The money shall be paid back again with advantage.
Be with me betimes in the morning, and so, good
morrow, Peto.

PETO Good morrow, good my lord.   *Exeunt*

---

521 dinnertime i.e. midday   **522 answer thee** respond to your charges, account for himself to you
523 withal with   **528 answerable** held responsible   **530 morrow** morning   **532 oily** greasy/cunning,
slippery   **533 Paul's** St Paul's Cathedral, the tallest landmark in London at this time   **541 2s 2d** two
shillings and two pence   **543 ob** abbreviation of 'obolus', i.e. halfpenny   **544 But** merely
545 intolerable deal excessive quantity   **546 close** hidden, safe   **advantage** a better opportunity
549 charge of foot command of an infantry company   **550 twelvescore** i.e. 240 yards   **551 money** i.e.
that was stolen   **advantage** interest   **552 betimes** early

Act 3 Scene 1   *running scene 8*

Enter Hotspur, Worcester, Lord Mortimer and Owen
Glendower

MORTIMER These promises are fair, the parties sure,
        And our induction full of prosperous hope.
HOTSPUR Lord Mortimer, and cousin Glendower,
        Will you sit down?
5   And uncle Worcester — a plague upon it,
        I have forgot the map!
GLENDOWER No, here it is.   *Shows a map*
        Sit, cousin Percy, sit, good cousin Hotspur —
        For by that name as oft as Lancaster
10   Doth speak of you, his cheeks look pale and with
        A rising sigh he wisheth you in heaven.
HOTSPUR And you in hell, as oft as he hears Owen
        Glendower spoke of.
GLENDOWER I cannot blame him: at my nativity
15   The front of heaven was full of fiery shapes,
        Of burning cressets, and at my birth
        The frame and foundation of the earth
        Shaked like a coward.
HOTSPUR Why, so it would have done at the same
20   season, if your mother's cat had but kittened, though
        yourself had never been born.
GLENDOWER I say the earth did shake when I was born.
HOTSPUR And I say the earth was not of my mind,
        If you suppose as fearing you it shook.
25 **GLENDOWER** The heavens were all on fire, the earth did
          tremble.
HOTSPUR O, then the earth shook to see the heavens on
        fire,
        And not in fear of your nativity.
        Diseasèd nature oftentimes breaks forth
        In strange eruptions; and the teeming earth
30   Is with a kind of colic pinched and vexed
        By the imprisoning of unruly wind

3.1 *Location: unspecified; probably in Glendower's house* **1 promises** i.e. of support **sure** secure,
reliable **2 induction** beginning **prosperous hope** hope of prospering **9 Lancaster** i.e. King Henry;
Glendower deliberately refers to him by his former title (Duke of Lancaster) **15 front** forehead, face
16 cressets torches (literally fires burning in iron baskets), hence meteors (signs of ill omen) **24 as fearing
you** because it feared you **29 eruptions** outbreaks of disease/natural or meteorological disturbances
teeming fertile, breeding **30 colic** severe stomach pains

Within her womb, which, for enlargement striving,
Shakes the old beldam earth and tumbles down
Steeples and moss-grown towers. At your birth
35   Our grandam earth, having this distemperature,
In passion shook.
GLENDOWER   Cousin, of many men
I do not bear these crossings. Give me leave
To tell you once again that at my birth
40   The front of heaven was full of fiery shapes,
The goats ran from the mountains, and the herds
Were strangely clamorous to the frighted fields.
These signs have marked me extraordinary,
And all the courses of my life do show
45   I am not in the roll of common men.
Where is the living, clipped in with the sea
That chides the banks of England, Scotland and
    Wales,
Which calls me pupil, or hath read to me?
And bring him out that is but woman's son
50   Can trace me in the tedious ways of art
And hold me pace in deep experiments.
HOTSPUR   I think there's no man speaks better Welsh.
I'll to dinner.
MORTIMER   Peace, cousin Percy, you will make him mad.
55   **GLENDOWER**   I can call spirits from the vasty deep.
HOTSPUR   Why, so can I, or so can any man.
But will they come when you do call for them?
GLENDOWER   Why, I can teach thee, cousin, to command
    the devil.
HOTSPUR   And I can teach thee, cousin, to shame the
    devil
60   By telling truth: tell truth and shame the devil.
If thou have power to raise him, bring him hither,
And I'll be sworn I have power to shame him hence.
O, while you live, tell truth and shame the devil!

32 **womb** bowels/stomach   **enlargement** release   33 **beldam** old woman, grandmother   34 **moss-grown** overgrown with moss, old   35 **grandam** grandmother   **distemperature** bodily disturbance   36 **passion** suffering, bodily affliction   38 **crossings** contradictions   42 **clamorous** noisy   **frighted fields** fields full of fear   43 **marked me** marked me out as   44 **courses** events   45 **roll** list   46 **the living** any person living   **clipped in with** surrounded by   47 **chides** beats, contends with   48 **read to** i.e. instructed, educated   50 **trace** follow   **tedious** time-consuming, lengthy, complex   **art** scholarship/magic, occult arts   51 **hold me pace** keep up with me   **deep experiments** profound, learned investigations   52 **Welsh** i.e. nonsense, gibberish   55 **call** summon, invoke (Hotspur shifts the sense to 'call out to')   **vasty deep** immense abyss   60 **tell . . . devil** proverbial

MORTIMER Come, come, no more of this unprofitable
      chat.
65   **GLENDOWER** Three times hath Henry Bullingbrook made
      head
      Against my power: thrice from the banks of Wye
      And sandy-bottomed Severn have I sent him
      Bootless home and weather-beaten back.
HOTSPUR Home without boots, and in foul weather too!
70   How scapes he agues, in the devil's name?
GLENDOWER Come, here's the map: shall we divide our
      right
      According to our threefold order ta'en?
MORTIMER The archdeacon hath divided it
      Into three limits very equally:
75   England, from Trent and Severn hitherto,
      By south and east is to my part assigned:
      All westward, Wales beyond the Severn shore,
      And all the fertile land within that bound,
      To Owen Glendower: and, dear coz, to you
80   The remnant northward, lying off from Trent.
      And our indentures tripartite are drawn,
      Which being sealèd interchangeably —
      A business that this night may execute—
      Tomorrow, cousin Percy, you and I
85   And my good lord of Worcester will set forth
      To meet your father and the Scottish power,
      As is appointed us, at Shrewsbury.
      My father Glendower is not ready yet,
      Nor shall we need his help these fourteen days.—
90   Within that space you may have drawn together   *To Glendower*
      Your tenants, friends and neighbouring gentlemen.
GLENDOWER A shorter time shall send me to you, lords.
      And in my conduct shall your ladies come,
      From whom you now must steal and take no leave,
95   For there will be a world of water shed
      Upon the parting of your wives and you.

---

65 made head advanced   **66 power** army   **Wye** river on the Welsh-English border   **68 Bootless**
unsuccessful, without gain (Hotspur plays on the literal sense)   **70 agues** violent fevers characterized by
shaking   **71 right** just claim (to land)   **72 threefold order ta'en** three-way agreement   **73 archdeacon**
not identified; chronicle sources suggest Archdeacon of Bangor   **74 limits** regions   **75 Trent . . . hitherto**
the rivers Trent and Severn up to this point (presumably Mortimer indicates the map)   **81 indentures**
tripartite contracts drawn up in triplicate   **drawn** drawn up   **82 sealèd interchangeably** each party has
a copy signed and sealed by all   **83 this . . . execute** can be done tonight   **87 appointed** agreed by
Shrewsbury town on the Welsh-English border   **88 father** father-in-law   **90 space** period of time
93 in my conduct escorted by me   **94 steal** slip away   **95 a . . . water** i.e. many tears

HOTSPUR Methinks my moiety, north from Burton here,   *Looks at map*
In quantity equals not one of yours:
See how this river comes me cranking in,
100   And cuts me from the best of all my land
A huge half-moon, a monstrous cantle out.
I'll have the current in this place dammed up,
And here the smug and silver Trent shall run
In a new channel, fair and evenly.
105   It shall not wind with such a deep indent,
To rob me of so rich a bottom here.
GLENDOWER Not wind? It shall, it must. You see it doth.
MORTIMER Yea, but
Mark how he bears his course, and runs me up
110   With like advantage on the other side,
Gelding the opposèd continent as much
As on the other side it takes from you.
WORCESTER Yea, but a little charge will trench him here
And on this north side win this cape of land,
115   And then he runs straight and even.
HOTSPUR I'll have it so. A little charge will do it.
GLENDOWER I'll not have it altered.
HOTSPUR Will not you?
GLENDOWER No, nor you shall not.
120   HOTSPUR Who shall say me nay?
GLENDOWER Why, that will I.
HOTSPUR Let me not understand you, then. Speak it in
Welsh.
GLENDOWER I can speak English, lord, as well as you,
For I was trained up in the English court;
125   Where, being but young, I framed to the harp
Many an English ditty lovely well
And gave the tongue a helpful ornament;
A virtue that was never seen in you.
HOTSPUR Marry,
130   And I am glad of it with all my heart.

---

97 moiety share, portion   **Burton** Derbyshire town of Burton-upon-Trent   **99 comes . . . in** twists sharply into my section; Hotspur objects that the river turns north from Burton and deprives him of the fertile lands of Lincolnshire and part of Nottinghamshire   **101 cantle out** corner or portion cut off   **103 smug** smooth   **105 deep indent** sharp angled section, indentation   **106 bottom** river valley   **109 he** it (the river Trent)   **runs me** runs   **110 like advantage** the same effect   **111 Gelding** depriving, cutting (land) off from   **opposèd continent** land on the opposite side   **113 charge** cost/gunpowder used in blasting   **trench** create a trench or channel   **114 cape** spur, projecting piece   **122 Let . . . Welsh** i.e. say it in Welsh (which I don't understand) so that I won't understand (and take offence)   **125 being but young** since I was young at the time   **framed to** composed for   **126 ditty** poem, ballad   **lovely** beautifully   **127 gave . . . ornament** adorned the English language with music and poetry/decorated the words with the music/improved the sound of the language with my Welsh accent   **128 virtue** accomplishment, skill

I had rather be a kitten and cry mew
Than one of these same metre ballad-mongers.
I had rather hear a brazen candlestick turned,
Or a dry wheel grate on the axle-tree,
135   And that would set my teeth nothing on edge,
Nothing so much as mincing poetry:
'Tis like the forced gait of a shuffling nag.
GLENDOWER Come, you shall have Trent turned.
HOTSPUR I do not care: I'll give thrice so much land
140   To any well-deserving friend;
But in the way of bargain, mark ye me,
I'll cavil on the ninth part of a hair.
Are the indentures drawn? Shall we be gone?
GLENDOWER The moon shines fair, you may away by
night.
145   I'll haste the writer and withal
Break with your wives of your departure hence.
I am afraid my daughter will run mad,
So much she doteth on her Mortimer.   *Exit*
MORTIMER Fie, cousin Percy, how you cross my father!
150   **HOTSPUR** I cannot choose: sometime he angers me
With telling me of the mouldwarp and the ant,
Of the dreamer Merlin and his prophecies,
And of a dragon and a finless fish,
A clip-winged griffin and a moulten raven,
155   A couching lion and a ramping cat,
And such a deal of skimble-skamble stuff
As puts me from my faith. I tell you what,
He held me last night at least nine hours
In reck'ning up the several devils' names
160   That were his lackeys: I cried 'Hum', and 'Well, go to',

---

132 metre ballad-mongers sellers of predictably rhymed popular ballads   **133 brazen** brass   **turned** i.e. on a lathe (which made an unpleasant grating noise)   **134 dry** unoiled   **axle-tree** axle   **136 Nothing ... as** nothing like as much as   **mincing** affectedly dainty   **137 nag** feeble old horse   **141 in ... bargain** when it comes to bargaining   **142 cavil on** dispute insistently over   **143 drawn** drawn up   **145 haste the writer** hurry the writer of the indentures   **withal** at the same time   **146 Break with** speak to, inform   **148 doteth on** loves very dearly, is infatuated with   **149 cross** antagonize   **150 choose** help it   **151 mouldwarp** mole; according to Holinshed's *Chronicles* the division of the map was arranged in accordance with a prophecy that imaged Henry IV as a mole and the others as dragon, lion and wolf   **152 dreamer** visionary   **Merlin** wizard and prophet at the legendary court of King Arthur   **154 clip-winged** with its wings clipped, i.e. prevented from flying   **griffin** mythical beast, half-lion, half-eagle   **moulten** having moulted, lost its feathers   **155 couching** lying down (form of 'couchant', a heraldic term)   **ramping** rearing, standing on its hind legs (form of 'rampant', a heraldic term)   **156 skimble-skamble** incoherent, nonsensical   **157 puts ... faith** makes me forget or disbelieve my religion   **159 reck'ning up** listing, recounting   **several** various   **160 lackeys** servants, followers   **'Hum'** non-committal sound expressing agreement   **'Well, go to'** i.e. you don't say, well I never

But marked him not a word. O, he is as tedious
As a tired horse, a railing wife,
Worse than a smoky house. I had rather live
With cheese and garlic in a windmill far,
165   Than feed on cates and have him talk to me
In any summer-house in Christendom.

MORTIMER In faith, he was a worthy gentleman,
Exceeding well read, and profited
In strange concealments, valiant as a lion
170   And wondrous affable and as bountiful
As mines of India. Shall I tell you, cousin?
He holds your temper in a high respect
And curbs himself even of his natural scope
When you do cross his humour — 'faith, he does.
175   I warrant you, that man is not alive
Might so have tempted him as you have done,
Without the taste of danger and reproof:
But do not use it oft, let me entreat you.

WORCESTER In faith, my lord, you are too wilful-blame,   *To Hotspur*
180   And since your coming hither have done enough
To put him quite besides his patience.
You must needs learn, lord, to amend this fault:
Though sometimes it show greatness, courage,
   blood —
And that's the dearest grace it renders you —
185   Yet oftentimes it doth present harsh rage,
Defect of manners, want of government,
Pride, haughtiness, opinion and disdain,
The least of which haunting a nobleman
Loseth men's hearts and leaves behind a stain
190   Upon the beauty of all parts besides,
Beguiling them of commendation.

HOTSPUR Well, I am schooled. Good manners be your
   speed!
Here come our wives, and let us take our leave.

---

161 marked him took no notice of   **162 railing** complaining, scolding   **164 cheese ... windmill** i.e. poor food in uncomfortable, noisy accommodation   **165 cates** delicacies   **166 summer-house** rich man's country house   **167 In faith** truly   **168 profited ... concealments** proficient in secret arts   **171 India** i.e. the West Indies   **172 temper** temperament, character   **173 scope** freedom of expression   **174 do ... humour** antagonize him   **176 tempted** provoked   **177 taste ... reproof** experiencing harm and rebuke **178 use it oft** do it often   **179 wilful-blame** blameworthy for being obstinately self-willed   **181 besides** out of   **182 must needs** must   **183 show** is evidence of   **blood** spirit   **184 dearest grace** most valuable advantage   **renders** offers   **185 present** represent, demonstrate   **186 want of government** lack of self-control   **187 opinion** arrogance, conceit   **188 haunting** being associated with   **189 Loseth** causes him to lose   **190 parts besides** other qualities   **191 Beguiling** depriving   **192 schooled** instructed/admonished   **be your speed** bring you good fortune

Enter Glendower with the Ladies

MORTIMER This is the deadly spite that angers me:
195   My wife can speak no English, I no Welsh.

GLENDOWER My daughter weeps. She'll not part with
          you,
        She'll be a soldier too, she'll to the wars.

MORTIMER Good father, tell her that she and my aunt
          Percy
        Shall follow in your conduct speedily.

*Glendower speaks to her in Welsh, and she answers him in
the same*

200 **GLENDOWER** She is desperate here: a peevish self-willed
          harlotry,
        One that no persuasion can do good upon.
                        The Lady speaks in Welsh

MORTIMER I understand thy looks: that pretty Welsh
        Which thou pour'st down from these swelling
          heavens
        I am too perfect in, and, but for shame,
205   In such a parley should I answer thee.
                        The Lady [speaks] again in Welsh
        I understand thy kisses and thou mine,
        And that's a feeling disputation.
        But I will never be a truant, love,
        Till I have learned thy language, for thy tongue
210   Makes Welsh as sweet as ditties highly penned,
        Sung by a fair queen in a summer's bow'r,
        With ravishing division, to her lute.

GLENDOWER Nay, if thou melt, then will she run mad.
        The Lady speaks again in Welsh

MORTIMER O, I am ignorance itself in this!

215 **GLENDOWER** She bids you on the wanton rushes lay you
          down
        And rest your gentle head upon her lap,
        And she will sing the song that pleaseth you

---

194 spite vexation, regret   **198 aunt Percy** more confusion between the two Edmund Mortimers: Lady Percy (Hotspur's wife) was in fact the sister of the Mortimer married to Glendower's daughter and aunt of the younger man   **199 in your conduct** under your escort   **200 desperate here** recklessly determined on this point (her decision not to leave Mortimer)   **peevish self-willed harlotry** obstinate headstrong hussy   **202 pretty Welsh** i.e. her eloquent tears   **203 swelling heavens** i.e. her eyes filled with tears   **204 too perfect** only too accomplished, fluent   **205 parley** language, conversation (perhaps, picking up on **soldier**, with a sense of 'military negotiation')   **207 feeling disputation** moving, heartfelt discussion/conversation conducted through touch   **208 truant** negligent student   **210 highly penned** elaborately composed   **212 division** ornamentation, variation (specifically, passage in which a series of short notes elaborates on a longer passage)   **213 melt** give way to your feelings, weep   **214 this** i.e. Welsh   **215 wanton rushes** luxuriant floor covering of reeds

And on your eyelids crown the god of sleep,
Charming your blood with pleasing heaviness,
220 Making such difference 'twixt wake and sleep
As is the difference betwixt day and night
The hour before the heavenly-harnessed team
Begins his golden progress in the east.

MORTIMER With all my heart I'll sit and hear her sing:
225 By that time will our book, I think, be drawn.

GLENDOWER Do so,
And those musicians that shall play to you
Hang in the air a thousand leagues from hence,
And straight they shall be here: sit, and attend.

230 HOTSPUR Come, Kate, thou art perfect in lying down:
come, quick, quick, that I may lay my head in thy
lap.

LADY PERCY Go, ye giddy goose.   *The music plays*

HOTSPUR Now I perceive the devil understands Welsh,
235 and 'tis no marvel he is so humorous. By'r lady, he's
a good musician.

LADY PERCY Then would you be nothing but musical, for
you are altogether governed by humours. Lie still, ye
thief, and hear the lady sing in Welsh.

240 HOTSPUR I had rather hear Lady, my brach, howl in
Irish.

LADY PERCY Wouldst have thy head broken?

HOTSPUR No.

LADY PERCY Then be still.

245 HOTSPUR Neither, 'tis a woman's fault.

LADY PERCY Now God help thee!

HOTSPUR To the Welsh lady's bed.

LADY PERCY What's that?

HOTSPUR Peace, she sings.
Here the Lady sings a Welsh song

250 HOTSPUR Come, I'll have your song too.   *To Lady Percy*

---

218 **crown** give power to   219 **heaviness** drowsiness   222 **heavenly-harnessed team** horses that drew the sun god's chariot   223 **progress** course/royal journey   225 **book** indentures, legal contracts   **drawn** drawn up   228 **Hang . . . air** i.e. they're spirits   **thousand leagues** three thousand miles   229 **straight** straight away   230 **perfect in** expert at, practised at   **lying down** with sexual connotations (continued in **lap**)   234 **devil understands Welsh** i.e. because the supposed spirits have answered Glendower's call and music is playing   235 **humorous** capricious, whimsical   238 **humours** moods, whims (thought to be generated by bodily fluids or 'humours')   240 **brach** bitch, female dog (called **Lady**)   **Irish** designed as insult here; may possibly suggest his bitch's breed   242 **broken** beaten, grazed   244 **still** quiet, calm   245 **Neither** i.e. I won't do that either   **woman's fault** i.e. being silent (or sexually passive) is a woman's trait; may play on 'broken head' as 'broken maidenhead' (lost virginity), perhaps with **fault** quibbling on its sense of 'vagina/sinful sexual yielding'

LADY PERCY Not mine, in good sooth.

HOTSPUR Not yours, in good sooth?

You swear like a comfit-maker's wife.

'Not you, in good sooth', and 'As true as I live',

255   And 'As God shall mend me' and 'As sure as day!'

And givest such sarcenet surety for thy oaths,

As if thou never walk'st further than Finsbury.

Swear me, Kate, like a lady as thou art,

A good mouth-filling oath, and leave 'in sooth',

260   And such protest of pepper-gingerbread,

To velvet-guards and Sunday-citizens.

Come, sing.

LADY PERCY I will not sing.

HOTSPUR 'Tis the next way to turn tailor, or be red-

265   breast teacher. An the indentures be drawn, I'll away

within these two hours, and so, come in when ye

will.   *Exit*

GLENDOWER Come, come, Lord Mortimer, you are as

slow

As hot Lord Percy is on fire to go.

270   By this our book is drawn, we'll but seal,

And then to horse immediately.

MORTIMER With all my heart.   *Exeunt*

Act 3 Scene 2   *running scene 9*

Enter the King, Prince of Wales and others

KING HENRY IV Lords, give us leave. The Prince of Wales

and I

Must have some private conference. But be near at

hand,

For we shall presently have need of you. *Exeunt Lords*

I know not whether heaven will have it so,

5   For some displeasing service I have done,

That in his secret doom, out of my blood

---

251 **sooth** truth   253 **comfit-maker's** confectioner's; Hotspur makes fun of a genteel oath and offers several more   256 **sarcenet surety** flimsy assurance   **sarcenet** fine silken cloth   257 **Finsbury** Finsbury Fields, popular place of recreation just outside the city of London   258 **Swear me** swear/swear for me   260 **protest of pepper-gingerbread** i.e. mild oaths   **pepper-gingerbread** in which pepper was partly substituted for ginger, making the gingerbread less spicy and pungent   261 **velvet-guards** velvet trimmings on clothes, or those who wore them   **Sunday-citizens** those keeping their best clothes for Sunday   264 **tailor** tailors were supposed to be enthusiastic singers   **be red-breast teacher** teach singing to robins (small red-breasted birds)   270 **this** this time   **but seal** just put our seals on the documents   **3.2** *Location: the royal court*   1 **give us leave** please leave us alone   6 **doom** judgement   **blood** family, offspring

He'll breed revengement and a scourge for me.
But thou dost in thy passages of life
Make me believe that thou art only marked
10 For the hot vengeance and the rod of heaven
To punish my mistreadings. Tell me else,
Could such inordinate and low desires,
Such poor, such bare, such lewd, such mean attempts,
Such barren pleasures, rude society,
15 As thou art matched withal and grafted to,
Accompany the greatness of thy blood
And hold their level with thy princely heart?
PRINCE HENRY So please your majesty, I would I could
Quit all offences with as clear excuse
20 As well as I am doubtless I can purge
Myself of many I am charged withal:
Yet such extenuation let me beg,
As, in reproof of many tales devised,
Which oft the ear of greatness needs must hear
25 By smiling pick-thanks and base news-mongers,
I may, for some things true, wherein my youth
Hath faulty wand'red and irregular,
Find pardon on my true submission.
KING HENRY IV Heaven pardon thee! Yet let me wonder, Harry,
30 At thy affections, which do hold a wing
Quite from the flight of all thy ancestors.
Thy place in council thou hast rudely lost,
Which by thy younger brother is supplied,
And art almost an alien to the hearts
35 Of all the court and princes of my blood.
The hope and expectation of thy time
Is ruined, and the soul of every man
Prophetically do forethink thy fall.
Had I so lavish of my presence been,

---

7 **scourge** punishment of divine origin/punishing whip   8 **passages** course through, way of   9 **only marked For** solely designated to be   10 **rod** i.e. of punishment   11 **mistreadings** wrongful steps, sins   **else** how else   12 **inordinate** immoderate, disorderly   13 **bare** wretched, paltry/undisguised   **lewd** vulgar, low   **attempts** undertakings   14 **rude society** vulgar, uncivilized companionship   15 **withal** with   **grafted** united   17 **hold their level** think themselves equal to   19 **Quit** acquit myself of   **clear** honest   20 **doubtless** sure   23 **reproof** refutation, disproof   24 **greatness** the great, the high-ranking   25 **pick-thanks** flatterers and informers   **news-mongers** tellers of tales, gossips   26 **things true** genuine misdemeanours   27 **faulty . . . irregular** gone astray off the proper path   28 **true submission** honest admission   29 **wonder** express surprise   30 **affections** tastes, inclinations   **hold a wing** fly   32 **rudely** violently, in an uncivilized manner (according to an apocryphal tale, the prince was expelled from the King's Privy Council for hitting the Lord Chief Justice)   33 **supplied** filled   34 **alien** stranger   36 **time** youth, life   38 **forethink** expect/prophesy

40   So common-hackneyed in the eyes of men,
        So stale and cheap to vulgar company,
        Opinion, that did help me to the crown,
        Had still kept loyal to possession
        And left me in reputeless banishment,
45   A fellow of no mark nor likelihood.
        By being seldom seen, I could not stir
        But like a comet I was wondered at,
        That men would tell their children, 'This is he.'
        Others would say, 'Where? Which is Bullingbrook?'
50   And then I stole all courtesy from heaven,
        And dressed myself in such humility
        That I did pluck allegiance from men's hearts,
        Loud shouts and salutations from their mouths,
        Even in the presence of the crownèd king.
55   Thus I did keep my person fresh and new;
        My presence, like a robe pontifical,
        Ne'er seen but wondered at: and so my state,
        Seldom but sumptuous, showed like a feast
        And won by rareness such solemnity.
60   The skipping king, he ambled up and down
        With shallow jesters and rash bavin wits,
        Soon kindled and soon burnt, carded his state,
        Mingled his royalty with carping fools,
        Had his great name profanèd with their scorns
65   And gave his countenance, against his name,
        To laugh at gibing boys and stand the push
        Of every beardless vain comparative;
        Grew a companion to the common streets,
        Enfeoffed himself to popularity,
70   That, being daily swallowed by men's eyes,
        They surfeited with honey and began
        To loathe the taste of sweetness, whereof a little

40 **common-hackneyed** cheapened by habitual exposure (from 'hackney', a horse for hire)   42 **Opinion** public opinion   43 **Had . . . possession** would have remained loyal to the holder of the crown (Richard II, deposed by Henry)   44 **reputeless** inglorious, shameful/anonymous, unacknowledged   45 **mark** significance   **likelihood** prospect of success   50 **stole . . . heaven** adopted a manner of heavenly graciousness   56 **pontifical** belonging to a bishop   57 **state** magnificence, kingship   58 **Seldom** infrequently seen   **feast** special occasion, celebration   59 **solemnity** ceremonious dignity   60 **skipping** frivolous   **up and down** i.e. aimlessly   61 **rash bavin** quickly burnt up   **bavin** brushwood or kindling soon ignited and burnt   62 **carded his state** destroyed his dignity, kingly status (to 'card' is either to mix or to comb impurities from wool)   63 **carping** chattering (Quarto has 'capring', so most editors print 'capering')   64 **scorns** foolishness, mockeries/contemptuous way of speaking   65 **against his name** to the detriment of his royal reputation   66 **gibing** mocking, taunting   **stand the push** expose himself to the proximity/mockery of   67 **beardless vain comparative** immature, worthless maker of mocking comparisons   69 **Enfeoffed** committed, bound (literally, to vow loyalty to a lord in return for land)   71 **surfeited** grew overindulged and sick   72 **loathe . . . sweetness** i.e. they got sick of the sight of him

More than a little is by much too much.
So when he had occasion to be seen,
75 He was but as the cuckoo is in June,
Heard, not regarded, seen, but with such eyes
As, sick and blunted with community,
Afford no extraordinary gaze,
Such as is bent on sun-like majesty
80 When it shines seldom in admiring eyes.
But rather drowsed and hung their eyelids down,
Slept in his face and rendered such aspect
As cloudy men use to do to their adversaries,
Being with his presence glutted, gorged and full.
85 And in that very line, Harry, standest thou,
For thou hast lost thy princely privilege
With vile participation. Not an eye
But is a-weary of thy common sight,
Save mine, which hath desired to see thee more,
90 Which now doth that I would not have it do,
Make blind itself with foolish tenderness.
PRINCE HENRY I shall hereafter, my thrice-gracious lord,
Be more myself.
KING HENRY IV For all the world
95 As thou art to this hour was Richard then,
When I from France set foot at Ravenspurgh,
And even as I was then is Percy now.
Now, by my sceptre and my soul to boot,
He hath more worthy interest to the state
100 Than thou, the shadow of succession;
For of no right, nor colour like to right,
He doth fill fields with harness in the realm,
Turns head against the lion's armèd jaws,
And, being no more in debt to years than thou,
105 Leads ancient lords and reverend bishops on
To bloody battles and to bruising arms.
What never-dying honour hath he got

75 **cuckoo...June** i.e. commonplace by midsummer, not noticed any longer   77 **community**
familiarity   78 **extraordinary gaze** special notice   82 **face** i.e. presence   **rendered such aspect** with
such an expression   83 **cloudy** sullen, gloomy   **use to** habitually   85 **line** category   87 **vile**
participation associating with commoners and base, vulgar people   88 **common** widespread, public/cheap,
vulgar   91 **tenderness** i.e. tears of affection   93 **Be more myself** act in a manner more befitting my
position   94 **For...world** i.e. in every way   99 **He...state** He (Percy) has a more honourable claim to the
crown   100 **shadow of succession** mere shadow of a proper heir   101 **of** having   **colour like to**
semblance, pretext of   102 **harness** armour, i.e. armed men   103 **Turns head** directs his attention/leads
his army   **lion's** i.e. the king's (the lion is a traditional symbol of royalty)   104 **in...years** older
(historically Hotspur was actually twenty-three years older than the prince)   105 **ancient** long-established
106 **bruising** damaging, crushing

Against renownèd Douglas, whose high deeds,
Whose hot incursions and great name in arms
110   Holds from all soldiers chief majority
And military title capital
Through all the kingdoms that acknowledge Christ!
Thrice hath the Hotspur, Mars in swaddling clothes,
This infant warrior, in his enterprises
115   Discomfited great Douglas, ta'en him once,
Enlargèd him and made a friend of him,
To fill the mouth of deep defiance up
And shake the peace and safety of our throne.
And what say you to this? Percy, Northumberland,
120   The archbishop's grace of York, Douglas, Mortimer,
Capitulate against us and are up.
But wherefore do I tell these news to thee?
Why, Harry, do I tell thee of my foes,
Which art my near'st and dearest enemy?
125   Thou that art like enough, through vassal fear,
Base inclination and the start of spleen,
To fight against me under Percy's pay,
To dog his heels and curtsy at his frowns,
To show how much thou art degenerate.
130   **PRINCE HENRY** Do not think so. You shall not find it so.
And heaven forgive them that so much have swayed
Your majesty's good thoughts away from me!
I will redeem all this on Percy's head
And in the closing of some glorious day
135   Be bold to tell you that I am your son,
When I will wear a garment all of blood
And stain my favours in a bloody mask,
Which, washed away, shall scour my shame with it.
And that shall be the day, whene'er it lights,
140   That this same child of honour and renown,
This gallant Hotspur, this all-praisèd knight,

---

108 whose i.e. Hotspur's   **high** illustrious, noble   **109 hot incursions** fierce attacks   **110 chief . . . capital** military fame and pre-eminence   **113 Mars** Roman god of war   **swaddling clothes** wrappings for babies (refers to Hotspur's youth)   **114 enterprises** military undertakings   **115 Discomfited** defeated   **ta'en him once** captured him on one occasion   **116 Enlargèd** released   **117 fill . . . up** complete the number of opponents/add to the roar of opposition   **121 Capitulate** have formed a league, draw up agreements   **up** i.e. in arms   **124 dearest** most precious, loved/worst, most bitter   **125 like** likely   **vassal** base, servile   **126 Base inclination** taste for the inferior/acceding to base motives   **start of spleen** rush of anger   **128 curtsy** bow, show respect   **133 redeem . . . head** atone for my sins with Percy's head/make Percy pay for all this   **134 in . . . day** at the end of some victorious battle   **137 favours** facial features/chivalric tokens worn to symbolize pledges or great feats   **bloody mask** face made unrecognizable because covered in blood/mass, covering of blood   **138 scour** cleanse, get rid of   **139 lights** arrives/dawns

And your unthought-of Harry chance to meet.
For every honour sitting on his helm,
Would they were multitudes, and on my head
145 My shames redoubled! For the time will come,
That I shall make this northern youth exchange
His glorious deeds for my indignities.
Percy is but my factor, good my lord,
To engross up glorious deeds on my behalf,
150 And I will call him to so strict account,
That he shall render every glory up,
Yea, even the slightest worship of his time,
Or I will tear the reckoning from his heart.
This, in the name of heaven, I promise here:
155 The which if I perform and do survive
I do beseech your majesty may salve
The long-grown wounds of my intemperature.
If not, the end of life cancels all bonds,
And I will die a hundred thousand deaths
160 Ere break the smallest parcel of this vow.
KING HENRY IV A hundred thousand rebels die in this:
Thou shalt have charge and sovereign trust herein.
Enter Blunt
How now, good Blunt? Thy looks are full of speed.
BLUNT So hath the business that I come to speak of.
165 Lord Mortimer of Scotland hath sent word
That Douglas and the English rebels met
The eleventh of this month at Shrewsbury.
A mighty and a fearful head they are,
If promises be kept on every hand,
170 As ever offered foul play in a state.
KING HENRY IV The Earl of Westmorland set forth today,
With him my son, Lord John of Lancaster,
For this advertisement is five days old.
On Wednesday next, Harry, thou shalt set forward:
175 On Thursday we ourselves will march.
Our meeting is Bridgnorth, and, Harry, you shall
    march

---

142 unthought-of ignored, associated with no great expectations **143 helm** helmet **148 factor** agent, commercial broker **149 engross up** accumulate, buy up **152 worship...time** honour gained in his lifetime **153 reckoning** account, bill **156 salve** apply healing ointment to **157 intemperature** intemperance, lack of restraint/diseased body, disordered health **160 parcel** part **162 charge** command (of troops) **sovereign** supreme, royal (perhaps continuing the disease imagery with play on the sense of 'healing') **163 speed** urgency **168 head** military force **169 If...hand** if all who have promised to join them do so **173 advertisement** announcement, news **176 Bridgnorth** small Shropshire town on the River Severn, south of Shrewsbury

Through Gloucestershire, by which account,
Our business valuèd, some twelve days hence
Our general forces at Bridgnorth shall meet.
180   Our hands are full of business: let's away.
Advantage feeds him fat while men delay.   *Exeunt*

Act 3 Scene 3   *running scene 10*

Enter Falstaff and Bardolph

FALSTAFF Bardolph, am I not fallen away vilely since this
last action? Do I not bate? Do I not dwindle? Why my
skin hangs about me like an old lady's loose gown.
I am withered like an old apple-john. Well, I'll repent,
5   and that suddenly, while I am in some liking. I shall be
out of heart shortly, and then I shall have no strength
to repent. An I have not forgotten what the inside of a
church is made of, I am a peppercorn, a brewer's
horse. The inside of a church! Company, villainous
10   company, hath been the spoil of me.
BARDOLPH Sir John, you are so fretful, you cannot live
long.
FALSTAFF Why, there is it: come sing me a bawdy song,
make me merry. I was as virtuously given as a
15   gentleman need to be; virtuous enough: swore little,
diced not — above seven times a week, went to a
bawdy-house not above once in a quarter — of an
hour, paid money that I borrowed — three of four
times, lived well and in good compass: and now I live
20   out of all order, out of compass.
BARDOLPH Why, you are so fat, Sir John, that you must
needs be out of all compass, out of all reasonable
compass, Sir John.
FALSTAFF Do thou amend thy face, and I'll amend my
25   life: thou art our admiral, thou bearest the lantern in

178 **our business valuèd** according to this reckoning   181 **Advantage**...**fat** opportunity (for rebellion)
increases   3.3 *Location: the tavern in Eastcheap*   1 **fallen away vilely** horribly shrunken   2 **action**
engagement, battle (i.e. the robbery on Gad's Hill)   **bate** decrease   4 **apple-john** type of apple said to be in
best eating condition when shrivelled   5 **suddenly** immediately   **in some liking** in the mood/in good
physical condition   6 **out of heart** disheartened/out of condition   **strength** i.e. physical or spiritual
8 **peppercorn** i.e. small and shrivelled   **brewer's horse** i.e. old and worn out   11 **fretful** restless, anxious/
frayed, worn   13 **there is it** i.e. exactly, that's the situation   14 **given** inclined   17 **bawdy-house**
brothel   19 **compass** measure, moderation/circumference (referring to his wide girth), belt   25 **admiral**
flagship with a **lantern** to guide the rest of the fleet

the poop, but 'tis in the nose of thee; thou art the
Knight of the Burning Lamp.

BARDOLPH Why, Sir John, my face does you no harm.

FALSTAFF No, I'll be sworn, I make as good use of it as
30 many a man doth of a death's-head or a *memento
mori*: I never see thy face but I think upon hellfire
and Dives that lived in purple, for there he is in his
robes, burning, burning. If thou wert any way given
to virtue, I would swear by thy face; my oath should
35 be 'By this fire', but thou art altogether given over;
and wert indeed, but for the light in thy face, the son
of utter darkness. When thou ran'st up Gad's Hill in
the night to catch my horse, if I did not think that
thou hadst been an *ignis fatuus* or a ball of wildfire,
40 there's no purchase in money. O, thou art a
perpetual triumph, an everlasting bonfire-light!
Thou hast saved me a thousand marks in links and
torches, walking with thee in the night betwixt
tavern and tavern. But the sack that thou hast drunk
45 me would have bought me lights as good cheap as
the dearest chandler's in Europe. I have maintained
that salamander of yours with fire any time this two
and thirty years. Heaven reward me for it!

BARDOLPH I would my face were in your belly!

50 **FALSTAFF** So should I be sure to be heart-burned.

Enter Hostess [Quickly]

How now, Dame Partlet the hen! Have you inquired
yet who picked my pocket?

HOSTESS QUICKLY Why, Sir John, what do you think, Sir
John? Do you think I keep thieves in my house?
55 I have searched, I have inquired, so has my husband,
man by man, boy by boy, servant by servant. The
tithe of a hair was never lost in my house before.

---

26 poop stern or rear of a ship   **nose** i.e. because it is red from drinking   **27 Knight...Lamp** mock-
chivalric title parodying heroic names in tales of romance   **30 death's-head** skull (i.e. emblem of mortality,
often carved into a stone set in a ring)   *memento mori* object used to symbolize death (Latin: 'reminder of
death')   **32 Dives...purple** refers to Christ's parable of Dives, the rich man clothed in purple who goes to
hell for allowing the pauper, Lazarus, to starve (Luke 16:19–31)   **35 given over** lost to virtue, committed to
sin   **39 *ignis fatuus*** will-o'-the-wisp, marsh gas which gives off phosphorescent light and misleads night
wanderers   **ball of wildfire** will-o'-the-wisp/ball of lightning/skin disease characterized by vivid
eruptions   **40 purchase** value   **41 bonfire-light** Folio spells 'Bone-fire-Light', suggesting both etymology
and original pronunciation   **42 links** torches   **44 drunk me** drunk (me is emphatic)   **45 good cheap**
cheap   **46 chandler's** candle-maker's   **47 salamander** lizard-like creature supposed to live in fire
49 I...belly! proverbial retort (compares to modern 'Get stuffed!')   **50 be heart-burned** have indigestion/
my heart would be literally on fire   **51 Dame Partlet** traditional name for a hen   **57 tithe** tenth part

FALSTAFF Ye lie, hostess: Bardolph was shaved and lost
many a hair; and I'll be sworn my pocket was picked.
60   Go to, you are a woman, go.
HOSTESS QUICKLY Who, I? I defy thee. I was never called
so in mine own house before.
FALSTAFF Go to, I know you well enough.
HOSTESS QUICKLY No, Sir John, you do not know me, Sir
65   John. I know you, Sir John: you owe me money, Sir
John, and now you pick a quarrel to beguile me of it.
I bought you a dozen of shirts to your back.
FALSTAFF Dowlas, filthy dowlas: I have given them away
to bakers' wives, and they have made bolters of them.
70   **HOSTESS QUICKLY** Now, as I am a true woman, holland
of eight shillings an ell. You owe money here besides,
Sir John, for your diet and by-drinkings, and money
lent you, four and twenty pounds.
FALSTAFF He had his part of it, let him pay.   *Points to Bardolph*
75   **HOSTESS QUICKLY** He? Alas, he is poor, he hath nothing.
FALSTAFF How? Poor? Look upon his face. What call you
rich? Let them coin his nose, let them coin his cheeks.
I'll not pay a denier. What, will you make a younker
of me? Shall I not take mine ease in mine inn but
80   I shall have my pocket picked? I have lost a seal-ring
of my grandfather's worth forty mark.
HOSTESS QUICKLY I have heard the prince tell him,
I know not how oft, that that ring was copper!
FALSTAFF How? The prince is a jack, a sneak-cup. An if
85   he were here, I would cudgel him like a dog, if he
would say so.
*Enter the Prince marching [with Peto], and Falstaff meets
him playing on his truncheon like a fife*
How now, lad? Is the wind in that door? Must we all
march?
BARDOLPH Yea, two and two, Newgate fashion.

---

58 was shaved had his beard cut/went bald through syphilis/had his head shaved to get rid of lice/was
robbed; **hair** may play on 'whore'   **60 woman** i.e. inadequate/deceitful/promiscuous   **63 know** am
acquainted with/have sexual knowledge of   **66 beguile** cheat   **67 to your back** for you to wear
68 Dowlas coarse linen (from Doulas in Brittany)   **69 bolters** cloths used for sifting flour   **70 holland** fine
linen (originally from Holland)   **71 ell** a measure of length (forty-five inches)   **72 diet and by-drinkings**
meals and drinks in between meals   **78 denier** small coin worth one tenth of a penny   **younker**
fashionable and gullible young man, easily duped   **79 take mine ease** relax   **80 seal-ring** engraved ring
used for sealing documents with wax, frequently an heirloom   **81 forty mark** a substantial sum of money; a
mark was worth two thirds of a pound   **84 jack** knave, rascal   **sneak-cup** sneaky person, knave/one who
sneaks drinks from others' cups   **truncheon** cudgel (symbol of his new military office)   **87 Is . . . door?** i.e.
is that the situation   **door** direction   **89 two . . . fashion** prisoners were shackled together and led in pairs
to Newgate, the City prison

90   **HOSTESS QUICKLY** My lord, I pray you hear me.

    PRINCE HENRY What say'st thou, Mistress Quickly? How
      does thy husband? I love him well. He is an honest
      man.

    HOSTESS QUICKLY Good my lord, hear me.

95   **FALSTAFF** Prithee let her alone, and list to me.

    PRINCE HENRY What say'st thou, Jack?

    FALSTAFF The other night I fell asleep here behind the
      arras and had my pocket picked. This house is turned
      bawdy-house: they pick pockets.

100   **PRINCE HENRY** What didst thou lose, Jack?

    FALSTAFF Wilt thou believe me, Hal, three or four bonds
      of forty pound apiece, and a seal-ring of my
      grandfather's?

    PRINCE HENRY A trifle, some eight-penny matter.

105   **HOSTESS QUICKLY** So I told him, my lord; and I said I
      heard your grace say so. And, my lord, he speaks
      most vilely of you, like a foul-mouthed man as he is,
      and said he would cudgel you.

    PRINCE HENRY What? He did not?

110   **HOSTESS QUICKLY** There's neither faith, truth, nor
      womanhood in me else.

    FALSTAFF There's no more faith in thee than a stewed
      prune, nor no more truth in thee than in a drawn fox.
      And for womanhood, Maid Marian may be the

115   deputy's wife of the ward to thee. Go, you nothing, go.

    HOSTESS QUICKLY Say, what thing? What thing?

    FALSTAFF What thing? Why, a thing to thank heaven on.

    HOSTESS QUICKLY I am no thing to thank heaven on,
      I would thou shouldst know it. I am an honest man's

120   wife, and, setting thy knighthood aside, thou art a
      knave to call me so.

    FALSTAFF Setting thy womanhood aside, thou art a
      beast to say otherwise.

    HOSTESS QUICKLY Say, what beast, thou knave, thou?

125   **FALSTAFF** What beast? Why, an otter.

    PRINCE HENRY An otter, Sir John? Why an otter?

---

99 pick pockets plays on the sense of 'plunder vaginas'   **101 bonds** deeds promising the bearer payment
112 stewed prune commonly available in brothels, hence 'whore/pimp'   **113 drawn fox** hunted fox
(**drawn** from cover and dependent on its cunning for safety)   **114 Maid Marian** a disreputable character in
morris dances and May games, played by a boy in female clothing   **115 deputy's . . . ward** wife of the
deputy of the ward (an administrative district), i.e. a respectable woman   **to** compared to   **nothing** thing of
no significance/vagina ('no thing')   **117 thing** whore/vagina   **on** for   **120 thy knighthood** the respect
usually due to one who is a knight   **125 otter** an aquatic mammal whose exact nature and type was a
subject of debate

FALSTAFF Why? She's neither fish nor flesh; a man knows not where to have her.

HOSTESS QUICKLY Thou art an unjust man in saying so;
130   thou or any man knows where to have me, thou knave, thou!

PRINCE HENRY Thou say'st true, hostess, and he slanders thee most grossly.

HOSTESS QUICKLY So he doth you, my lord, and said this
135   other day you owed him a thousand pound.

PRINCE HENRY Sirrah, do I owe you a thousand pound?

FALSTAFF A thousand pound, Hal? A million. Thy love is worth a million: thou ow'st me thy love.

HOSTESS QUICKLY Nay, my lord, he called you Jack, and
140   said he would cudgel you.

FALSTAFF Did I, Bardolph?

BARDOLPH Indeed, Sir John, you said so.

FALSTAFF Yea, if he said my ring was copper.

PRINCE HENRY I say 'tis copper. Dar'st thou be as good as
145   thy word now?

FALSTAFF Why, Hal, thou know'st, as thou art but a man, I dare, but as thou art a prince, I fear thee as I fear the roaring of the lion's whelp.

PRINCE HENRY And why not as the lion?

150   **FALSTAFF** The king himself is to be feared as the lion: dost thou think I'll fear thee as I fear thy father? Nay, if I do, let my girdle break.

PRINCE HENRY O, if it should, how would thy guts fall about thy knees! But, sirrah, there's no room for faith,
155   truth, nor honesty in this bosom of thine: it is all filled up with guts and midriff. Charge an honest woman with picking thy pocket? Why, thou whoreson, impudent, embossed rascal, if there were anything in thy pocket but tavern-reck'nings, memorandums of
160   bawdy-houses, and one poor penny-worth of sugar-candy to make thee long-winded: if thy pocket were enriched with any other injuries but these, I am a villain. And yet you will stand to it, you will not pocket up wrong. Art thou not ashamed?

---

128 have place, categorize/have sex with   **148 whelp** cub, offspring   **152 let … break** the breaking of one's belt (**girdle**) proverbially signified bad luck   **158 embossed** swollen/foaming at the mouth with exhaustion like a hunted animal   **rascal** rogue/young, inferior deer   **159 memorandums** bills, invoices **160 sugar-candy … long-winded** sugar was used to improve stamina   **162 injuries** items whose loss you claim has caused you injury   **163 stand to it** insist, maintain your grievance   **164 pocket up** accept (plays on literal sense of 'pocket')

165 **FALSTAFF** Dost thou hear, Hal? Thou know'st in the
state of innocency Adam fell, and what should poor
Jack Falstaff do in the days of villainy? Thou seest
I have more flesh than another man, and therefore
more frailty. You confess then, you picked my
170 pocket?

PRINCE HENRY It appears so by the story.

FALSTAFF Hostess, I forgive thee. Go, make ready
breakfast, love thy husband, look to thy servants
and cherish thy guests. Thou shalt find me tractable
175 to any honest reason: thou seest I am pacified still.
Nay, prithee be gone.— *Exit Hostess*
Now Hal, to the news at court: for the robbery, lad,
how is that answered?

PRINCE HENRY O, my sweet beef, I must still be good
180 angel to thee. The money is paid back again.

FALSTAFF O, I do not like that paying back, 'tis a double
labour.

PRINCE HENRY I am good friends with my father and
may do anything.

185 **FALSTAFF** Rob me the exchequer the first thing thou
dost, and do it with unwashed hands too.

BARDOLPH Do, my lord.

PRINCE HENRY I have procured thee, Jack, a charge of foot.

FALSTAFF I would it had been of horse. Where shall
190 I find one that can steal well? O, for a fine thief, of
two-and-twenty or thereabout! I am heinously
unprovided. Well, God be thanked for these rebels,
they offend none but the virtuous. I laud them,
I praise them.

195 **PRINCE HENRY** Bardolph.

BARDOLPH My lord?

PRINCE HENRY Go bear this letter to Lord John of
Lancaster, *Gives letters*
To my brother John. This to my lord of
Westmorland.— [*Exit Bardolph*]
Go, Peto, to horse, for thou and I

---

168 **flesh . . . frailty** Falstaff plays with the biblical saying 'the flesh is frail' (Matthew 26:41 and elsewhere)
175 **still** always   178 **answered** accounted for   179 **sweet beef** plump, fresh, unsalted beef   **good angel** guardian angel   181 **double labour** i.e. first taking it, then returning it   185 **exchequer** royal treasury   186 **with unwashed hands** straight away/without scruple   188 **charge of foot** command of an infantry company   192 **unprovided** ill-equipped (for villainous exploits)   193 **they . . . virtuous** i.e. by causing war, which provides opportunities for theft and profiteering   **laud** celebrate, praise

200   Have thirty miles to ride yet ere dinner time.—
                                                    [*Exit Peto*]
         Jack, meet me tomorrow in the Temple hall
         At two o'clock in the afternoon.
         There shalt thou know thy charge and there receive
         Money and order for their furniture.
205   The land is burning, Percy stands on high,
         And either they or we must lower lie.
                                             [*Exit Prince Henry*]
    FALSTAFF Rare words! Brave world! Hostess, my
         breakfast, come!
         O, I could wish this tavern were my drum!   *Exit*

Act 4 Scene 1   *running scene 11*

Enter Harry Hotspur, Worcester and Douglas

    HOTSPUR Well said, my noble Scot. If speaking truth
         In this fine age were not thought flattery,
         Such attribution should the Douglas have,
         As not a soldier of this season's stamp
5   Should go so general current through the world.
         By heaven, I cannot flatter: I defy
         The tongues of soothers. But a braver place
         In my heart's love hath no man than yourself.
         Nay, task me to my word, approve me, lord.
10   **DOUGLAS** Thou art the king of honour:
         No man so potent breathes upon the ground
         But I will beard him.
    Enter a Messenger   **With letters**
    HOTSPUR Do so, and 'tis well.—
         What letters hast there? — I can but thank you.
15   **MESSENGER** These letters come from your father.
    HOTSPUR Letters from him? Why comes he not himself?
    MESSENGER He cannot come, my lord, he is grievous
         sick.

---

201 Temple hall the Inner Temple at one of the London Inns of Court (where young men studied law)
203 charge company, regiment   **204 furniture** equipment   **207 Rare** marvellous   **Brave** splendid
208 tavern...drum Falstaff wishes he might remain at the inn; a **drum** summoned soldiers to battle
(possible pun on **tavern**/'taborin', a type of drum)   **4.1** *Location: the rebel camp near Shrewsbury*
2 fine over-refined   **3 attribution** honour, praise   **4 As not a** that no other   **season's stamp** year's
design or mint (coinage term)   **5 general current** generally accepted (continues coining imagery)   **6 defy**
reject, challenge   **7 soothers** flatterers   **braver** more honourable   **9 task** hold   **approve me** prove,
test   **11 breathes...ground** lives   **12 beard** i.e. challenge, defy (literally, pull insultingly by the beard)
14 but only

HOTSPUR How? Has he the leisure to be sick now
    In such a jostling time? Who leads his power?
20   Under whose government come they along?
MESSENGER His letters bears his mind, not I his mind.
WORCESTER I prithee tell me, doth he keep his bed?
MESSENGER He did, my lord, four days ere I set forth,
    And at the time of my departure thence
25   He was much feared by his physician.
WORCESTER I would the state of time had first been
      whole
    Ere he by sickness had been visited:
    His health was never better worth than now.
HOTSPUR Sick now? Droop now? This sickness doth
      infect
30   The very life-blood of our enterprise,
    'Tis catching hither, even to our camp.
    He writes me here that inward sickness —
    And that his friends by deputation could not
    So soon be drawn, nor did he think it meet
35   To lay so dangerous and dear a trust
    On any soul removed but on his own.
    Yet doth he give us bold advertisement,
    That with our small conjunction we should on,
    To see how fortune is disposed to us,
40   For, as he writes, there is no quailing now,
    Because the king is certainly possessed
    Of all our purposes. What say you to it?
WORCESTER Your father's sickness is a maim to us.
HOTSPUR A perilous gash, a very limb lopped off:
45   And yet, in faith, it is not. His present want
    Seems more than we shall find it. Were it good
    To set the exact wealth of all our states
    All at one cast? To set so rich a main
    On the nice hazard of one doubtful hour?
50   It were not good, for therein should we read

19 jostling clashing, contentious **power** army **20 government** leadership **21 bears** contain/reveal
I his mind this Folio reading makes sense, though it is cheeky for the messenger to answer back in this way;
most modern editors emend to 'not I, my lord'. **22 keep** keep to **25 He . . . by** his health was much feared
for **26 would** wish **state of time** present situation **whole** sound, healthy **28 better worth** more
important **31 catching hither** contagious even here **32 inward sickness** possibly an incomplete line,
or one that expresses Hotspur's hasty manner of speaking **33 by deputation** through those acting on his
behalf **34 drawn** drawn together, assembled **meet** fitting, appropriate **35 dear** important **37 bold
advertisement** resolute advice/advice to be resolute **38 conjunction** combined forces **on** proceed
41 possessed informed **43 maim** serious injury **45 present want** absence now **46 more . . . it** worse
than it will actually prove to be **47 set** hazard, stake **48 cast** throw of the dice **main** army/gambling
stake **49 nice hazard** delicate risk/precarious game of dice **doubtful** uncertain **50 read** discern

The very bottom and the soul of hope,
The very list, the very utmost bound
Of all our fortunes.

DOUGLAS 'Faith, and so we should,
55   Where now remains a sweet reversion,
We may boldly spend upon the hope of what
Is to come in.
A comfort of retirement lives in this.

HOTSPUR A rendezvous, a home to fly unto,
60   If that the devil and mischance look big
Upon the maidenhead of our affairs.

WORCESTER But yet I would your father had been here.
The quality and hair of our attempt
Brooks no division: it will be thought
65   By some, that know not why he is away,
That wisdom, loyalty and mere dislike
Of our proceedings kept the earl from hence.
And think how such an apprehension
May turn the tide of fearful faction
70   And breed a kind of question in our cause,
For well you know, we of the off'ring side
Must keep aloof from strict arbitrement,
And stop all sight-holes, every loop from whence
The eye of reason may pry in upon us:
75   This absence of your father draws a curtain,
That shows the ignorant a kind of fear
Before not dreamt of.

HOTSPUR You strain too far.
I rather of his absence make this use:
80   It lends a lustre and more great opinion,
A larger dare to our great enterprise,
Than if the earl were here, for men must think,
If we without his help can make a head
To push against the kingdom, with his help
85   We shall o'erturn it topsy-turvy down.
Yet all goes well, yet all our joints are whole.

---

51 **very bottom** full extent   52 **list** limit   **bound** extent, boundary   55 **reversion** back-up, something to
be relied on (literally, future inheritance)   58 **retirement** something to fall back on/peace, seclusion
59 **rendezvous** retreat, refuge   60 **big** threateningly, menacingly   61 **maidenhead** beginning, first trial
(literally, virginity)   63 **hair** nature   64 **Brooks** tolerates   66 **loyalty** i.e. to the king   **mere** absolute
68 **apprehension** thought, perception   69 **fearful faction** (rebel) alliances that generate fear/frightened
groups (of rebel sympathizers)   70 **question** doubt, mistrust   71 **off'ring** challenging, aggressing
72 **strict arbitrement** close scrutiny, rigorous judgement   73 **loop** loophole, aperture   75 **draws** opens
78 **strain too far** exaggerate   79 **make this use** find this advantage   80 **opinion** renown, prestige
81 **dare** boldness   83 **make a head** raise an army   86 **Yet** still   **joints** limbs

DOUGLAS As heart can think. There is not such a word
    Spoke of in Scotland as this dream of fear.
Enter Sir Richard Vernon
HOTSPUR My cousin Vernon, welcome, by my soul.
90 VERNON Pray God my news be worth a welcome, lord.
    The Earl of Westmorland, seven thousand strong,
    Is marching hitherwards, with him Prince John.
HOTSPUR No harm: what more?
VERNON And further, I have learned,
95   The king himself in person hath set forth,
    Or hitherwards intended speedily,
    With strong and mighty preparation.
HOTSPUR He shall be welcome too. Where is his son,
    The nimble-footed madcap Prince of Wales,
100   And his comrades that daffed the world aside
    And bid it pass?
VERNON All furnished, all in arms,
    All plumed like estridges that with the wind
    Bated like eagles having lately bathed,
105   Glittering in golden coats like images,
    As full of spirit as the month of May,
    And gorgeous as the sun at midsummer,
    Wanton as youthful goats, wild as young bulls.
    I saw young Harry with his beaver on,
110   His cuisses on his thighs, gallantly armed,
    Rise from the ground like feathered Mercury,
    And vaulted with such ease into his seat,
    As if an angel dropped down from the clouds,
    To turn and wind a fiery Pegasus
115   And witch the world with noble horsemanship.
HOTSPUR No more, no more. Worse than the sun in
      March,
    This praise doth nourish agues. Let them come.
    They come like sacrifices in their trim,
    And to the fire-eyed maid of smoky war

---

87 As . . . think i.e. as can possibly be wished   **93 No harm** i.e. that doesn't matter   **96 intended** is about to leave   **97 preparation** equipped military force   **100 daffed** tossed carelessly   **102 furnished** equipped **103 estridges** ostriches (presumably the men's helmets are adorned with feathers)   **104 Bated** fluttered **105 golden coats** sleeveless outer garments richly adorned with heraldic arms, worn over armour **images** gilded statues/emblems   **107 gorgeous** brightly coloured, magnificent   **108 Wanton** wild, frolicsome, carefree   **109 beaver** helmet (technically, the visor)   **110 cuisses** thigh armour **111 feathered Mercury** Roman messenger of the gods, usually depicted with wings on cap and sandals **112 seat** i.e. saddle   **114 wind** wheel about, turn   **Pegasus** winged horse in Greek mythology **115 witch** bewitch   **117 agues** violent fevers thought to be bred or worsened by the early spring **sun 118 trim** finery, adornment (like animals garlanded for sacrifice)   **119 maid . . . war** Bellona, the Roman goddess of war

120   All hot and bleeding will we offer them:
    The mailèd Mars shall on his altar sit
    Up to the ears in blood. I am on fire
    To hear this rich reprisal is so nigh
    And yet not ours. Come, let me take my horse,
125   Who is to bear me like a thunderbolt
    Against the bosom of the Prince of Wales.
    Harry to Harry, shall hot horse to horse
    Meet and ne'er part till one drop down a corpse!
    O, that Glendower were come!
130 **VERNON** There is more news:
    I learned in Worcester, as I rode along,
    He cannot draw his power this fourteen days.
DOUGLAS That's the worst tidings that I hear of yet.
WORCESTER Ay, by my faith, that bears a frosty sound.
135 **HOTSPUR** What may the king's whole battle reach unto?
VERNON To thirty thousand.
HOTSPUR Forty let it be.
    My father and Glendower being both away,
    The powers of us may serve so great a day.
140   Come, let us take a muster speedily:
    Doomsday is near; die all, die merrily.
DOUGLAS Talk not of dying. I am out of fear
    Of death or death's hand for this one-half year. *Exeunt*

Act 4 Scene 2   *running scene 12*

Enter Falstaff and Bardolph

FALSTAFF Bardolph, get thee before to Coventry. Fill me
    a bottle of sack. Our soldiers shall march through,
    we'll to Sutton Coldfield tonight.
BARDOLPH Will you give me money, captain?
5 **FALSTAFF** Lay out, lay out.
BARDOLPH This bottle makes an angel.

---

121 **mailèd Mars** Roman god of war, clad in armour   123 **reprisal** prize   131 **Worcester** English town on the River Severn   132 **draw...days** gather his forces for a fortnight   135 **What...unto?** What is the total number of the king's troops?   139 **powers of us** forces we have   **serve** suffice for   140 **muster** roll-call   141 **Doomsday** Judgement Day   142 **out of** free from   143 **this one-half year** six months; Douglas does not expect to die within this period   **4.2** *Location: the road (they are travelling, probably along the Roman road Watling Street from London to Shrewsbury via Coventry, a Midlands town near Stratford-upon-Avon)*   1 **get thee before** you go on ahead   3 **Sutton Coldfield** Warwickshire town twenty miles north-west of Coventry   5 **Lay out** pay for it yourself   6 **makes** brings the amount you owe me to (Falstaff responds to the sense of 'creates')   **angel** a gold coin variously worth between 6s 8d and 10s

FALSTAFF An if it do, take it for thy labour. And if it
make twenty, take them all, I'll answer the coinage.
Bid my lieutenant Peto meet me at the town's end.

10   BARDOLPH I will, captain. Farewell.   *Exit*

FALSTAFF If I be not ashamed of my soldiers, I am a
soused gurnet. I have misused the king's press
damnably. I have got, in exchange of a hundred and
fifty soldiers, three hundred and odd pounds. I press

15   me none but good householders, yeoman's sons,
inquire me out contracted bachelors, such as had been
asked twice on the banns, such a commodity of warm
slaves as had as lieve hear the devil as a drum; such as
fear the report of a caliver worse than a struck fowl or

20   a hurt wild duck. I pressed me none but such toasts-
and-butter, with hearts in their bellies no bigger than
pins' heads, and they have bought out their services.
And now my whole charge consists of ancients,
corporals, lieutenants, gentlemen of companies, slaves

25   as ragged as Lazarus in the painted cloth, where the
glutton's dogs licked his sores; and such as indeed
were never soldiers, but discarded unjust servingmen,
younger sons to younger brothers, revolted tapsters
and ostlers trade-fallen, the cankers of a calm world

30   and long peace, ten times more dishonourable ragged
than an old-faced ancient; and such have I, to fill up
the rooms of them that have bought out their services,
that you would think that I had a hundred and fifty
tattered prodigals lately come from swine-keeping,

35   from eating draff and husks. A mad fellow met me on

---

8 answer the coinage be responsible for the validity of the coins   **12 soused gurnet** type of pickled
fish/drunkard   **press** power of conscription   **13 I . . . pounds** Falstaff has allowed those who can afford it to
buy their way out of being soldiers   **of** for   **15 good** substantial, wealthy   **yeomen's sons** the sons of
freeholders of small landed estates   **16 inquire me out** ask for, seek   **contracted** engaged (to be married)
17 banns public notice of the intention to marry, announced in church on three successive Sundays; the
bachelors here are to be married soon   **commodity** portion, quantity   **warm** comfortably off/sexually
eager   **18 lieve** soon   **drum** i.e. customarily sounded to enlist recruits or call men to battle   **19 caliver**
musket, lightweight firearm   **20 toasts-and-butter** milksops, pampered fellows   **21 hearts . . . heads** i.e.
those with little appetite for fighting   **22 bought . . . services** bribed Falstaff to be exempted from military
service   **23 charge** command, unit   **ancients** ensigns, i.e. soldiers who carried military banners (plays on
the sense of 'elderly people')   **24 gentlemen of companies** gentlemen soldiers without formal rank
25 Lazarus . . . sores refers to the biblical story of the beggar Lazarus and the contemptuous rich man (Luke
16:19–21)   **painted cloth** cheap wall-hanging depicting the biblical tale   **27 discarded unjust servingmen** dismissed dishonest servants   **28 younger . . . brothers** i.e. those with no hope of a substantial
inheritance   **revolted tapsters** apprentice barmen who have run away from their masters   **29 ostlers**
trade-fallen out-of-work stablemen   **cankers** ulcers/parasites   **31 ancient** military banner   **32 rooms**
places   **34 prodigals** in the biblical parable, the prodigal (extravagant) son wasted his inheritance and was
reduced to feeding with the pigs   **35 draff and husks** pigswill and corn husks

the way and told me I had unloaded all the gibbets
and pressed the dead bodies. No eye hath seen such
scarecrows. I'll not march through Coventry with
them, that's flat. Nay, and the villains march wide
40   betwixt the legs, as if they had gyves on; for indeed,
I had the most of them out of prison. There's not a
shirt and a half in all my company, and the half shirt
is two napkins tacked together and thrown over the
shoulders like a herald's coat without sleeves, and the
45   shirt, to say the truth, stolen from my host of Saint
Albans, or the red-nose innkeeper of Daventry. But
that's all one, they'll find linen enough on every
hedge.

Enter the Prince and the Lord of Westmorland

PRINCE HENRY How now, blown Jack? How now, quilt?
50   **FALSTAFF** What, Hal? How now, mad wag? What a devil
dost thou in Warwickshire? — My good lord of
Westmorland, I cry you mercy: I thought your
honour had already been at Shrewsbury.

WESTMORLAND 'Faith, Sir John, 'tis more than time that
55   I were there, and you too, but my powers are there
already. The king, I can tell you, looks for us all: we
must away all tonight.

FALSTAFF Tut, never fear me. I am as vigilant as a cat to
steal cream.

60   **PRINCE HENRY** I think to steal cream indeed, for thy theft
hath already made thee butter. But tell me, Jack,
whose fellows are these that come after?

FALSTAFF Mine, Hal, mine.

PRINCE HENRY I did never see such pitiful rascals.

65   **FALSTAFF** Tut, tut, good enough to toss: food for powder,
food for powder. They'll fill a pit as well as better.
Tush, man, mortal men, mortal men.

WESTMORLAND Ay, but, Sir John, methinks they are
exceeding poor and bare, too beggarly.

---

36 gibbets gallows   **40 gyves** leg-irons, shackles   **44 herald's ... sleeves** the tabard was a sleeveless
outer garment open down the sides   **45 Saint Albans** town along Watling Street about twenty-five miles
north of London   **46 Daventry** Northamptonshire town south-east of Coventry   **47 find ... hedge** i.e.
they'll steal clothes left to dry on hedgerows   **49 blown** swollen/short of breath   **quilt** padded covering/fat
man (plays on Falstaff's name, Jack, which could also mean a padded tunic worn instead of armour   **52 cry
you mercy** beg your pardon   **56 looks for** expects   **58 fear** doubt   **61 butter** i.e. fat   **65 toss** throw
away/impale on a pike   **food for powder** cannon-fodder   **66 pit** mass grave   **as well as better** just as
well as better men would   **67 Tush** exclamation of contempt   **69 bare** poorly clothed/inadequately
equipped (Falstaff shifts the sense to 'bare-boned, thin')

70   **FALSTAFF** Faith, for their poverty, I know not where they
        had that; and for their bareness, I am sure they never
        learned that of me.
    PRINCE HENRY No, I'll be sworn, unless you call three
        fingers on the ribs bare. But, sirrah, make haste.
75   Percy is already in the field.
    FALSTAFF What, is the king encamped?
    WESTMORLAND He is, Sir John. I fear we shall stay too
        long.
    FALSTAFF Well,
80   To the latter end of a fray and the beginning of a feast
        Fits a dull fighter and a keen guest.   *Exeunt*

Act 4 Scene 3   *running scene 13*

Enter Hotspur, Worcester, Douglas and Vernon

    HOTSPUR We'll fight with him tonight.
    WORCESTER It may not be.
    DOUGLAS You give him then advantage.
    VERNON Not a whit.
5   **HOTSPUR** Why say you so? Looks he not for supply?
    VERNON So do we.
    HOTSPUR His is certain, ours is doubtful.
    WORCESTER Good cousin, be advised, stir not tonight.
    VERNON Do not, my lord.
10   **DOUGLAS** You do not counsel well:
        You speak it out of fear and cold heart.
    VERNON Do me no slander, Douglas: by my life,
        And I dare well maintain it with my life,
        If well-respected honour bid me on,
15   I hold as little counsel with weak fear
        As you, my lord, or any Scot that this day lives.
        Let it be seen tomorrow in the battle
        Which of us fears.
    DOUGLAS Yea, or tonight.
20   **VERNON** Content.
    HOTSPUR Tonight, say I.

---

73 three . . . ribs three fingers' depth of fat covering his ribs; a 'finger' measured three quarters of an
inch   **75 field** battlefield   **77 stay** delay   **80 To . . . guest** i.e. the end of a fight and the beginning of a feast
is the best time to arrive for one keener on eating than fighting (proverbial)   **4.3** *Location: the rebel
camp near Shrewsbury*   **1 him** i.e. the king   **3 then** in that case, if you wait   **5 Looks . . . supply?** Is he
not expecting reinforcements?   **13 maintain** justify, support, prove   **14 well-respected** well-considered
bid me on urges me forward   **15 counsel** conference

VERNON Come, come it may not be. I wonder much,
    Being men of such great leading as you are,
    That you foresee not what impediments
25   Drag back our expedition: certain horse
    Of my cousin Vernon's are not yet come up,
    Your uncle Worcester's horse came but today,
    And now their pride and mettle is asleep,
    Their courage with hard labour tame and dull,
30   That not a horse is half the half of himself.
HOTSPUR So are the horses of the enemy
    In general, journey-bated and brought low.
    The better part of ours are full of rest.
WORCESTER The number of the king exceedeth ours:
35   For God's sake, cousin, stay till all come in.
                       The trumpet sounds a parley
Enter Sir Walter Blunt
BLUNT I come with gracious offers from the king,
    If you vouchsafe me hearing and respect.
HOTSPUR Welcome, Sir Walter Blunt, and would to God
    You were of our determination.
40   Some of us love you well, and even those some
    Envy your great deservings and good name,
    Because you are not of our quality,
    But stand against us like an enemy.
BLUNT And heaven defend but still I should stand so,
45   So long as out of limit and true rule
    You stand against anointed majesty.
    But to my charge: the king hath sent to know
    The nature of your griefs, and whereupon
    You conjure from the breast of civil peace
50   Such bold hostility, teaching his duteous land
    Audacious cruelty. If that the king
    Have any way your good deserts forgot,
    Which he confesseth to be manifold,
    He bids you name your griefs, and with all speed
55   You shall have your desires with interest,

---

23 leading leadership   **25 Drag** hold   **expedition** speedy action   **horse** horses, cavalry   **28 pride and mettle** spirit and liveliness   **30 That…himself** so that none of the horses is even a quarter of its normal strength   **32 journey-bated** exhausted by travelling   *parley* trumpet summons to negotiation between enemy forces   **37 vouchsafe** permit   **respect** consideration   **39 determination** mind, conviction   **40 even those some** those very people   **42 quality** party   **44 defend** forbid   **45 out of limit** past the bounds of natural order and allegiance   **46 anointed** i.e. rightful, legitimate (having been marked with holy oil as part of the coronation ceremony)   **47 charge** duty, task   **48 griefs** grievances, complaints   **whereupon** on what grounds   **49 conjure** call forth (with connotations of magical invocation and bewitchment)   **51 If that** if   **52 deserts** deservings, merits   **55 with interest** and more in addition

And pardon absolute for yourself and these
Herein misled by your suggestion.
HOTSPUR The king is kind, and well we know the king
Knows at what time to promise, when to pay.
60 My father, my uncle and myself
Did give him that same royalty he wears,
And when he was not six and twenty strong,
Sick in the world's regard, wretched and low,
A poor unminded outlaw sneaking home,
65 My father gave him welcome to the shore.
And when he heard him swear and vow to God
He came but to be Duke of Lancaster,
To sue his livery and beg his peace,
With tears of innocency and terms of zeal,
70 My father, in kind heart and pity moved,
Swore him assistance and performed it too.
Now when the lords and barons of the realm
Perceived Northumberland did lean to him,
The more and less came in with cap and knee,
75 Met him in boroughs, cities, villages,
Attended him on bridges, stood in lanes,
Laid gifts before him, proffered him their oaths,
Gave him their heirs, as pages followed him
Even at the heels in golden multitudes.
80 He presently, as greatness knows itself,
Steps me a little higher than his vow
Made to my father, while his blood was poor,
Upon the naked shore at Ravenspurgh,
And now, forsooth, takes on him to reform
85 Some certain edicts and some strait decrees
That lay too heavy on the commonwealth,
Cries out upon abuses, seems to weep
Over his country's wrongs, and by this face,
This seeming brow of justice, did he win

---

57 suggestion prompting, incitement   **62 was...strong** had fewer than twenty-six followers
63 Sick...regard suffering poor public reputation   **64 unminded** disregarded   **outlaw** Richard II had
banished Henry Bullingbrook; he returned following his father's death and Richard's seizure of his land and
titles   **68 sue his livery** legally claim his right to inherit his father's lands and title   **beg his peace** seek
reconciliation with King Richard   **69 terms of zeal** i.e. eager assurances of loyalty   **74 more...knee**
those of higher and lower social status offered him allegiance – with cap in hand and knees bent in a bow/
kneeling   **76 Attended** awaited/accompanied   **lanes** paths/rows   **78 heirs...followed** punctuated thus
in Folio, but most editors emend to 'heirs as pages, followed', thus altering the sense   **79 golden** splendidly
or brightly dressed/celebratory, joyous/rich, abundant   **80 presently** soon   **greatness knows itself** those
in power come to understand their situation   **81 Steps...higher** becomes more ambitious
82 his...poor he was still humble/before he was king   **84 forsooth** in truth, perhaps used ironically
here   **85 strait** harsh, strict   **87 Cries...abuses** condemns corruption, draws attention to wrongs

90   The hearts of all that he did angle for.
        Proceeded further — cut me off the heads
        Of all the favourites that the absent king
        In deputation left behind him here,
        When he was personal in the Irish war.
95 **BLUNT** Tut, I came not to hear this.
    HOTSPUR Then to the point.
        In short time after, he deposed the king.
        Soon after that, deprived him of his life,
        And in the neck of that, tasked the whole state.
100   To make that worse, suffered his kinsman March —
        Who is, if every owner were placed,
        Indeed his king — to be engaged in Wales,
        There without ransom to lie forfeited,
        Disgraced me in my happy victories,
105   Sought to entrap me by intelligence,
        Rated my uncle from the council board,
        In rage dismissed my father from the court,
        Broke oath on oath, committed wrong on wrong,
        And in conclusion drove us to seek out
110   This head of safety; and withal to pry
        Into his title, the which we find
        Too indirect for long continuance.
    BLUNT Shall I return this answer to the king?
    HOTSPUR Not so, Sir Walter. We'll withdraw awhile.
115   Go to the king, and let there be impawned
        Some surety for a safe return again,
        And in the morning early shall my uncle
        Bring him our purpose. And so farewell.
    BLUNT I would you would accept of grace and love.
120 **HOTSPUR** And't may be so we shall.
    BLUNT Pray heaven you do.   *Exeunt*

---

91 cut . . . favourites Richard's favourite courtiers were beheaded   **cut me** cut (**me** is emphatic)   **93 In deputation** as his deputies   **94 was personal in** went in person to   **99 in . . . of** on the strength of/ immediately after   **tasked** taxed   **100 March** the Earl of March, Edmund Mortimer   **101 if . . . placed** if every claimant were entitled to occupy their rightful position   **102 engaged** held hostage   **103 forfeited** abandoned   **104 Disgraced . . . victories** i.e. by demanding my prisoners, the King turned my triumphs into disgrace   **105 intelligence** spying   **106 Rated** chided angrily, dismissed   **110 head of safety** defensive army   **withal** furthermore   **pry . . . title** examine his claim (to the throne)   **112 indirect** insufficiently direct in the line of succession/devious, irregular   **for long continuance** to last long   **115 impawned** pledged, held in pawn   **116 surety** guarantee   **119 accept . . . love** i.e. be reconciled

Act 4 Scene 4

Enter the Archbishop of York and Sir Michael

ARCHBISHOP OF YORK Hie, good Sir Michael; bear this   *Gives a letter*
    sealèd brief
    With wingèd haste to the Lord Marshal,
    This to my cousin Scroop, and all the rest
    To whom they are directed. If you knew
5   How much they do import, you would make haste.
SIR MICHAEL My good lord,
    I guess their tenor.
ARCHBISHOP OF YORK Like enough you do.
    Tomorrow, good Sir Michael, is a day
10   Wherein the fortune of ten thousand men
    Must bide the touch, for, sir, at Shrewsbury,
    As I am truly given to understand,
    The king with mighty and quick-raisèd power
    Meets with Lord Harry. And I fear, Sir Michael,
15   What with the sickness of Northumberland,
    Whose power was in the first proportion,
    And what with Owen Glendower's absence thence,
    Who with them was rated firmly too
    And comes not in, o'er-ruled by prophecies,
20   I fear the power of Percy is too weak
    To wage an instant trial with the king.
SIR MICHAEL Why, my good lord, you need not fear.
    There is Douglas and Lord Mortimer.
ARCHBISHOP OF YORK No, Mortimer is not there.
25 **SIR MICHAEL** But there is Mordake, Vernon, Lord Harry
    Percy,
    And there is my lord of Worcester and a head
    Of gallant warriors, noble gentlemen.
ARCHBISHOP OF YORK And so there is. But yet the king
    hath drawn

4.4 *Location: unspecified; presumably in the Archbishop of York's palace*   ***Sir Michael*** presumably a priest or a knight; 'sir' can be a courtesy title for clergymen   **1 Hie** go quickly   **brief** letter, dispatch   **4 directed** addressed   **5 much … import** much information they contain/important they are   **7 tenor** substance, drift   **8 Like** likely   **11 bide the touch** be put to the test (as gold is tested with a touchstone)   **14 Lord Harry** i.e. Hotspur   **16 power … proportion** army was of the greatest size/importance   **18 rated firmly** considered to be strong, a powerful source of support   **19 comes not in** does not participate   **o'er-ruled by prophecies** i.e. he is staying away due to unfavourable predictions of events   **21 instant trial** immediate test of strength   **26 head** force, army

The special head of all the land together:

30   The Prince of Wales, Lord John of Lancaster,
         The noble Westmorland and warlike Blunt;
         And many more corrivals and dear men
         Of estimation and command in arms.

SIR MICHAEL Doubt not, my lord, he shall be well
         opposed.

35   **ARCHBISHOP OF YORK** I hope no less, yet needful 'tis to
         fear.
         And, to prevent the worst, Sir Michael, speed;
         For if Lord Percy thrive not, ere the king
         Dismiss his power, he means to visit us,
         For he hath heard of our confederacy,

40   And 'tis but wisdom to make strong against him:
         Therefore make haste. I must go write again
         To other friends, and so farewell, Sir Michael. *Exeunt*

Act 5 Scene 1   *running scene 15*

*Enter the King, Prince of Wales, Lord John of Lancaster, Earl
of Westmorland, Sir Walter Blunt and Falstaff*

KING HENRY IV How bloodily the sun begins to peer
         Above yon busky hill! The day looks pale
         At his distemperature.

PRINCE HENRY The southern wind

5   Doth play the trumpet to his purposes,
         And by his hollow whistling in the leaves
         Foretells a tempest and a blust'ring day.

KING HENRY IV Then with the losers let it sympathize,
         For nothing can seem foul to those that win.
                                        The trumpet sounds

Enter Worcester [and Vernon]

10   How now, my lord of Worcester? 'Tis not well
         That you and I should meet upon such terms
         As now we meet. You have deceived our trust,
         And made us doff our easy robes of peace,
         To crush our old limbs in ungentle steel:

15   This is not well, my lord, this is not well.

---

29 **special head** exceptional military leadership   32 **corrivals** partners   **dear** honourable/valuable
33 **estimation** worth, reputation   37 **thrive** flourish, succeed   39 **confederacy** league, conspiracy (with
the rebels)   40 **make strong** strengthen our defences   5.1 *Location: the king's camp near
Shrewsbury*   2 **busky** bush-covered   3 **distemperature** unhealthy, unnatural appearance   5 **the
trumpet** part of trumpeter or herald   9 **foul** gloomy, bad (weather)   13 **doff** take off   **easy** comfortable
14 **ungentle steel** hard, uncomfortable steel armour

What say you to it? Will you again unknit
This churlish knot of all-abhorrèd war?
And move in that obedient orb again
Where you did give a fair and natural light,
20   And be no more an exhaled meteor,
A prodigy of fear and a portent
Of broachèd mischief to the unborn times?
WORCESTER Hear me, my liege:
For mine own part, I could be well content
25   To entertain the lag-end of my life
With quiet hours, for I do protest,
I have not sought the day of this dislike.
KING HENRY IV You have not sought it? How comes it,
      then?
FALSTAFF Rebellion lay in his way, and he found it.
30   **PRINCE HENRY** Peace, chewet, peace!
WORCESTER It pleased your majesty to turn your looks
Of favour from myself and all our house;
And yet I must remember you, my lord,
We were the first and dearest of your friends.
35   For you my staff of office did I break
In Richard's time, and posted day and night
To meet you on the way, and kiss your hand,
When yet you were in place and in account
Nothing so strong and fortunate as I.
40   It was myself, my brother and his son,
That brought you home and boldly did outdare
The danger of the time. You swore to us,
And you did swear that oath at Doncaster,
That you did nothing of purpose gainst the state,
45   Nor claim no further than your new-fall'n right,
The seat of Gaunt, dukedom of Lancaster.
To this we swore our aid. But in short space
It rained down fortune show'ring on your head,
And such a flood of greatness fell on you —
50   What with our help, what with the absent king,

---

16 unknit undo   **17 churlish** rude, ungracious, base   **18 orb** orbit, sphere   **20 exhaled meteor** meteors
were believed to be formed of vapours drawn from the earth ('exhaled') by the sun; they were considered bad
omens   **21 prodigy** omen/unnatural thing   **22 broachèd** already begun   **mischief** evil, calamity
unborn times future   **25 entertain** occupy   **lag-end** latter part   **27 dislike** animosity, discord
30 chewet chough, jackdaw, i.e. chatterer/minced meat or fish pie   **33 remember** remind   **35 staff of
office** Worcester had been steward of the king's household   **36 posted** rode speedily   **39 Nothing**
nowhere near   **41 brought** escorted, accompanied   **outdare** defy   **43 Doncaster** town in the north-east
of England   **44 did . . . state** had no intention of threatening the realm   **45 new-fall'n right** recently
inherited title (after his father's death)   **46 seat** estate   **Gaunt** John of Gaunt, Henry's father

What with the injuries of wanton time,
The seeming sufferances that you had borne,
And the contrarious winds that held the king
So long in the unlucky Irish wars
55   That all in England did repute him dead —
And from this swarm of fair advantages
You took occasion to be quickly wooed
To gripe the general sway into your hand,
Forgot your oath to us at Doncaster,
60   And being fed by us, you used us so
As that ungentle gull, the cuckoo's bird,
Useth the sparrow, did oppress our nest,
Grew by our feeding to so great a bulk
That even our love durst not come near your sight
65   For fear of swallowing. But with nimble wing
We were enforced, for safety sake, to fly
Out of your sight and raise this present head,
Whereby we stand opposèd by such means
As you yourself have forged against yourself
70   By unkind usage, dangerous countenance,
And violation of all faith and troth
Sworn to us in your younger enterprise.
KING HENRY IV These things indeed you have articulated,
Proclaimed at market-crosses, read in churches,
75   To face the garment of rebellion
With some fine colour that may please the eye
Of fickle changelings and poor discontents,
Which gape and rub the elbow at the news
Of hurly-burly innovation:
80   And never yet did insurrection want
Such water-colours to impaint his cause,
Nor moody beggars, starving for a time
Of pell-mell havoc and confusion.

---

51 **injuries** abuses, wrongdoing **wanton** ungoverned, poorly managed 52 **seeming sufferances** apparent wrongs 53 **contrarious** opposing, unfavourable 54 **unlucky** ill-fated 55 **repute** believe him to be 57 **occasion** the opportunity **wooed** persuaded 58 **gripe** grip, grasp **general sway** overall power 61 **ungentle gull** cruel/dishonourable young bird **cuckoo's . . . sparrow** the cuckoo lays its eggs in other birds' nests to be hatched and fed; cuckoo chicks are much bigger and eventually take over the nest 64 **our love** those of us who loved you **durst not** did not dare 65 **swallowing** being eaten 68 **opposèd . . . means** in opposition to you as a result of such factors 70 **unkind** cruel/unnatural 71 **troth** honesty, integrity 72 **younger** earlier, original 75 **face** adorn, cover 76 **colour** hue/pretexts, pretence 77 **changelings** turncoats, changeable people **discontents** discontented persons 78 **rub the elbow** hug themselves in pleasure 79 **hurly-burly** chaotic **innovation** novelty, change, revolution 80 **want** need, lack 81 **water-colours** watery deceptions **impaint** paint, colour 82 **moody** sullen, angry 83 **havoc** plundering, violent disorder

PRINCE HENRY In both our armies there is many a soul
85   Shall pay full dearly for this encounter,
        If once they join in trial. Tell your nephew,
        The Prince of Wales doth join with all the world
        In praise of Henry Percy: by my hopes —
        This present enterprise set off his head —
90   I do not think a braver gentleman,
        More active-valiant or more valiant-young,
        More daring or more bold, is now alive
        To grace this latter age with noble deeds.
        For my part, I may speak it to my shame,
95   I have a truant been to chivalry,
        And so I hear he doth account me too.
        Yet this before my father's majesty:
        I am content that he shall take the odds
        Of his great name and estimation,
100   And will, to save the blood on either side,
        Try fortune with him in a single fight.
KING HENRY IV And, Prince of Wales, so dare we venture
            thee,
        Albeit considerations infinite
        Do make against it. No, good Worcester, no,
105   We love our people well; even those we love
        That are misled upon your cousin's part.
        And, will they take the offer of our grace,
        Both he and they and you, yea, every man
        Shall be my friend again and I'll be his.
110   So tell your cousin, and bring me word
        What he will do. But if he will not yield,
        Rebuke and dread correction wait on us
        And they shall do their office. So, be gone,
        We will not now be troubled with reply.
115   We offer fair, take it advisedly.
                        Exeunt Worcester [and Vernon]
PRINCE HENRY It will not be accepted, on my life.
        The Douglas and the Hotspur both together
        Are confident against the world in arms.

---

84 **both our** i.e. the king's and the rebels'   86 **trial** battle   88 **by my hopes** i.e. of salvation   89 **set...
head** not counted against him   90 **braver** finer/more courageous   93 **latter** recent, present   97 **this** I say
this   98 **odds** advantages   99 **estimation** reputation   102 **venture** hazard, risk   103 **Albeit** despite the
fact that   104 **make** weigh, argue   106 **cousin's** relative's (i.e. nephew's)   107 **grace** pardon
112 **Rebuke** shame, disgrace   **dread correction** terrible punishment   **wait on us** are at my command
113 **office** duty, task   115 **fair** fairly, fair terms   **take it advisedly** consider it carefully

KING HENRY IV Hence, therefore, every leader to his
        charge,
120   For on their answer will we set on them;
        And God befriend us as our cause is just!

                        Exeunt all but Prince and Falstaff

FALSTAFF Hal, if thou see me down in the battle and
        bestride me, so; 'tis a point of friendship.

PRINCE HENRY Nothing but a colossus can do thee that
125   friendship. Say thy prayers, and farewell.

FALSTAFF I would it were bedtime, Hal, and all well.

PRINCE HENRY Why, thou ow'st heaven a death.

                        [*Exit Prince Henry*]

FALSTAFF 'Tis not due yet. I would be loath to pay him
        before his day. What need I be so forward with him
130   that calls not on me? Well, 'tis no matter, honour
        pricks me on. But how if honour prick me off when I
        come on? How then? Can honour set to a leg? No. Or
        an arm? No. Or take away the grief of a wound? No.
        Honour hath no skill in surgery, then? No. What is
135   honour? A word. What is that word 'honour'? Air. A
        trim   reckoning!   Who   hath   it?   He   that   died
        o'Wednesday. Doth he feel it? No. Doth he hear it?
        No. Is it insensible, then? Yea, to the dead. But will it
        not live with the living? No. Why? Detraction will not
140   suffer it. Therefore I'll none of it. Honour is a mere
        scutcheon: and so ends my catechism.   *Exit*

Act 5 Scene 2   *running scene 16*

Enter Worcester and Sir Richard Vernon

WORCESTER O, no, my nephew must not know, Sir
        Richard,
        The liberal kind offer of the king.

VERNON 'Twere best he did.

---

119 **charge** command/company, unit/responsibility   120 **on their answer** once we've had their answer,
i.e. refusal of the terms   123 **bestride** stand astride a fallen man in order to defend him   **so** thus –
presumably Falstaff demonstrates the gesture   124 **colossus** giant; the Colossus of Rhodes, a gigantic
statue of Apollo, supposedly stood astride the entrance to the harbour   127 **death** proverbial; puns on
'debt'   129 **forward** eager   131 **pricks** spurs   **prick me off** marks me down (for a dead man)
132 **set . . . leg** join together, set a broken leg   133 **grief** pain   136 **trim** fine, neat   138 **insensible** cannot
be felt by the senses   139 **Detraction** slander   141 **scutcheon** heraldic shield, decorated with coats of
arms and often used at funerals   **catechism** set series of questions and answers (used as a form of
instruction by the Church)   5.2   *Location: the rebel camp near Shrewsbury, then the battlefield*

WORCESTER Then we are all undone.

5   It is not possible, it cannot be,
       The king would keep his word in loving us.
       He will suspect us still and find a time
       To punish this offence in other faults.
       Supposition all our lives shall be stuck full of eyes;
10   For treason is but trusted like the fox,
       Who, ne'er so tame, so cherished and locked up,
       Will have a wild trick of his ancestors.
       Look how he can, or sad or merrily,
       Interpretation will misquote our looks,
15   And we shall feed like oxen at a stall,
       The better cherished, still the nearer death.
       My nephew's trespass may be well forgot,
       It hath the excuse of youth and heat of blood,
       And an adopted name of privilege,
20   A hare-brained Hotspur, governed by a spleen:
       All his offences live upon my head
       And on his father's. We did train him on,
       And, his corruption being ta'en from us,
       We as the spring of all, shall pay for all.
25   Therefore, good cousin, let not Harry know,
       In any case, the offer of the king.

VERNON Deliver what you will, I'll say 'tis so.
       Here comes your cousin.

Enter Hotspur [and Douglas]

HOTSPUR My uncle is returned.
30   Deliver up my lord of Westmorland.—
       Uncle, what news?

WORCESTER The king will bid you battle presently.

DOUGLAS Defy him by the lord of Westmorland.

HOTSPUR Lord Douglas, go you and tell him so.

35 **DOUGLAS** Marry, and shall, and very willingly.

Exit Douglas

WORCESTER There is no seeming mercy in the king.

---

4 undone ruined **7 still** always **9 Supposition** notions, uncertainty, speculation **stuck...eyes** always watching, suspicious **11 ne'er so tame** however tame he appears **12 trick** trait **13 Look... can** however one appears **or sad** either sad **14 misquote** falsely report, misinterpret **16 The...death** refers to the fact that **oxen** are fattened up before being killed **17 trespass** wrongdoing, transgression **19 adopted...privilege** nickname which gives him licence (i.e. **Hotspur**, signifying rash impulsiveness) **20 hare-brained** reckless, rash **spleen** violent bad temper (from the abdominal organ regarded as the location of strong emotion) **21 live upon** shall be blamed on **22 train** lead **23 ta'en** derived, caught (like an infectious disease) **24 spring** source **26 In any case** whatever happens **27 Deliver...so** say what you like, I'll agree **30 Deliver up** release – Westmorland has been held as surety for Worcester's safe return **32 battle** to engage in battle **33 Defy him by** send our defiant response through **36 seeming** apparent

HOTSPUR Did you beg any? God forbid!
WORCESTER I told him gently of our grievances,
 Of his oath-breaking, which he mended thus,
40 By now forswearing that he is forsworn.
 He calls us rebels, traitors, and will scourge
 With haughty arms this hateful name in us.
Enter Douglas
DOUGLAS Arm, gentlemen, to arms! For I have thrown
 A brave defiance in King Henry's teeth,
45 And Westmorland that was engaged did bear it,
 Which cannot choose but bring him quickly on.
WORCESTER The Prince of Wales stepped forth before
  the king,
 And, nephew, challenged you to single fight.
HOTSPUR O, would the quarrel lay upon our heads,
50 And that no man might draw short breath today
 But I and Harry Monmouth! Tell me, tell me,
 How showed his talking? Seemed it in contempt?
VERNON No, by my soul. I never in my life
 Did hear a challenge urged more modestly,
55 Unless a brother should a brother dare
 To gentle exercise and proof of arms.
 He gave you all the duties of a man,
 Trimmed up your praises with a princely tongue,
 Spoke your deservings like a chronicle,
60 Making you ever better than his praise
 By still dispraising praise valued with you.
 And, which became him like a prince indeed,
 He made a blushing cital of himself,
 And chid his truant youth with such a grace
65 As if he mastered there a double spirit
 Of teaching and of learning instantly.
 There did he pause. But let me tell the world,
 If he outlive the envy of this day,

---

38 **gently** with dignity, like a gentleman 39 **mended** improved on, contributed to 40 **forswearing** ...
forsworn falsely swearing that he had not broken his word 41 **scourge** punish 43 **Arm** prepare, put on
your armour 45 **engaged** held as hostage **bear** convey 49 **would** ... **heads** if only the quarrel was
just between the two of us 50 **draw short breath** become out of breath (from fighting)/die
51 **Monmouth** nickname for the prince; the name of the town on the Welsh-English border where he was
born 54 **urged** proposed 56 **gentle** honourable/not excessively violent **proof of arms** trial of fighting
skills 57 **duties of** respect due to 58 **Trimmed** ... **praises** adorned his praise of you 59 **chronicle**
factual historical account 60 **Making** ... **you** increasing your worth since no praise of his could do justice
to your merits 63 **blushing cital** modest account 64 **chid** rebuked, condemned **truant** neglectful,
misspent 65 **double** ... **instantly** two sides of himself, both teacher and pupil, at the same time 68 **envy**
malice, hostility

England did never owe so sweet a hope,
70 So much misconstrued in his wantonness.
HOTSPUR Cousin, I think thou art enamourèd
On his follies: never did I hear
Of any prince so wild a liberty.
But be he as he will, yet once ere night
75 I will embrace him with a soldier's arm,
That he shall shrink under my courtesy.
Arm, arm with speed. And, fellows, soldiers, friends,
Better consider what you have to do
Than I, that have not well the gift of tongue,
80 Can lift your blood up with persuasion.

Enter a Messenger

MESSENGER My lord, here are letters for you.
HOTSPUR I cannot read them now.
O, gentlemen, the time of life is short!
To spend that shortness basely were too long,
85 If life did ride upon a dial's point,
Still ending at the arrival of an hour.
And if we live, we live to tread on kings,
If die, brave death, when princes die with us!
Now, for our consciences, the arms are fair,
90 When the intent for bearing them is just.

Enter another Messenger

MESSENGER My lord, prepare, the king comes on apace.
HOTSPUR I thank him, that he cuts me from my tale,
For I profess not talking. Only this:
Let each man do his best. And here I draw a sword
95 Whose worthy temper I intend to stain
With the best blood that I can meet withal
In the adventure of this perilous day.
Now, *Esperance*! Percy! And set on.
Sound all the lofty instruments of war,
100 And by that music let us all embrace,

---

69 owe own **70 wantonness** wild, dissolute behaviour **72 On** of **73 so ... liberty** who indulged in so
much lawless freedom, wild behaviour **76 shrink ... courtesy** be overwhelmed by my degree of courtesy/
collapse, be wounded by me **78 Better ... persuasion** you are better off thinking for yourselves about
what you have to do than expecting me, who lacks the gift of eloquence, to try to rouse your spirits
84 To ... hour a life spent basely goes on for too long even if it only lasts an hour **85 If** even if **dial's
point** hand of a clock **88 brave** glorious **89 fair** justifiable **91 apace** swiftly **92 cuts me** forces me to
break off **93 profess not** don't claim to be expert at **95 temper** character/degree of hardness
97 adventure risky venture **98 *Esperance*!** hope (French; part of the Percy family motto)
99 instruments i.e. trumpets, drums

For, heaven to earth, some of us never shall
A second time do such a courtesy.
They embrace [and exeunt]. The trumpets sound. The King
entereth with his power. Alarum unto the battle. Then enter
Douglas and Sir Walter Blunt [dressed like the King]
BLUNT What is thy name, that in battle thus
Thou crossest me? What honour dost thou seek
105   Upon my head?
DOUGLAS Know then, my name is Douglas,
And I do haunt thee in the battle thus
Because some tell me that thou art a king.
BLUNT They tell thee true.
110 **DOUGLAS** The Lord of Stafford dear today hath bought
Thy likeness, for instead of thee, King Harry,
This sword hath ended him. So shall it thee,
Unless thou yield thee as a prisoner.
BLUNT I was not born to yield, thou haughty Scot,
115   And thou shalt find a king that will revenge
Lord Stafford's death.   *Fight. Blunt is slain*
Then enters Hotspur
HOTSPUR O Douglas, had'st thou fought at Holmedon
thus,
I never had triumphed o'er a Scot.
DOUGLAS All's done, all's won, here breathless lies the
king.
120 **HOTSPUR** Where?
DOUGLAS Here.
HOTSPUR This, Douglas? No. I know this face full well:
A gallant knight he was, his name was Blunt,
Semblably furnished like the king himself.
125 **DOUGLAS** Ah, fool, go with thy soul, whither it goes!
A borrowed title hast thou bought too dear.
Why didst thou tell me that thou wert a king?
HOTSPUR The king hath many marching in his coats.

---

101 heaven to earth I'll wager heaven against earth (i.e. something eternal and valuable against something transitory and unimportant) **[and exeunt]** most editions introduce a scene break here, but Folio does not have one and the action continues, with the imaginary location shifting seamlessly from rebel camp to battlefield ***Alarum*** call to battle (played on a trumpet) **[dressed like the King]** wearing the king's colours, Blunt is acting as a decoy. Most editors introduce a scene break at this stage direction, since the stage is momentarily bare and the imaginary location shifts from the rebel camp to the battlefield, but in the early texts and on stage the action is continuous **107 haunt** follow **110 dear** at great cost **bought Thy likeness** paid for appearing like you (i.e. Stafford was also dressed like the king) **117 Holmedon** town in Northumberland **122 full** extremely **124 Semblably furnished** similarly dressed and armed **128 marching...coats** wearing the same clothing as him **coats** sleeveless outer garments adorned with heraldic arms, worn over armour

DOUGLAS Now, by my sword, I will kill all his coats.

130   I'll murder all his wardrobe, piece by piece,

Until I meet the king.

HOTSPUR Up, and away!

Our soldiers stand full fairly for the day.   *Exeunt*

Alarum, and enter Falstaff, solus

FALSTAFF Though I could scape shot-free at London, I

135   fear the shot here: here's no scoring but upon the pate.

Soft! Who are you? Sir Walter Blunt. There's honour

for you! Here's no vanity! I am as hot as molten

lead, and as heavy too; heaven keep lead out of me! I

need no more weight than mine own bowels. I have

140   led my ragamuffins where they are peppered: there's

not three of my hundred and fifty left alive, and they

for the town's end, to beg during life. But who comes

here?

Enter the Prince

PRINCE HENRY What, stand'st thou idle here? Lend me

    thy sword.

145   Many a nobleman lies stark and stiff

Under the hoofs of vaunting enemies,

Whose deaths are unrevenged. Prithee

Lend me thy sword.

FALSTAFF O Hal, I prithee give me leave to breathe

150   awhile. Turk Gregory never did such deeds in arms as

I have done this day. I have paid Percy, I have made

him sure.

PRINCE HENRY He is, indeed, and living to kill thee. I

prithee lend me thy sword.

155 FALSTAFF Nay, Hal, if Percy be alive, thou get'st not my

sword; but take my pistol, if thou wilt.

PRINCE HENRY Give it me. What, is it in the case?

FALSTAFF Ay, Hal, 'tis hot. There's that will sack a city.

    The Prince draws out a bottle of sack

PRINCE HENRY What, is it a time to jest and dally now?

    Exit. [He] throws it at him [as he leaves]

---

133 **stand . . . day** seem likely to win the battle   *solus* alone   134 **shot-free** without paying the tavern bill/without getting shot   135 **scoring** adding to tavern bill/being wounded   **pate** head 137 **Here's no vanity!** There's no self-conceit or concern for frivolity in death!   **molten** melted   138 **keep lead** i.e. bullets   139 **bowels** guts, stomach   140 **ragamuffins** i.e. his ragged company of soldiers **peppered** shot and killed; this would enable Falstaff to pocket his soldiers' pay   142 **town's end** outskirts of the town where beggars congregate   146 **vaunting** bragging, vainglorious   150 **Turk Gregory** Pope Gregory VII or XIII; both had violent reputations   **Turk** violent barbarian   151 **paid** repaid, settled with (i.e. killed)   152 **sure** i.e. dead, but the prince shifts the sense to 'out of danger'   157 **case** holster 158 **hot** Falstaff claims it has recently been fired frequently   **sack** destroy   **out** i.e. from Falstaff's holster

160 **FALSTAFF** If Percy be alive, I'll pierce him. If he do come
in my way, so: if he do not, if I come in his willingly,
let him make a carbonado of me. I like not such
grinning honour as Sir Walter hath. Give me life,
which if I can save, so: if not, honour comes
165 unlooked for, and there's an end.   *Exit*

Act 5 Scene 3   *running scene 16 continues*

Alarum. Excursions. Enter the King, the Prince, Lord John of
Lancaster and Earl of Westmorland   **The Prince has been wounded**

KING HENRY IV I prithee,
    Harry, withdraw thyself, thou bleed'st too much.
    Lord John of Lancaster, go you with him.
PRINCE JOHN Not I, my lord, unless I did bleed too.
5 **PRINCE HENRY** I beseech your majesty, make up,
    Lest your retirement do amaze your friends.
KING HENRY IV I will do so.
    My lord of Westmorland, lead him to his tent.
WESTMORLAND Come, my lord, I'll lead you to your tent.
10 **PRINCE HENRY** Lead me, my lord? I do not need your
      help;
    And heaven forbid a shallow scratch should drive
    The Prince of Wales from such a field as this,
    Where stained nobility lies trodden on,
    And rebels' arms triumph in massacres!
15 **PRINCE JOHN** We breathe too long: come, cousin
      Westmorland,
    Our duty this way lies. For heaven's sake, come.
              [*Exeunt Lancaster and Westmorland*]
PRINCE HENRY By heaven, thou hast deceived me,
    Lancaster.
    I did not think thee lord of such a spirit:
    Before, I loved thee as a brother, John;
20   But now, I do respect thee as my soul.

---

160 pierce pronounced 'perse' – the word puns on 'Percy'   **161 so** so be it/thus – presumably miming his
action   **162 carbonado** dish of scored, grilled meat   **163 grinning honour** i.e. the sort of honour Blunt has
earned, whose expression is now fixed as death stiffens his facial muscles   **164 so** all well and good
165 unlooked for without being sought, unexpectedly   **an end** death/of my speech   **5.3** *Location: the*
battlefield at Shrewsbury   **Excursions** outbursts of fighting moving across the stage   **5 make up**
advance, bring up your forces   **6 retirement** retreat, insufficiently aggressive strategy   **amaze** alarm,
bewilder   **13 stained** bloodstained (may play on sense of 'dishonoured')   **15 breathe** rest, pause

KING HENRY IV I saw him hold Lord Percy at the point
With lustier maintenance than I did look for
Of such an ungrown warrior.

PRINCE HENRY O, this boy lends mettle to us all!   *Exit*
Enter Douglas

25 **DOUGLAS** Another king? They grow like Hydra's heads.
I am the Douglas, fatal to all those
That wear those colours on them. What art thou,
That counterfeit'st the person of a king?

KING HENRY IV The king himself, who, Douglas, grieves
at heart

30 So many of his shadows thou hast met
And not the very king. I have two boys
Seek Percy and thyself about the field:
But, seeing thou fall'st on me so luckily,
I will assay thee, so defend thyself.

35 **DOUGLAS** I fear thou art another counterfeit,
And yet, in faith, thou bear'st thee like a king.
But mine I am sure thou art, whoe'er thou be,
And thus I win thee.
                                    They fight, the King being in danger
Enter Prince

PRINCE HENRY Hold up thy head, vile Scot, or thou art
like

40 Never to hold it up again! The spirits
Of valiant Shirley, Stafford, Blunt, are in my arms;
It is the Prince of Wales that threatens thee,
Who never promiseth but he means to pay.
                                    They fight. Douglas flieth
Cheerly, my lord. How fares your grace?

45 Sir Nicholas Gawsey hath for succour sent,
And so hath Clifton: I'll to Clifton straight.

KING HENRY IV Stay, and breathe awhile.
Thou hast redeemed thy lost opinion,
And showed thou mak'st some tender of my life,

50 In this fair rescue thou hast brought to me.

---

21 point i.e. of his sword   **22 lustier maintenance** more vigorous bearing   **23 ungrown** immature;
historically, John was thirteen at the time of the battle   **24 mettle** courage, spirit   **25 Hydra's heads** in
Greek mythology, the Hydra was a monster that grew two heads for every one that was cut off   **27 colours**
i.e. the king's   **28 counterfeit'st** impersonates   **30 shadows** reflections/those in disguise, actors   **31 very**
real, true   **32 Seek** who seek   **34 assay** test   **37 mine** my victim, conquest   **39 like** likely   **41 are** . . .
arms lend strength to my arms   **43 pay** settle the debt/kill   *flieth* runs away   **44 Cheerly** expression of
encouragement   **48 opinion** reputation   **49 mak'st** . . . **life** have some care for my life

PRINCE HENRY O heaven! They did me too much injury
    That ever said I hearkened to your death.
    If it were so, I might have let alone
    The insulting hand of Douglas over you,
55   Which would have been as speedy in your end
    As all the poisonous potions in the world
    And saved the treacherous labour of your son.
KING HENRY IV Make up to Clifton, I'll to Sir Nicholas
    Gawsey.   *Exit*

Enter Hotspur

HOTSPUR If I mistake not, thou art Harry Monmouth.
60   **PRINCE HENRY** Thou speak'st as if I would deny my
    name.
HOTSPUR My name is Harry Percy.
PRINCE HENRY Why, then I see
    A very valiant rebel of that name.
    I am the Prince of Wales; and think not, Percy,
65   To share with me in glory any more:
    Two stars keep not their motion in one sphere,
    Nor can one England brook a double reign,
    Of Harry Percy and the Prince of Wales.
HOTSPUR Nor shall it, Harry, for the hour is come
70   To end the one of us; and would to heaven
    Thy name in arms were now as great as mine!
PRINCE HENRY I'll make it greater ere I part from thee,
    And all the budding honours on thy crest
    I'll crop, to make a garland for my head.
75   **HOTSPUR** I can no longer brook thy vanities.   *Fight*

Enter Falstaff

FALSTAFF Well said, Hal! To it Hal! Nay, you shall find
    no boy's play here, I can tell you.

*Enter Douglas, he fights with Falstaff, who falls down as if he
were dead*

                            [*Exit Douglas*]

The Prince killeth Percy [*Hotspur*]

HOTSPUR O, Harry, thou hast robbed me of my youth!
    I better brook the loss of brittle life
80   Than those proud titles thou hast won of me.

---

52 hearkened waited eagerly for, sought   **54 insulting** threatening, harmful/boastful, contemptuous
58 Make up to move your forces forwards   **66 motion** course, trajectory, orbit   **sphere** orbit; stars and
planets were thought to be contained within crystalline spheres   **67 brook** endure   **71 name in arms**
military reputation   **73 budding . . . crest** literally, chivalric favours decorating his helmet; figuratively, his
glorious reputation   **75 vanities** vain boasts   **76 said** done   ***killeth*** i.e. fatally wounds   **79 brittle**
fragile   **80 titles** claims to honour

They wound my thoughts worse than the sword my
　　flesh:
But thought's the slave of life, and life, time's fool;
And time that takes survey of all the world
Must have a stop. O, I could prophesy,
85　But that the earth and the cold hand of death
Lies on my tongue. No, Percy, thou art dust
And food for—　　　　　　　　　　　　　　*Dies*
PRINCE HENRY For worms, brave Percy. Farewell, great
　　heart!
Ill-weaved ambition, how much art thou shrunk?
90　When that this body did contain a spirit,
A kingdom for it was too small a bound,
But now two paces of the vilest earth
Is room enough. This earth that bears thee dead
Bears not alive so stout a gentleman.
95　If thou wert sensible of courtesy,
I should not make so great a show of zeal,
But let my favours hide thy mangled face,　　*Covers Hotspur's face*
And, even in thy behalf, I'll thank myself
For doing these fair rites of tenderness.
100　Adieu, and take thy praise with thee to heaven!
Thy ignominy sleep with thee in the grave,
But not remembered in thy epitaph!—
What? Old acquaintance? Could not all this flesh　*He sees Falstaff on*
Keep in a little life? Poor Jack, farewell!　　　*the ground*
105　I could have better spared a better man.
O, I should have a heavy miss of thee,
If I were much in love with vanity!
Death hath not struck so fat a deer today,
Though many dearer, in this bloody fray.
110　Embowelled will I see thee by and by:
Till then in blood by noble Percy lie.　　　　*Exit*
Falstaff riseth up
FALSTAFF Embowelled! If thou embowel me today, I'll
　　give you leave to powder me and eat me too
　　tomorrow. 'Twas time to counterfeit, or that hot

---

84 prophesy conventional belief held that the dying were able to foretell the future　**89 Ill-weaved**
devious, tangled　**91 too…bound** insufficient to contain it　**94 stout** strong, valiant　**95 sensible**
aware　**96 show of zeal** expression of feeling　**97 favours** chivalric tokens worn on his helmet
101 ignominy shame　**106 heavy…thee** miss you greatly (**heavy** plays on the sense of 'weighty, fat')
109 dearer more noble/more valuable　**110 Embowelled** disembowelled (in preparation for embalming)
111 in blood in his own blood (plays on hunting term; a **deer** that was **in blood** was vigorous and full of
life)　**113 powder** embalm/preserve in salt (like venison)

115   termagant Scot had paid me scot and lot too.
       Counterfeit? I am no counterfeit; to die, is to be a
       counterfeit, for he is but the counterfeit of a man who
       hath not the life of a man. But to counterfeit dying,
       when a man thereby liveth, is to be no counterfeit,
120   but the true and perfect image of life indeed. The
       better part of valour is discretion, in the which better
       part I have saved my life. I am afraid of this
       gunpowder Percy, though he be dead. How, if he
       should counterfeit too and rise? I am afraid he would
125   prove the better counterfeit: therefore I'll make him
       sure, yea, and I'll swear I killed him. Why may not he
       rise as well as I? Nothing confutes me but eyes, and
       nobody sees me. Therefore, sirrah, with a new   *Stabs him*
       wound in your thigh, come you along with me.
                            Takes Hotspur on his back
       Enter Prince and John of Lancaster
130 **PRINCE HENRY** Come, brother John, full bravely hast
            thou fleshed
       Thy maiden sword.
    PRINCE JOHN But, soft! Who have we here?
       Did you not tell me this fat man was dead?
    PRINCE HENRY I did. I saw him dead,
135   Breathless and bleeding on the ground.—
       Art thou alive? Or is it fantasy   *To Falstaff*
       That plays upon our eyesight? I prithee speak.
       We will not trust our eyes without our ears.
       Thou art not what thou seem'st.
140 **FALSTAFF** No, that's certain: I am not a double man. But
       if I be not Jack Falstaff, then am I a jack. There is   *Throws the*
       Percy. If your father will do me any honour, so: if not, *body down*
       let him kill the next Percy himself. I look to be either
       earl or duke, I can assure you.
145 **PRINCE HENRY** Why, Percy I killed myself and saw thee
       dead.
    FALSTAFF Didst thou? Lord, Lord, how the world is given
       to lying! I grant you I was down and out of breath,
       and so was he. But we rose both at an instant and

---

115 termagant savage, violent   **scot and lot** in full   **121 discretion** good judgement   **123 gunpowder**
i.e. fiery, explosive   **127 confutes** refutes, contradicts   **130 fleshed** initiated into fighting (plays on sense
'sexual initiated'; from the practice of feeding hunting dogs raw meat to excite them)   **131 maiden** virgin,
previously unused   **sword** with phallic connotations   **136 fantasy** illusion, imagination   **140 double
man** ghost/two men (referring to the fact he carries Hotspur on his back)   **141 jack** knave   **149 at an
instant** simultaneously

150 fought a long hour by Shrewsbury clock. If I may be
believed, so: if not, let them that should reward
valour bear the sin upon their own heads. I'll take't
on my death, I gave him this wound in the thigh: if
the man were alive and would deny it, I would make
155 him eat a piece of my sword.

PRINCE JOHN This is the strangest tale that e'er I heard.

PRINCE HENRY This is the strangest fellow, brother
John.—
Come, bring your luggage nobly on your back.   *To Falstaff*
For my part, if a lie may do thee grace,
160 I'll gild it with the happiest terms I have.—
                                                                A retreat is sounded
The trumpets sound retreat, the day is ours.—
Come, brother, let's to the highest of the field,
To see what friends are living, who are dead.
                                          Exeunt [Prince Henry and Lancaster]

FALSTAFF I'll follow, as they say, for reward. He that
165 rewards me, heaven reward him! If I do grow great
again, I'll grow less, for I'll purge, and leave sack, and
live cleanly as a nobleman should do.   *Exit*

Act 5 Scene 4   *running scene 16 continues*

*The trumpets sound. Enter the King, Prince of Wales, Lord
John of Lancaster, Earl of Westmorland [and others], with
Worcester and Vernon prisoners*

KING HENRY IV Thus ever did rebellion find rebuke.
Ill-spirited Worcester, did we not send grace,
Pardon and terms of love to all of you?
And wouldst thou turn our offers contrary?
5 Misuse the tenor of thy kinsman's trust?
Three knights upon our party slain today,
A noble earl and many a creature else
Had been alive this hour,

---

150 **Shrewsbury clock** perhaps referring to an actual clock (e.g. the church clock), or a metaphorical
phrase   152 **take't...death** swear as though I were about to die and my soul depended upon it
158 **luggage** i.e. Hotspur   159 **do thee grace** bring you honour   160 **gild** embellish   **happiest** most
favourable   ***retreat*** specific trumpet call signalling retreat   161 **the...ours** we have won
162 **highest** highest vantage point   165 **do...less** become a powerful nobleman/I'll slim down
166 **purge** repent, purify myself/take laxatives or emetics to cause weight loss   **leave** give up
5.4   1 **rebuke** punishment   2 **Ill-spirited** wicked, evil-hearted   **grace** good will, forgiveness   4 **turn...
contrary** report the opposite   5 **Misuse** abuse   **tenor** character, nature   6 **upon our party** on our side

If like a Christian thou hadst truly borne
10   Betwixt our armies true intelligence.

WORCESTER What I have done my safety urged me to,
      And I embrace this fortune patiently,
      Since not to be avoided it falls on me.

KING HENRY IV Bear Worcester to death and Vernon too:
15   Other offenders we will pause upon.
                          Exeunt Worcester and Vernon, [guarded]
      How goes the field?

PRINCE HENRY The noble Scot, Lord Douglas, when he
          saw
      The fortune of the day quite turned from him,
      The noble Percy slain, and all his men
20   Upon the foot of fear, fled with the rest;
      And falling from a hill, he was so bruised
      That the pursuers took him. At my tent
      The Douglas is, and I beseech your grace
      I may dispose of him.

25 KING HENRY IV With all my heart.

PRINCE HENRY Then, brother John of Lancaster, to you
      This honourable bounty shall belong:
      Go to the Douglas, and deliver him
      Up to his pleasure, ransomless and free:
30   His valour shown upon our crests today
      Hath taught us how to cherish such high deeds
      Even in the bosom of our adversaries.

KING HENRY IV Then this remains, that we divide our
          power.—
      You, son John, and my cousin Westmorland
35   Towards York shall bend you with your dearest
          speed,
      To meet Northumberland and the prelate Scroop,
      Who, as we hear, are busily in arms.—

---

10 true intelligence honest information   **11 safety** concern for personal safety   **14 death** execution
15 pause upon think about, consider their fates   **16 field** battlefield   **20 Upon . . . fear** running away in
fear   **22 took** seized, arrested   **24 dispose of** decide what to do with   **27 honourable bounty** the honour
of this act of generosity   **29 to his pleasure** to do as he pleases   **30 crests** helmets   **31 high** noble
32 Even . . . adversaries in Quarto, **PRINCE JOHN** replies before the king's closing speech: 'I thank your
grace for this high courtesy, / Which I shall give away immediately.' ('give away': undertake, pass on
[to Douglas])   **33 power** army   **35 bend you** direct your course   **dearest** utmost   **36 prelate**
ecclesiastical dignitary (i.e. the Archbishop of York, Richard **Scroop**)   **37 busily in arms** engaged in
preparing for battle

Myself and you, son Harry, will towards Wales,
To fight with Glendower and the Earl of March.
40   Rebellion in this land shall lose his way,
Meeting the check of such another day.
And since this business so fair is done,
Let us not leave till all our own be won.   *Exeunt*

---

41 check curb, reprimand   **such another day** another battle like today's   **42 fair** successfully   **43 leave** stop   **all...won** everything that rightfully belongs to us is under our control (**won** puns on 'one')

TEXTUAL NOTES

Q = First Quarto text of 1598
Q5 = Fifth Quarto text of 1613
Q7 = Seventh Quarto text of 1632
F = First Folio text of 1623
F2 = a correction introduced in the Second Folio text of 1632
F3 = a correction introduced in the Third Folio text of 1663–64
Ed = a correction introduced by a later editor
SD = stage direction
SH = speech heading (i.e. speaker's name)

List of parts = Ed

BARDOLPH = F. Q = *Bardoll*
1.1.64 Stained = Q. F = Strain'd **66 welcome** = Q. F = welcomes **76 In**...**is** = Ed. F *includes at end of king's speech, making his answer his own rhetorical question*
1.2.0 SD *Falstaff* = Ed. F = *Falstaffe and Pointz (it is conceivable that Poins enters here and remains silently in the background during the first 74 lines of dialogue, but more likely that he enters when his name is mentioned at line 72)* **42 of Hybla** = Q. *Not in* F **80 similes** = Q5. F = smiles **89 for**...**it** = F. Q = for wisedome cries out in the streets and no man regards it **105 Poins** *set as a speech heading in* F **121 had been** = Q. F = had **160 Peto, Bardolph** = Ed. F = *Haruey, Rossill (Shakespeare's original names for these characters)* **213 foil** = Q. F = soyle
1.3.24 name = Q. *Not in* F **27 As**...**son** = F. Q = As is deliuered to your maiestie. / Either enuie therefore, or misprision, / Is guiltie of this fault, and not my sonne *(F is more likely to be purposeful revision than compositorial error)* **43 bore** = Q. F = bare **45 corpse** *spelled* Coarse *in* F **68 this** = F. Q = his **78 yet he doth**= Q. F = yet doth **136 downfall** = F. Q = down-trod **164 wore** = F. Q = weare **239 poisoned him** = F. Q = him poisoned **256 candy** = Q. F = caudie **303 Lord** = Ed. F = loe
2.1.34 SH FIRST CARRIER = Ed. F = *Car.*
2.2.0 SD *and Bardolph* *(not in* F *but implied by Q's 'and Peto &c.')* **10 thief's** = Q. F = Theefe **12 square** *spelled* squire *in* F **28 me my** = Q. F = my **50 SH BARDOLPH** = Ed. F = *Bardolfe,* what newes? *(continuation of Poins' speech)* **51 SH GADSHILL** = Ed. F = *Bar.* **76 SH FIRST TRAVELLER** = Ed. F = *Tra.* **82 Ah, whoreson** = Ed. F = a whorson
2.3.1 SH HOTSPUR = Ed. *Not in* F **17 our friends** = Q. F = our Friend **59 beads** = Q. F = beds **113 well believe** = Q. F = will beleeue **115 far will** = Q. F = farre wilt
2.4.116 and foot them = Q. *Not in* F **125 with lime in't** F *(uncorrected) reads* with in't F *(corrected) reads* with lime **144 SH POINS** = Q. F = *Prin.* **193 ward** = Q. F = word **224 the** = F. Q = their **238 plentiful** = Q. F = plentie **328 talon** *spelled* Talent *in* F **332 Braby** = F. Q = Bracy **333 That** = Q. F = The **340 that** = Q. F = the **393 tristful** = Ed. F = trustfull **407 sun** *spelled* Sonne *in* F **485 most** = Q. F = most most **550 march** = Q. F = Match
3.1.46 the = F. Q = he **67 sent** = Q. F = hent **193 our** = F. Q = your **220 'twixt** = Q. F = betwixt **228 hence** = Q. F = thence

122

3.2.154 heaven ... survive = F. Q = God *I* promise heere, / The which if he be pleasd I shall
  performe *(F alteration due to 1606 Parliamentary 'Act to restrain the Abuses of Players')*

3.3.24 my = Q. F = thy **36 son** *spelled* Sunne *in* F **57 tithe** = Ed. F = tight **84 sneak-cup** =
  F. Q = sneakeup **135 owed** *spelled* ought *in* F **173 and cherish** = F. Q = cherish *(F sets
  this speech as verse, though it is prose in Q; seems to have been added in an attempt to create a
  pentameter line)*

4.1.21 I his mind = F. Q = I my mind. Ed = I, my lord **63 hair** = Q. F = Heire **81 our** = Q. F
  = your **88 as** = Q. F = At **dream** = F. Q = tearme **92 with him** = Q. F = with **127 hot**
  = Q. F = not

4.2.3 Coldfield = Ed. F = cop-hill **19 fowl** = Q. F = Foole **34 tattered** = F3. F = totter'd

4.4.0 SD *Michael* *spelled* Michell *in* F

5.1.47 swore = Q. F = sware **72 your younger** = Q. F = yonger **138 Is it** = F. Q = tis

5.2.8 other = Q. F = others **31 news** = Q. F = newe- **52 talking** = F. Q = tasking **73 a
  liberty** = Q. F = at Liberty **79 Than** = Q. F = That **89 are** = Q. F = is **140 ragamuffins**
  = Ed. F = rag of Muffins **145 lies** = Q. F = likes

5.3.6 Lest your = Q. F = Least you **63 that** = F. Q = the **93 thee dead** = Q7. Q/F = the
  dead **129 with me** = Q. F = me

OATHS FROM THE QUARTO

The following oaths were altered in the Folio text as a result of the Parliamentary Act to Restrain the Abuses of Players (spelling has been modernized in this list):

	QUARTO	FOLIO
1.2.20	No, by my troth, not so much	No, not so much
1.2.40	By the Lord, thou say'st true, lad	Thou say'st true, lad
1.2.65	By the Lord, I'll be a brave judge	I'll be a brave judge
1.2.74–5	Zblood,* I am as melancholy as a gibcat	I am as melancholy as a gib cat
1.2.83	I would to God thou and I knew	I would thou and I knew
1.2.96	By the Lord, an I do not	An I do not
1.2.100	Zounds,** where thou wilt, lad	Where thou wilt, lad
1.2.136	Not I, by my faith	Not I
1.2.144	By the Lord, I'll be traitor then	I'll be a traitor then
1.2.149–50	Well, God give thee the spirit . . . and him the . . .	Well, mayst thou have the spirit . . . and he the . . .

* **Zblood** God's blood.
** **Zounds** God's wounds.

124

	QUARTO	*FOLIO*
1.3.132	Zounds, I will speak of him	Yes, I will speak of him
1.3.219	By God, he shall not have a Scot	By heaven, he shall not have a Scot
1.3.253	Zblood, when you and he came back	When you and he came back
1.3.264	I have done, i'faith	I have done, in sooth
2.1.17	By the mass, there is ne'er a king	There is ne'er a king
2.1.27	God's body, the turkeys	The turkeys
2.1.37	Nay, by God, soft, I know	Nay, soft, I pray ye; I know
2.1.80	and yet, zounds, I lie	And yet, I lie
2.1.89	Nay, by my faith, I think you are	Nay, I think rather you are
2.2.34	Zblood, I'll not bear mine own flesh	I'll not bear mine own flesh
2.2.63	Zounds, will they not rob us	Will they not rob us
2.3.16	By the Lord, our plot	I protest, our plot
2.3.22	Zounds, an I were	By this hand if I were
2.3.82–3	In faith I'll know your business	In sooth, I'll know your business
2.3.90	In faith I'll break	Indeed, I'll break
2.4.9	upon their salvation	upon their confidence
2.4.12	a good boy, by the Lord, so they call me	a good boy
2.4.133	I could sing psalms or anything	I could sing all manner of songs
2.4.144	Zounds, ye fat paunch	Ye fat paunch

	QUARTO	**FOLIO**
2.4.144	call me coward, by the Lord, I'll stab thee	call me coward, I'll stab thee
2.4.188	Pray God	Pray heaven
2.4.235–6	Zounds, an I were at the strappado	No. Were I at the strappado
2.4.244	Zblood, you starveling	Away, you starveling
2.4.266	By the Lord, I knew ye as well as he	I knew ye as well as he
2.4.274	But by the Lord, lads	But, lads
2.4.282	O Jesu, my lord the prince	My lord the prince
2.4.296	Now sirs, by our lady, you fought fair	Now, sirs: you fought fair
2.4.301	Faith, tell me now	Tell me now
2.4.369	Not a whit, i'faith	Not a whit
2.4.388	O Jesu, this is excellent sport	This is excellent sport
2.4.395	O Jesu, he doth it as like	O rare, he doth it as like
2.4.445	Zblood, my lord, they are false	I'faith, my lord, they are false
2.4.446	for a young prince, i'faith	for a young prince
2.4.474	God help the wicked	heaven help the wicked
2.4.485	O Jesu, my lord, my lord	O, my lord, my lord
3.2.4	I know not whether God will have it so	. . . whether heaven will . . .
3.2.29	God pardon	Heaven pardon
3.2.131	And God forgive	And heaven forgive
3.2.154	This, in the name of God, I promise here	. . . in the name of heaven . . .

	QUARTO	FOLIO
3.3.35	By this fire, that's God's angel	By this fire
3.3.48	God reward me for it.	Heaven reward me for it!
3.3.49	Zblood, I would my face were	I would my face were
3.3.50	Godamercy,* so should I	So should I
3.3.61	I defy thee: God's light, I was never	I defy thee. I was never
3.3.82	O Jesu, I have heard	I have heard
3.3.84–5	Zblood and he	An if he
3.3.87	in that door i'faith	in that door
3.3.117	Why a thing to thank God on.	Why, a thing to thank heaven on.
3.3.118	I am no thing to thank God on,	I am no thing to thank heaven on,
3.3.152	I pray God my girdle break	let my girdle break
4.1.6	By God I cannot flatter	By heaven, I cannot flatter
4.1.18	Zounds, how has he the leisure	How? Has he the leisure
4.3.44	And God defend,	And heaven defend
4.3.121	Pray God you do	Pray heaven you do
5.1.127	Why, thou owest God a death	Why, thou ow'st heaven a death
5.2.138	God keep lead out of me	heaven keep lead out of me!
5.2.155	Nay before God Hal, if Percy	Nay, Hal, if Percy

* **Godamercy** God have mercy.

	QUARTO	FOLIO
5.3.11	And God forbid	And heaven forbid
5.3.16	for God's sake come	For heaven's sake, come
5.3.17	By God thou hast	By heaven, thou hast
5.3.51	O God, they did me too much injury,	O heaven! They did me ...
5.3.70	and would to God,	and would to heaven
5.3.113	Zblood, 'twas time to counterfeit	'Twas time to counterfeit
5.3.121	Zounds I am afraid of this gunpowder	I am afraid of this gunpowder
5.3.123	by my faith I am afraid he	I am afraid he
5.3.153–4	zounds I would make him eat	I would make him eat
5.3.164	God reward him	heaven reward him!

SCENE-BY-SCENE ANALYSIS

ACT 1 SCENE 1

King Henry despairs at the civil unrest that has dominated his reign. He describes the 'civil butchery', establishing the motif of 'blood' that highlights both the violent conflict and the theme of lineage and inheritance. He declares his intention to lead a long-planned Crusade to the Holy Land. He talks of the Crucifixion, 'fourteen hundred years ago', and of the 'twelvemonth' plan he has had to make his Crusade, establishing the motif of time which functions to place the events of the play in a wider historical context, as well as drawing attention to the brevity of individual man's existence within this.

Westmorland informs Henry that the English forces, led by the 'noble Mortimer' have been defeated by the Welsh rebels, led by Glendower. Henry realizes he must put his plans for a Crusade aside, and Westmorland tells him of more fighting between Scottish insurgents and 'the gallant Hotspur ... / Young Harry Percy'. Henry updates Westmorland: Hotspur defeated the 'bold Scots' and took many noble prisoners: 'an honourable spoil'. This emphasizes the theme of 'honour', further reinforced by Henry's comparisons between Hotspur and his own son, Prince Henry (also called Harry): the shared name establishes the deliberate paralleling and comparison between the two young men.

Lineage and father–son relationships are addressed as the king envies Hotspur's father, Lord Northumberland, whose son is 'the theme of honour's tongue', while 'riot and dishonour stain the brow' of his own. He also comments, however, on Hotspur's 'pride' in only sending one noble prisoner to the king and keeping the rest. Westmorland suggests that this is due to the influence of his uncle,

Worcester, who is 'Malevolent' towards the king. Henry has sent for Hotspur to explain his actions.

ACT 1 SCENE 2

Lines 1–109: Providing a comic contrast to the political/military concerns of the previous scene, Prince Henry and Falstaff exchange rapid-fire, quick-witted banter. Henry comments on his friend's corrupt lifestyle spent drinking and visiting brothels. Despite the accusation that Falstaff is 'fat-witted', his responses show that he can be quick and entertaining in his use of language, although both men speak in prose, reflecting the 'low' nature of their subject matter. Falstaff is revealed as a robber and a freeloader, but he appears good-natured and fond of Prince Henry, sometimes addressing him in a paternal tone that serves to highlight the estranged relationship between the prince and his father. Falstaff refers to the future, when Henry will be king, reminding the audience of the obligations of birth and rank that Henry is neglecting.

Lines 110–192: They are joined by Poins, who reveals that he plans to rob a party of travelling pilgrims and traders, all 'with fat purses', the next morning. Falstaff agrees to join him, but Henry refuses. Poins asks Falstaff to leave them while he convinces Henry to participate. Poins explains that he has planned 'a jest': Falstaff, Peto, Bardolph and Gadshill will commit the robbery, after which Poins and Henry will rob them of their ill-gotten gains. Henry objects that the others will know them by their horses, 'and by every other appointment', raising the question of appearance and identity. Poins suggests they leave their horses and disguise their 'outward garments' with outfits of buckram. Henry agrees to the plan and Poins goes to prepare.

Lines 193–215: Henry's soliloquy reveals a different side to his character. Speaking in blank verse, an indication of his noble status, he compares himself to the sun (a repeated image, associated with royalty), which has permitted 'the base contagious clouds / To smother up his beauty from the world'. Using repeated images of concealment, disguise and revelation, he explains that he is hiding his true character in order to appear even greater when the world witnesses his 'reformation'. Despite revealing a strong sense of his social status and responsibility, he is deliberately deceiving his friends and family and seems more concerned with creating a 'glittering' appearance than with his obligations.

ACT 1 SCENE 3

Lines 1–124: At court Hotspur has responded to King Henry's summons, accompanied by his father, Northumberland, and his uncle, Worcester. The king announces that he has been too 'temperate', and that Hotspur has taken advantage of his 'patience'. He declares that from now on he will be 'Mighty and to be feared'. Worcester argues that their family does not deserve to be punished, particularly as they helped Henry to achieve his 'greatness'. Henry sends Worcester out and Northumberland pleads on his son's behalf, arguing that there has been some 'envy or misprision' in the representation of his actions over the prisoners. Hotspur offers an explanation that shows his eloquence, but acknowledges his potentially rash temper. He tells Henry that, 'dry with rage and extreme toil' after the lengthy battle, with his wounds still raw and 'smarting', he was approached by a courtier, a 'popinjay', whose foppish behaviour and demands for the prisoners at that moment provoked him into rudeness. Sir Walter Blunt suggests that under such circumstances, Hotspur's actions might be overlooked, but Henry is still angry, revealing that Hotspur retains the prisoners and refuses to return them unless the king ransoms Mortimer, Hotspur's brother-in-law, from Glendower. Citing Mortimer's marriage to Glendower's daughter as evidence of treachery, Henry refuses to ransom 'revolted Mortimer'. Hotspur furiously defends his brother-in-law, describing his bravery in the 'bloody' battle with Glendower and accusing the king of slander. Henry forbids Hotspur to mention Mortimer again and, demanding the immediate delivery of the prisoners, he leaves.

Lines 125–310: Hotspur announces that even if 'the devil come and roar for them' he will not hand over the prisoners. His father urges him to calm down as Worcester returns, but Hotspur ignores him, calling Henry an 'unthankful king'. Hotspur describes Henry's reaction to the mention of Mortimer, and Worcester reveals that Richard II (who was deposed by Henry, and murdered shortly after) named Mortimer as his successor. Hotspur now understands Henry's reluctance to help Mortimer, but is angry with his family for their role in deposing 'that sweet lovely rose', Richard, and replacing him with 'this thorn, this canker, Bullingbrook', and with Henry for his ingratitude for the 'shames' that the family has undergone on his behalf.

Worcester tries to tell Hotspur of a 'deep and dangerous' plan, but Hotspur ignores him, continuing to rail against Henry. Northumberland tells his son that he is 'wasp-tongued and impatient'. Eventually, Worcester is able to outline his plan to ally with the Scottish and Welsh forces against Henry. He advises Hotspur to release his Scottish prisoners without ransom and to form an alliance with the Earl of Douglas. Worcester tells Northumberland to enlist the help of the Archbishop of York, Lord Scroop, whose brother was executed by Henry. Worcester himself will go to Wales to Glendower and Mortimer, promising to arrange a meeting of all of their 'powers'.

ACT 2 SCENE 1

At an inn-yard on the London–Canterbury road, two Carriers are preparing their horses. Once again, the motif of time is dominant, establishing the night setting of the scene and reinforcing the wider temporal concerns of the play. The Carriers are interrupted by Gadshill, asking for a lantern but, suspicious of his motives, they refuse and leave. The references to darkness emphasize secrecy and deception: both the comic deception of Falstaff by Poins, and the more serious plotting against King Henry. The inn's chamberlain arrives and informs Gadshill that there are wealthy guests preparing to leave. Gadshill sets off to organize the robbery.

ACT 2 SCENE 2

Further down the highway, Poins tells Henry, Peto and Bardolph that he has hidden Falstaff's horse for a joke. They stand aside as Falstaff approaches, angrily calling for Poins. Henry tells Falstaff to be quiet and pretends to go to find Poins, but joins the others in the darkness as they listen to Falstaff complaining and cursing them. They join him again, and Henry teases 'fat-guts' Falstaff as he demands the return of his horse. Gadshill arrives with the news that there is 'money of the king's' on its way down the hill. Henry says that he and Poins will go further down the lane to catch their victims if they should escape from the others, and they leave, exchanging an aside about their 'disguises'. Falstaff, Peto, Bardolph and Gadshill carry out the robbery, leaving with their victims. Henry and Poins return, disguised, and hide as the robbers re-enter, dividing up their profits. As Falstaff says that Poins and Henry will get nothing for being 'arrant cowards', the prince and his companion set upon them. Frightened, the robbers run away, leaving the loot behind. Henry laughs at the fact that Falstaff must walk home.

ACT 2 SCENE 3

Hotspur's serious plans contrast with the low and essentially comic plotting of the last two scenes, reinforcing the deliberate character-contrast with Prince Henry. Hotspur is reading a letter from an unnamed nobleman, who has declined to join the rebellion. Hotspur criticizes the letter-writer as a 'shallow cowardly hind', showing his quick temper and concerns with honour. Worried that the 'frosty-spirited rogue' will reveal the plot to the king, Hotspur decides that he must set off at once to join his fellow-conspirators. He is interrupted by his wife, Lady Percy, demanding to know what is wrong. She complains that he has been neglecting her: instead of 'pleasure and golden sleep' in bed, he disturbs her with nightmares, talking of 'prisoners' ransom and of soldiers slain'. She is worried that her brother, Mortimer, intends to stake his claim to the throne, and that Hotspur is involved. Although their exchange reveals a loving relationship, Henry is impatient, saying that he has no time for love. He tells her that she must not question him, as, although he knows her to be 'wise' and 'constant', she is a woman, and therefore not to be trusted. He consoles her with the promise that she shall soon join him.

ACT 2 SCENE 4

Lines 1–111: Prince Henry continues to lead a disreputable existence, ignoring his noble birth and responsibilities. In the Eastcheap tavern, he boasts to Poins of his drinking exploits. In order to 'drive away time' while they wait for Falstaff, he orders Poins to help him tease the young bartender, Francis. The prince mocks Francis for his limited use of language (forcing a contrast with the verbal dexterity of other characters in the play, such as himself, Falstaff and Hotspur) and for his hard-working nature. He moves on to criticize the similarly industrious character of 'the Hotspur of the north', one of his first acknowledgements of the political world outside his current life.

Lines 112–295: The others arrive and, as they drink, Henry and Falstaff banter rudely with each other, demonstrating the mixture of affection and contempt that the prince feels for Falstaff, and Falstaff's simultaneous lack of respect and awareness of Henry's royal status. Falstaff accuses the prince and Poins of being cowards for not taking part in the robbery. When Henry asks where the loot is, Falstaff tells how they were themselves robbed by 'a hundred' men. Dramatic irony compounds the humour as Falstaff boasts of how he fought off their attackers and only escaped 'by a miracle'. Encouraged by Poins and Henry, he continues to exaggerate, contradicting himself and inventing details, until the prince calls him a liar. They exchange insults until Henry reveals the truth: it was he and Poins who robbed them. Falstaff quickly recovers, claiming that he knew this, and that he did not fight back because he did not wish to kill 'the heir-apparent'. They are interrupted by Hostess Quickly who announces that a nobleman has brought Henry a message from the king. Falstaff goes to 'send him packing'.

Lines 296–484: Falstaff returns, and the prince immediately starts taunting him again, but Falstaff tells Henry that he has been summoned to court the following morning by his father. Falstaff tells Henry of the rebellion, and Hotspur's alliance with the Welsh and Scottish forces and urges him to prepare what he is going to say to the king the next day. In a meta-theatrical episode, they 'act out' Henry's coming interview with his father. Despite its comic overtones, this episode explores the relationships that Henry has with both Falstaff and his father. The questions that Falstaff puts to him as to whether the 'son of England' should 'prove a thief and take purses' emphasize the disparity between the prince's rank and duty and his current behaviour. When Falstaff uses his 'role' as king to recommend that Henry keeps Falstaff by him even when he banishes the others, Henry decides that they should swap places. He is playing the role of king, and abusing Falstaff, when a knocking is heard and Bardolph runs in.

Lines 485–554: Bardolph announces that the Watch are at the door. Hostess Quickly adds that they have come to search the house. The prince advises Falstaff to hide while he talks to the sheriff. Henry denies that Falstaff has been there, but promises to find him and send him to the sheriff, who leaves. Peto finds Falstaff snoring behind the arras and Henry goes through his pockets, finding only a bill for food and drink. Henry tells Peto that he will go and see the king in the morning, and warns him that they 'must all to the wars', joking that he will put Falstaff in command of an infantry company.

ACT 3 SCENE 1

Lines 1–148: The rebels meet in Wales to discuss their plans. They begin civilly, but Hotspur loses patience with Glendower's beliefs in astrological signs. Glendower claims that King Henry fears him because, at his birth, heaven was 'full of fiery shapes' and the earth 'Shaked like a coward', but Hotspur is rudely dismissive of these claims and mocks Glendower. Mortimer intervenes and they look at a map showing the potential division of land after the defeat of Henry. Mortimer announces that he, Hotspur and Worcester will set forth the next day to meet Northumberland and the Scottish armies at Shrewsbury, while Glendower gathers his forces to meet them 'in fourteen days'. Glendower promises to be with them quickly, and to bring their 'ladies' with him (Kate, Lady Percy, and his own daughter, wife of Mortimer). Hotspur, however, is still looking at the map and announces that he is not satisfied that his share is equal. Showing his lack of maturity, he goads Glendower and threatens to divert the course of the River Trent. In contrast to Hotspur, Glendower remains calm and agrees to a minor change in the map before leaving to find the ladies.

Lines 149–191: Mortimer rebukes Hotspur for his rudeness. Hotspur complains that Glendower angers him by talking about myths and magic and 'skimble-skamble stuff'. Worcester tells Hotspur that he must 'amend' his behaviour, providing an accurate analysis of his nephew's character: divided between 'greatness, courage, blood' and 'harsh rage . . . Pride, haughtiness, opinion and disdain'.

Lines 192–272: Glendower brings the ladies to bid goodbye. He translates the conversation between his daughter and Mortimer, as husband and wife do not speak each other's language. Their exchange is apparently romantic, however, and she sings him a parting song in Welsh. Hotspur mocks them as he and Lady Percy wrangle affectionately, perhaps showing a more genuine relationship than that of Mortimer and his wife. Mortimer and Hotspur leave.

ACT 3 SCENE 2

King Henry sends his lords away so that he can speak privately with Prince Henry. The king wonders whether God is punishing him through his son for some 'displeasing service' he has done in the past. Angry and disappointed, he rebukes Prince Henry for his lifestyle of 'barren pleasures and rude society'. Prince Henry claims that he has not behaved as badly as rumour suggests and asks for his father's pardon, but the king continues, pointing out that the prince's younger brother, Prince John, has had to take on his responsibilities. He argues that if he himself had been 'so common-hackneyed in the eyes of men' during his campaign for the throne, he would have lost the good opinion of the public, which was so important to his cause. In an emotional appeal, he compares Prince Henry's behaviour to that of Richard II, who 'Mingled his royalty with carping fools' and destroyed his popularity by being too much in the public eye. He talks about Hotspur, claiming that he 'hath more worthy interest to the state' than Prince Henry does, as he has shown courage and nobility in battle, even in his challenge to the king. He ends by saying that his son is just as likely to fight against him through 'fear' and 'Base inclination'. Moved, Henry begs him not to 'think so' and promises to redeem himself 'on Percy's head', washing away his own 'shame' with the blood of battle. His speech is eloquent and his use of blank verse and stirring imagery form a stark contrast with his speech and behaviour in previous scenes.

The king places Prince Henry in charge of the royal forces. Sir Walter Blunt brings news that the rebels are going to meet in Shrewsbury, and King Henry says that he knows this: Prince John has already set out. He announces that Prince Henry will set out 'on Wednesday next', that he will follow and that all their forces shall meet 'at Bridgnorth' in twelve days.

ACT 3 SCENE 3

In the Eastcheap tavern, Falstaff and Bardolph are involved in a humorous exchange. Hostess Quickly interrupts and Falstaff demands to know if she has caught whoever picked his pocket. She is indignant at the suggestion that there are thieves in her house, and reminds him that he owes her money. He claims that as well as his money, a seal-ring 'worth forty mark' has been stolen, but she tells everyone that the prince said that the ring was made of copper. Falstaff denounces Henry as a 'sneak-cup' and threatens to 'cudgel' him. As they bicker, Prince Henry arrives. They reveal their argument to him, Falstaff claiming that he has had 'three or four bonds of forty pound apiece, and a seal-ring' stolen, and the Hostess telling Henry that Falstaff spoke 'most vilely of him' and claimed that the prince owes him a thousand pounds. Falstaff jokes his way out of the accusations, and Henry reveals that it was he who went through Falstaff's pockets and found nothing of value. He asks Falstaff if he is 'not ashamed', but Falstaff is unrepentant, calling Hostess Quickly to prepare breakfast. Prince Henry reveals that he has paid back the sum taken in the robbery so Falstaff is no longer in trouble, and turns the conversation to the impending conflict, providing a serious conclusion to the boisterous comedy of the scene. Henry tells Falstaff that he has given him command of an infantry company, much to his lazy friend's disgust, but the humour that this generates is swiftly forgotten as the prince sustains his new, more serious character.

ACT 4 SCENE 1

The swift movement between the four scenes of this act emphasizes the increased pace of events.

Lines 1–88: Hotspur and Douglas are interrupted by a Messenger bringing news that Northumberland is 'grievous sick' and unable to lead his forces to join them. Northumberland's letter urges them to go into battle: in fact, they have no choice as the king is aware of their intentions and is preparing to fight. Worcester is concerned, but Hotspur remains optimistic, arguing that they will not be using all of their military strength at once, and will have 'a rendezvous, a home to fly unto' if they are unsuccessful. Douglas agrees, but Worcester worries that it will seem as though there is a division in the rebel forces, suggesting weakness. Hotspur bravely, if naively, retains his optimism.

Lines 89–143: Vernon brings news that Westmorland and Prince John are marching towards them with an army of seven thousand. The king has also set out 'With strong and mighty preparation'. Hotspur listens calmly then mockingly asks about Prince Henry,

'The nimble-footed madcap', showing contempt for the prince's lifestyle and reputation. Vernon reports, however, that Henry's forces are 'All furnished, all in arms', 'Glittering in golden coats', 'full of spirit', and 'gorgeous as the sun', evoking Henry's own image of himself at the end of Act 1 scene 2. Vernon recounts how the prince himself is like a 'feathered Mercury', riding on 'fiery Pegasus'. Angry at this praise of Henry, Hotspur declares himself 'on fire' to go into battle. He wants to meet the prince in single combat, 'Harry to Harry', symbolically emphasizing the dramatic paralleling of the two characters. He asks after Glendower, and Vernon reveals that the Welsh leader is not ready. Worcester and Douglas are disturbed by this news, but Hotspur urges them into battle, to 'die all, die merrily'.

ACT 4 SCENE 2

On the march to Shrewsbury, Falstaff sends Bardolph to buy wine. Falstaff reveals how he has 'misused' the power of conscription, making 'in exchange of a hundred and fifty soldiers, three hundred and odd pounds', by recruiting mostly wealthy men who can buy their way back out of service. Consequently, the troops he now has assembled consist of 'scarecrows' such as prisoners, 'servingmen ... revolted tapsters and ostlers trade-fallen'. While this provides comic relief from the preparations for battle, Falstaff's sustained dishonesty contrasts with Prince Henry's new found sense of duty and honour. Falstaff is joined by the prince and Westmorland, who criticize his troops. Falstaff comments callously that they are good enough for cannon fodder, and Henry urges him to hurry: the king and Hotspur are already encamped and ready for battle.

ACT 4 SCENE 3

The rebels argue over when to attack. A trumpet sounds a parley and Blunt brings a message from the king. Henry asks that the rebels 'name [their] griefs', promising to try to resolve matters and to pardon those who have stood against him. Hotspur launches into a long complaint, revealing the grievances of the Percy family against the king, detailing the help that they gave him in overthrowing Richard II and the king's subsequent ingratitude, such as his refusal to ransom Mortimer. When Blunt offers to relay this, however, Hotspur shows unusual restraint, saying that Worcester will be sent 'in the morning early' to talk with the king. He responds graciously to Blunt's wish for a peaceful solution.

ACT 4 SCENE 4

In a scene that foreshadows events in *Henry IV Part II*, the Archbishop of York sends letters to the Lord Marshall and Lord Scroop. He fears the outcome of a battle without Northumberland and Glendower's forces and is strengthening his defences in readiness against the king, who is aware of his role in the conspiracy.

ACT 5 SCENE 1

The pace of the previous act is sustained into Act 5, reinforcing the rapidity and confusion of the battle.

The king and prince discuss the worsening weather. Worcester is brought in and the king chastises him for deceiving his trust and bringing them to conflict. He gives Worcester the opportunity to 'unknit / This churlish knot of all-abhorrèd war', and Worcester responds that he is not the one responsible for the hostilities. He reiterates the complaints made by Hotspur in Act 4 scene 3, concerning the 'unkind usage' of the Percy family by the king. The king responds that this is merely an excuse with which to 'face the garment of rebellion'. Prince Henry offers to meet Hotspur in single combat to settle the matter, in order to prevent lives being lost in battle. He acknowledges Hotspur's bravery and nobility, and admits his own past failings as a 'truant to chivalry'. The king forbids this and again offers to pardon the rebels if they surrender now. Worcester goes to deliver this message, and the prince warns his father that the rebels will not accept his offer of peace. The king leaves to prepare. The prince and Falstaff say goodbye, and, once he is alone, Falstaff muses on the futility of honour if it leads to death, reasoning that 'honour' is merely 'a word'.

ACT 5 SCENE 2

Lines 1–42: Worcester tells Vernon that Hotspur must not learn of the king's offer. He argues that, whilst the king may forgive and forget Hotspur's 'trespass' as a youthful misdemeanour, he and Northumberland would be punished by Henry; thus selfishly placing his own concerns before the possibility of averting the war. Hotspur joins them and Worcester announces that the king will engage in battle, dishonestly claiming that he 'gently' told Henry of their 'grievances' and that the king called them traitors.

Lines 43–102: Douglas returns from sending Westmorland to the king with a message of defiance and Worcester tells Hotspur that Prince Henry offered to meet him in single combat. Hotspur is pleased with this idea, echoing Henry's honourable concern for the lives of his men. Vernon describes how Henry praised Hotspur and confessed his own 'truant youth', but Hotspur is unimpressed, expressing his intention to meet Henry on the battlefield. A messenger brings in letters, but Hotspur claims that 'the time of life is short' and that he cannot read them now. Another Messenger announces that the king is approaching and Hotspur leads the rebels to battle.

Lines 103–133: Douglas and Blunt enter, Blunt disguised as the king. They fight and Blunt is killed. Hotspur arrives and recognizes Blunt, revealing that Henry has many decoys on the battlefield. They head back to battle.

Lines 134–165: Falstaff enters, alone, and sees Blunt's body, remarking: 'There's honour for you!' Prince Henry finds him and demands his sword, chastising him for standing idle. Falstaff offers him a pistol, but the prince finds a bottle of wine in the holster. Disgusted, he leaves, and Falstaff reiterates his point that he would rather live than achieve honour in death.

ACT 5 SCENE 3

Lines 1–24: The king urges an injured Prince Henry to withdraw, accompanied by Prince John, but they refuse. Prince John and Westmorland return to the fight and the king and Prince Henry comment on John's bravery before the prince also returns to battle.

Lines 25–58: Douglas finds the king alone and, although uncertain whether it is another 'counterfeit', begins to fight him. The king is in danger of defeat when Prince Henry rejoins them, causing Douglas to flee. King Henry tells his son that he has 'redeemed' his 'lost opinion' before heading back into battle.

Lines 59–111: Hotspur arrives and the prince declares that one of the Harrys must die: 'Two stars keep not their motion in one sphere'. As they fight, Falstaff arrives, followed by Douglas. They also fight and Falstaff collapses as if dead. As Douglas leaves, Henry kills Hotspur and eulogizes over his body, acknowledging his bravery. He sees Falstaff, apparently dead, and delivers an ambiguous but fond eulogy, promising to return for both bodies later.

Lines 112–167: In a moment of bathos after the tensions of the scene, Falstaff sits up, revealing that he faked his death to avoid being killed. He decides to claim that Hotspur regained consciousness and that he, Falstaff, killed him. He stabs the body and is interrupted by the two princes, to whom he tells his unlikely tale. Unconvinced, Henry tells Falstaff he will back him in his claims if it will do his friend 'grace'. They leave as the retreat signals their victory over the rebels.

ACT 5 SCENE 4

The royal party enters, with Worcester and Vernon as prisoners. The king lays responsibility for the day's bloodshed on Worcester for not accepting his offer of peace, and condemns both rebels to death. Prince Henry reveals that he has Douglas prisoner and asks permission to release him in recognition of his bravery. The king agrees and issues his instructions: Prince John and Westmorland are to lead forces against Northumberland and Scroop, while he and Prince Henry march to Wales to fight Glendower. Despite the victory, the play ends as it began: with the country in civil conflict.

SYNOPSIS OF
HENRY IV PART II

In despair at the death of his son Hotspur, the Earl of Northumberland lends his support to a second rebellion, led by the Archbishop of York. As the threat of civil war looms over the country, King Henry IV grows sick, while also fearing that his son Prince Henry (known as Harry and, by Falstaff, as Hal) has returned to his old life with Falstaff and the other disreputable denizens of the Eastcheap tavern. Falstaff is sent on a recruiting expedition and renews old acquaintances in Gloucestershire. The rebel army is met by the King's forces, led this time by Hal's younger brother, Prince John of Lancaster. On his death-bed, King Henry is reconciled with his son, who has begun to distance himself from his former companions. A new, mature Hal accepts the crown as Henry V.

HENRY IV IN PERFORMANCE: THE RSC AND BEYOND

The best way to understand a Shakespeare play is to see it or ideally to participate in it. By examining a range of productions, we may gain a sense of the extraordinary variety of approaches and interpretations that are possible – a variety that gives Shakespeare his unique capacity to be reinvented and made 'our contemporary' four centuries after his death.

We begin with a brief overview of the play's theatrical and cinematic life, offering historical perspectives on how it has been performed. We then analyse in more detail a series of productions staged over the last half-century by the Royal Shakespeare Company. The sense of dialogue between productions that can only occur when a company is dedicated to the revival and investigation of the Shakespeare canon over a long period, together with the uniquely comprehensive archival resource of promptbooks, programme notes, reviews and interviews held on behalf of the RSC at the Shakespeare Birthplace Trust in Stratford-upon-Avon, allows an 'RSC stage history' to become a crucible in which the chemistry of the play can be explored.

We then go to the horse's mouth. Modern theatre is dominated by the figure of the director. He or she must hold together the whole play, whereas the actor must concentrate on his or her part. The director's viewpoint is therefore especially valuable. Shakespeare's plasticity is wonderfully revealed when we hear the directors of two highly successful productions answering the same questions in very different ways. And finally, we offer the actor's perspective: a view of the play through the eyes of Prince Hal.

FOUR CENTURIES OF *HENRY IV*: AN OVERVIEW

Henry IV Part I was probably written and performed between 1596 and 1597 with *Part II* following a year later. The first performances of which records survive were at court in 1612–13 when a total of twenty plays were presented to celebrate the marriage of James I's daughter Elizabeth to Frederick, the Elector of Palatine. They are listed as *The Hotspurre* and *Sir John Falstaffe*, and were only later identified as the two parts of Shakespeare's *Henry IV*. These alternative titles suggest that both were originally seen in terms of their star parts rather than as a political study of kingship with Prince Hal at the centre. As scholars and theatre historians have pointed out:

> That change of emphasis required a change of format. It takes both parts of *Henry IV* followed by *Henry V* to make Prince Hal into a fully-fledged hero, or anti-hero, and it was not until the mid-twentieth century that an influential cycle of these plays... was staged in the English theatre.[1]

Until this point the plays were performed individually and, although *Part II* was clearly designed as a sequel to *Part I* – probably in order to capitalize on the enormous and immediate popularity of the first play – there is little evidence to suggest that they were performed in sequence. Numerous contemporary references and reprints of the Quarto editions all point to their popularity and success, however. The writer Nicholas Breton mentions seeing 'the play of Ancient Pistol',[2] and Leonard Digges' prefatory poem to the 1640 edition of Shakespeare's poems provides further evidence of their popularity:

> ... let but Falstaff come,
> Hal, Poins, the rest, you scarce shall have a room,
> All is so pestered...

In his commendatory poem to the Folio edition of Beaumont and Fletcher (1647), Sir Thomas Palmer claims he could 'tell how long / Falstaff from cracking nuts have kept the throng'.

Falstaff was originally played either by company clown Will Kempe or comic actor Thomas Pope, while Prince Hal was almost certainly played by Richard Burbage, the leading tragedian with Shakespeare's acting company, the Lord Chamberlain's (later the King's) Men. John Lowin took over the role of Falstaff: 'before the Wars Lowin used to act, with mighty applause Falstaff'.[3] During the Interregnum from 1642 to 1660, the theatres were technically closed, although various means were employed to get around the prohibition on plays, such as the introduction of music and dancing into sketches from popular plays known as drolls; a collection of twenty-seven of these, *The Wits, or Sport Upon Sport*, by Francis Kirkman, was published in 1662 with three featuring episodes from Shakespeare's plays, including *The Bouncing Knight, or the Robbers Robbed*, centred on Falstaff's exploits. The frontispiece illustration places Falstaff and the Hostess in prominent positions.

Henry IV Part I continued to be popular after the Restoration and was one of the first plays performed by Thomas Killigrew's King's Company in 1660. Samuel Pepys' diary records his attendance at no fewer than four performances over the period 1660–68. The play's main attractions were still Hotspur and Falstaff. Thomas Betterton, the great Restoration actor-manager, played Hotspur in 1682, with 'wild impatient starts' and 'fierce and flashing fire',[4] but in the 1700 revival he took on the role of Falstaff. Thomas Davies records how 'the versatility of Betterton's genius was never more conspicuous than in his resigning the choleric Hotspur, in his declining years, and assuming the humour and gaiety of Falstaff, in which he is said to have been full as acceptable to the public as in the former'.[5] In contrast to most Shakespearean revivals in the period, it underwent relatively few changes apart from textual cuts of long political speeches, the Welsh dialogue and song, and much of the mock trial in the tavern. Betterton's continued popularity as Falstaff was largely responsible for a revival of *Part II* during the eighteenth century, in which the star turns were Falstaff and Justice Shallow.

In the next generation, James Quin, who had previously played Hotspur and the king, was the most notable Falstaff. David Garrick played Hotspur on five occasions, dressed 'in a laced frock and a

Ramilie wig',[6] but was plainly unsuited to the role, and the part was taken over by Spranger Barry. One of the theatrical highlights seems to have been Falstaff carrying Hotspur offstage:

> No joke ever raised such loud and repeated mirth, in the galleries, as Sir John's labour in getting the body of Hotspur on his back... Quin had little or no difficulty in perching Garrick upon his shoulders, who looked like a dwarf on the back of a giant. But oh! how he tugged and toiled to raise Barry from the ground![7]

His successor, John Henderson, reportedly had so much difficulty with his Hotspur that a small gang of 'Falstaff's ragamuffins' were used instead to bear the body offstage.[8] Other late eighteenth-century Falstaffs included at least one woman, Mrs Webb, who 'excelled in corpulent and grotesque characters' in Norwich in 1786.[9]

John Philip Kemble played Hotspur at Covent Garden in the early nineteenth century and his brother, Stephen, was one of a number of actors to play Falstaff without padding, although William Hazlitt remarked of his performance, 'Every fat man cannot represent a great man.'[10] The American actor James Henry Hackett played the part in England and America for forty years, and his Hotspurs included John Philip and Charles Kemble, as well as Edmund Kean and William Charles Macready. He received mixed reviews; *The Athenaeum* reported:

> His is the best Falstaff that has been seen for many a day, – which, however, is not saying much for it. But it has positive merits that deserve recognition. He did not... reach the full conception which Shakespeare has here embodied... but he aimed at it, and accomplished much; his soliloquy on honour, in particular, was well delivered, and, take him for all in all, we are disposed to give him a cordial welcome.[11]

His identification with the role was such that he became known as 'Falstaff Hackett'.

In 1821 a spectacular production of *Henry IV Part II* with Macready as King Henry and Charles Kemble as Prince Hal included a magnificent staging of the coronation procession as a tribute to the coronation of George IV. Kemble's production of *Part I* in 1824 with himself as Hotspur was mainly noted for the historical accuracy of costumes and sets, which included 'the King's Chamber in the old Palace of Westminster; the inn-yard at Rochester with the castle, by night; Hotspur's Camp; a distant view of Coventry; and Shrewsbury from the field of battle'.[12] Samuel Phelps' production at Sadler's Wells in 1846 was similarly spectacular:

> All has been done with a lavish and judicious hand, without a regard to cost or aught beside, save the desire of gratifying the public. The accoutrements, armour, and trappings worn by the several armies in the fourth and fifth acts are indeed splendid, and the minutest care has been shown in the arrangement of the costumes, even to the very crests of the different parties. The battle was admirably managed – the scenery was entirely new, and elicited much applause.[13]

The 1864 revival at Drury Lane which included the Glendower scene in full for the first time was distinguished by Phelps' Falstaff: 'He lays stress not on Falstaff's sensuality, but on the lively intellect that stands for soul as well as mind in his gross body', in a performance marked by 'a smooth delicate touch that stamps the knight distinctly as a man well born and bred'.[14] Phelps' remarkable doubling of the king and Justice Shallow in *Part II* later that year earned further praise.[15]

Herbert Beerbohm Tree's 1896 production at the Haymarket Theatre used a fuller text of the play and was well received by the critics, with the exception of George Bernard Shaw. William Archer praised the overall conception – 'There has been no nearer approach in our day to the complete performance of a Shakespearian drama.'[16] Of Tree's performance, *The Athenaeum* reported: 'it is the fat knight himself that comes before us'.[17] Shaw, however, thought that 'Mr Tree only wants one thing to make him an excellent Falstaff, and that is to get born over again as unlike himself as possible.'[18]

Victorian spectacle went out of fashion in the early twentieth century influenced by the ideas of William Poel and the English

Stage Society, which favoured performances on a thrust stage with minimal scenery and faster-paced, fluid action.

History does not update in the same way as the comedies and tragedies that have lent themselves to a variety of settings, costumes and periods. The effect on the history plays has been to emphasize

1. Herbert Beerbohm Tree as Falstaff in his 1896 production at the Haymarket Theatre. *The Athenaeum* reported: 'it is the fat knight himself that comes before us'.

their historicity. Between 1901 and 1906 Frank Benson staged a
cycle of Shakespeare's history plays for the first time at the Stratford-
upon-Avon festival season which omitted *Henry IV Part I* but
included *King John, Richard II, Henry IV Part II, Henry V, Henry VI
Part II,* and *Richard III*. W. B. Yeats was impressed by the way in
which 'play supports play'[19] when presented in this way. *Henry IV
Part I* was included in the new cycle in 1905, as was Marlowe's
Edward II. In 1921 Barry Jackson had staged both parts of *Henry IV*
on the same day (23 April) in Birmingham. The two parts
of *Henry IV* were the first plays performed after the opening of
the New Memorial Theatre in Stratford by the Prince of Wales in
1932 – *Part I* in the afternoon and *Part II* in the evening.

In 1935 Robert Atkins and Sydney Carroll staged a production of
Henry IV Part I with the popular vaudeville comedian George Robey
as Falstaff. Despite his lack of classical training many critics were
impressed by his performance; Herbert Farjeon reflected that 'We
learn from Mr Robey's Falstaff many things. One of them is that it is
a tremendous advantage to have Shakespeare's clowns . . . played by
men who are funny *before they begin* . . . Mr Sydney Carroll's brilliant
casting of Falstaff should put an end to the long dreary line of
legitimate actors who have made soggy hay of Shakespeare's
comics.'[20] However, *The New Statesman* regarded Robey's Falstaff as
an 'old soak rather than the fallen gentleman . . . nothing more than
a super-Bardolph'.[21]

John Burrell's production a decade later at the New Theatre was
warmly received:

> *Feliciter audax* [pleasingly audacious] is, indeed, the phrase for
> Mr Burrell's production. Choosing not to adopt the uninterrupted
> flow of the Elizabethan method, he closes each scene with a
> moment of dumb-show, shadowy and significant. I shall never
> forget Glendower, standing at the window (the actor is Harcourt
> Williams, who knows how to stand) – standing and staring after
> Hotspur as he gallops away, with the two women weeping at his
> feet while we know what they guess, that they will never see
> Hotspur again.[22]

2. Ralph Richardson as Falstaff and Laurence Olivier as Justice Shallow in John Burrell's 1945 New Theatre production: Ralph Richardson's Falstaff was universally admired, and Laurence Olivier triumphed as Hotspur in *Part I* and Justice Shallow in *Part II*.

Harcourt Williams' performance was not the only one to be widely praised. Ralph Richardson's Falstaff was universally admired:

> a grand buffoon and rapscallion in *Part I*, proceeded in *Part II* to a still richer understanding which could catch the sombre

illumination of 'Do not bid me remember mine end' and suggest, as Falstaffs rarely do, the attraction of the man for the Prince as well as the considerable brain behind the wit. This was a metamorphosis assisted by make-up but by no means entirely dependent on it: for Richardson's greatness – and I think the word is justifiable – in the part was a greatness of spirit that transcended the mere hulk of flesh.[23]

Laurence Olivier, meanwhile, played Hotspur in *Part I* and Justice Shallow in *Part II*, and triumphed in both.

But it was the 1951 presentation of the tetralogy of *Richard II*, *Henry IV Part I*, *Henry IV Part II* and *Henry V* by Anthony Quayle, John Kidd and Michael Redgrave at the Shakespeare Memorial Theatre which was to prove decisive in the plays'

3. The 1951 Shakespeare Memorial Theatre presented *Richard II*, *Henry IV Part I* and *Part II* and *Henry V* as a tetralogy: with Harry Andrews as Henry IV and Richard Burton as Hal.

fortunes. Anthony Quayle explained the thinking behind the productions:

> it seemed to us that the great epic theme of the Histories had become obscured through years of presenting the plays single, and many false interpretations had grown up, and come to be accepted, through star actors giving almost too persuasive and dominant performances of parts which the author intended to be by no means sympathetic.[24]

One critic suggested: 'One will never again think of these plays as single entities, and when they are played as such we shall feel them to have been lopped.'[25] Tanya Moiseiwitsch designed a single set of 'plain unvarnished oak' which could be 'embellished as the occasion demanded with props or with hangings' and 'provided three acting spaces and a large variety of entrances; it allowed the action to move in an uninterrupted flow'.[26] There *were* star performances though – 'Mr Redgrave's poetic Richard and dazzling Hotspur, Mr Quayle's splendidly rich Falstaff and Mr Richard Burton's sultry intriguing Hal', as well as 'Mr Harry Andrews's superb and masterly Bolingbroke';[27] the balance was shifted decisively away from Hotspur and Falstaff towards Hal.

Douglas Seale directed both parts of *Henry IV* at the Old Vic in 1955 in productions admired for being 'simple and direct and, while comparatively and mercifully static within each individual scene... they are driven with a brilliant sense of the narrative speed over all'.[28] Again, a strong cast achieved unanimous praise, from Paul Rogers' Falstaff – 'leaner and considerably dilapidated, is already some of the way downhill', to Robert Hardy's Prince – 'a very strong and charming performance', while 'John Neville makes a fine Hotspur and a whirlwind Pistol, and Paul Daneman an ominous Worcester followed, in a miraculous transformation, by an extremely funny Shallow, withered with senility and malice. Rachel Roberts and Gwen Cherrell draw fruitfully on Hogarth for Mistress Quickly and Doll Tearsheet.'[29]

It has become the norm since then for the two plays of *Henry IV* to be performed together, often within the context of a larger cycle of Shakespeare's history plays. The resources required for such ambitious projects are only realistically available to the national subsidized companies, and productions by the RSC (discussed below) have constituted the majority of these. In 1986 Michael Bogdanov and Michael Pennington formed the English Shakespeare Company with the aim of promoting and presenting the works of Shakespeare both nationally and internationally. The inaugural production, *The Henrys*, consisted of *Part I* and *Part II* of *Henry IV* plus *Henry V*. The following year they presented *The Wars of the Roses*, comprised of *Richard II*, *Henry IV Part I*, *Henry IV Part II*, *Henry V*, the three plays of *Henry VI* telescoped into two plays (*Henry VI: House of Lancaster*, *Henry VI: House of York*), and *Richard III*. The production toured successfully for two years, both within the UK and internationally. The company deliberately worked against the dominant mode of theatrical realism to present radical and exciting productions, designed to engage a modern audience:

> We would provide a space that would allow the plays to range over the centuries in imagery. We would free our, and the audiences' imaginations by allowing an eclectic mix of costumes and props, choosing a time and a place that was most appropriate for a character or a scene. Modern dress at one moment, medieval, Victorian or Elizabethan the next. We would use a kit of props ... [which], as far as possible, would remain on stage. The means of transformation from one scene to the next would remain visible. No tricks up our sleeves (until we needed one). We would create a style that was essentially rough theatre, but would add, when we needed it, a degree of sophistication.[30]

The relatively few American productions of *Henry IV* have concentrated historically on *Part I*, focusing on the roles of Hotspur and Falstaff. Stuart Vaughan directed both parts which played in repertory at New York's Phoenix Theater in 1960: the emphasis on Eric Berry's widely-praised, compelling Falstaff led to the accusation that it 'might accurately be called "The Decline and Fall of Sir John Falstaff, Fat Old Knight"'.[31] In 1993, Ron Daniels directed back-to-back stagings of *Part I* and *Part II* for the American

Repertory Theater, updated to an American Civil War setting which enjoyed a mixed critical reception:

> Mr Daniels has created a wildly anachronistic, culturally mixed salad in which different elements of Shakespeare's epic portrait are accorded theatrical analogues from wholly disparate historical moments. The result, given visual life by John Conklin's time-traveling, slightly ragged scenic shorthand, is less disjunctive than one might expect.[32]

Barbara Gaines' 1999 production of both plays at Chicago's Shakespeare Repertory Theater was widely praised for its simple staging and strong performances. In 2003 Dakin Matthews conflated the texts of both plays in a production at Lincoln Center's Vivian Beaumont Theater, directed by Jack O'Brien. The resulting adaptation lasted nearly four hours with two intervals, but compressed the action to create a fast-paced, fluid text. Kevin Kline's Falstaff was:

> made up to resemble a threadbare Santa Claus with a blimp of a prosthetic belly and a snowy beard, Mr Kline looks like the most traditional Falstaff imaginable. The wonderful surprise is how he deviates from the convention of bluster and braggadocio. Mr Kline has never had more of a chance to make a meal of the scenery. Instead, he delivers a finely measured performance that matches the actor's infinite resourcefulness with that of the character he plays.[33]

Remarkably, London's National Theatre did not stage a performance of *Henry IV* until Nicholas Hytner's production in 2005 played on a 'roughly arrow-shaped stage' in the large Olivier Theatre. The production managed 'to suggest the mighty sweep of the plays – their oscillation from uptight court to frowsty lowlife, from the frenetically urban to the peacefully pastoral, from the battlefield to the boozer – with depth and definition'.[34] Michael Gambon was praised for the way he:

> wonderfully incorporates the contradictions of Falstaff. He looks like the kind of wily, drunken bohemian tramp that Just William

would ill-advisedly let into the Brown household, where he would later be found comatose in the wine cellar. In the moveable feast of his accent, you hear the tones of a parvenu whose poshness is pretty precarious and inclined to slip into saloon-bar bravado. This is not a sentimentalised fat knight. He's utterly out for himself, and the last thing we're treated to in *Part 1* is the sight of him shamelessly robbing two venerable corpses.[35]

Matthew McFadyen made a 'shrewd witty prince', and David Bradley played the 'haunted cadaverous king', while:

The scenes in Gloucestershire are delectably comic, thanks to the great John Wood, whose Justice Shallow is a transcendent study in florid, nervously energetic self-delusion about a wild youth that he did not experience. He is delightfully partnered by Adrian Scarborough, who, as Silence, is like a little slip of death inadequately warmed up – until he gets a few glasses inside him, when he cannot be restrained from providing quavering, unwanted cabaret.[36]

The two parts of *Henry IV* with their broad cross-section of scenes and characters have come to be regarded as a sort of national epic firmly established at the heart of the Shakespearean repertory. The most remarkable film version is Orson Welles' 1966 film adaptation, *Chimes at Midnight*, in which the entire tetralogy from *Richard II* to *Henry V* is telescoped into less than two hours. In 1938 Welles directed an unsuccessful play called *Five Kings* in which he had gathered all the Falstaff material from the *Henrys* and *The Merry Wives of Windsor*. This formed the basis of Welles' film, shot while he was supposedly making *Treasure Island*. As Scott McMillin suggests, 'he was not interested in the historical epic formed by the histories; he was interested in Falstaff – or, perhaps more accurately, in a certain angle of vision which he thought of as Falstaffian'.[37] The star-studded cast included Jeanne Moreau, Margaret Rutherford, John Gielgud (as Henry IV), with Ralph Richardson as the narrator. The film's 'brilliance' lies in Welles' characteristically bravura film vocabulary and style. As McMillin puts it: 'If Falstaff had made films, he would have made something like this one.'[38]

The BBC Shakespeare version, by contrast, offers a conventional historical cycle of the second tetralogy (*Richard II*, *Henry IV Part I*, *Henry IV Part II*, *Henry V*) made for television and directed by David Giles. Anthony Quayle, who had played Falstaff so successfully in 1951, reprised the role. The narrow focus of television does not, however, lend itself easily to the broad sweep of history:

> If cycle-thinking puts the realm and its rulers ahead of Falstaff, and if the performance of Falstaff puts him well ahead of the realm and its rulers, trouble is brewing. Quayle's assured performance as Falstaff is the strongest element of the production, and the separate 'sphere of intelligence' provided by his addresses to the audience happily interrupts the dutiful effort to capture history in the space of the television studio. He is in better control of the medium – and this makes Prince Hal's efforts to take better control of the kingdom seem second-rate.[39]

The English Shakespeare Company's highly politicized, eclectic *Wars of the Roses* was recorded for television in 1989.

AT THE RSC

> The stage is the world, as in a mediaeval morality play. It may represent court, camp, tavern, England, France, but it is always the blank slate on which life writes its lessons for [Hal], the bare, mental arena in which the soul of a royal Everyman discovers his destiny and true friends.
> (Ronald Bryden)[40]

In mid-twentieth-century post-war Britain, Hal took centre stage in productions of *Henry IV Part I*. Caught between the mighty figures of Henry IV and Falstaff and the worlds of court and tavern, his education became the focal point of the play. Directors instilled an ambiguity into the proceedings, with Hal never truly revealing his nature but remaining enigmatic, and therefore slightly dangerous and anti-heroic. An adolescent under the sway of two highly charismatic father figures, manipulative and aware of the power he wields, critics and audiences have often found him a difficult character to like. Sympathy for Hal derives mainly from the portrayal of Henry IV and Falstaff. The prince attempts to learn from two men who are not what they seem to be; who present one face to the world and another to themselves. He inhabits two worlds, different in their emotional propensities and ethos, but equal in their duplicity.

When looking at RSC productions, the resulting influence of these environments on Hal can be seen reflected in the design concept chosen by directors. Pointing to an overarching theme, court and tavern were either designed as stylistically opposed or inextricably linked. With *Henry IV Part I* rarely performed on its own, the design of a production will often be part of a larger scheme, involving *Henry IV Part II*, *Richard II* and/or *Henry V*. Occasionally, they have been performed as part of the cycle of Shakespeare's histories (produced in 1963–65, 2000–01 and 2006–08), chronologically following through and encompassing the eight plays from *Richard II* to *Richard III*.

In 1964 *Henry IV Part I* and *Part II* were performed as part of a seven-play history cycle called the *Wars of the Roses* that examined the politics, the mechanics of power that moved behind Shakespeare's history plays. These:

> were bleakly anti-heroic, capable of making war seem devastating and inhuman. The younger theatregoers of 1963 did not share the end-of-war patriotism that had motivated the . . . 1951 Stratford series for the Festival of Britain. The sensibilities of the new audience were being shaped by Beckett, Osborne, Pinter, Brecht. This was not a crowd given to what they would have regarded as the sentiment and jingoism of the past . . . Peter Hall saw the dominant image as a mechanism of power:
>
>> Over the years I became more and more fascinated by the contortions of politicians and by the corrupting seductions experienced by anyone who wields power . . . I realised that the mechanism of power had not changed in centuries.

... [Designer, John] Bury saw the violence and power politics of the cycle as framed in steel:

> It was a period of armour and a period of the sword: they were plays about warfare, about power, about danger. One spent one's time either in armour, or piercing someone's armour – or being pierced ... We were trying to make a world: a dangerous world, a terrible world, in which all these happenings fit.[41]

The hard and heavy oppressive nature of the set complemented a darkly political reading of the play. The fragility of the characters and the dehumanizing effect of war were also reflected in the costumes, which assimilated the metal world:

> The stage floor was plated steel. The acting space for all seven plays was defined by two huge triangle-based metal-plated walls, which could be turned to present different faces and shifted to form different angles ... [For *Henry IV*] the dominant metallic textures were modified here and there by wood and cloth, and banners were used in the battle scenes, but austerity prevailed in the overall visual impression.[42]

When Bury joined the RSC in 1962, he brought with him a revolutionary concept – that a production's design should be based around a central 'image' which should be followed on in the costuming and sound of that production. He altered the use of stage space by using real materials that had texture, substance, and a natural sound when the actors worked on them. His style was a rejection of the romantic designs and costumes frequently seen in the 1950s.

As in so many of Shakespeare's plays, the physical and mental condition of the king is reflected in his state. The ill health of the 'body politic' was clearly visible in John Napier's design for the 1982 production. Picking up on the idea that 'We are all diseased', director Trevor Nunn:

> contrived to suggest that a whole range of minor figures suffered from the general malaise ... [The] set consisted of four tall wooden

structures, each built like the open-section interior of a three-storey square house ... each structure could be moved separately backwards or forwards, to build a different 'house' for each location. Often the structures were full of people, even as they were moved into place, particularly with the tavern-scenes, which became momentarily large portable pubs. At times, the scene practically seethed with extras, working hoists, trundling kegs, mounting ladders to paint signs, bustling about with sacks or trays of drinks, beating carpets, making beds ... these sets remained drab. The boards were twisted. They were hung with shields and lances, but all were painted black – the colour of the wood itself – and the dark heavy structures seemed gloomy and overpowering. The effect was enhanced by David Hersey's lighting: often a dim suffused light; at other times a bright overhead spotlight, leaving dingy shadows all around. In addition, Eastcheap extras often remained on the set, lounging up stairs, watching, during the intervening court scenes. The effect was to suggest a political world which was haunted by shabbiness.[43]

In keeping with the idea that *Henry IV* takes its form from the medieval morality play, Adrian Noble's designer, Bob Crowley, strongly marked out the symbolism of faith and sin, heaven and hell, in the set design in 1991. He 'sharply juxtaposed the excesses of the tavern with the calculation of the court':[44]

Julian Glover's King Henry and Robert Stephens's Falstaff form the opposing poles of Adrian Noble's production of *Henry IV Part 1*, the King stern, cold and authoritarian in grey and black, Falstaff warm, mercurial, libertarian, and faintly epicene in scarlet ... The King's bare court is furnished with hard chairs and severe tables; while soft fabrics and yielding sofas in glowing shades of red characterise the tavern scenes. The Eastcheap tavern erupts on us like a mediaeval vision of hell, a lurid maze of private rooms with sex visibly on sale.[45]

We could hardly be reminded more forcibly that Shakespeare's matchless history has its roots in mediaeval drama or that Hal is poised between an angry God in Henry and a ribald Satan in Falstaff.[46]

Meanwhile, the greed, the violence, the humble bustle, the sordid pastimes of ordinary English life go on. Shakespeare's greatness is at its most awesome when he shows you how the politics of the nobility is mirrored, refracted, parodied and complemented by the goings on in Eastcheap and Rochester. Noble has retained Act Two Scene One, in the inn at Rochester, which directors usually cut. Here the robbery is set up when Shakespeare's equivalent of the hotel manager tips off Gadshill as to which guests are carrying the loot. The underworld types are played without a touch of mockery. These are dangerous but ordinary people who have a living to make, and their lives are no laughing matter any more than the Percys'.[47]

When explaining his entrance as Falstaff, Desmond Barrit explained the idea for the design of *Henry IV* in 2000:

Up through the floor I pushed, by way of a sort of rubber flange that we came to know as the sphincter ... The idea of this curious entrance, of course, was symbolic: our production was part of the RSC's 'This England' project to present eight of Shakespeare's history plays, and the subject of those plays was this island, this England, this earth that we live on, and the director wanted Falstaff, as a man of the earth, to be seen to be born from the earth.[48]

In contrast to the history cycle of 1964, no design concept linked the plays. Each was individually conceived by separate directors and designers. This was criticized by some who felt that the continuity of the cycle was less apparent, and confusing, when the same actors in the same roles appeared in completely different times and settings. However, Es Devlin's set design for the two parts of Michael Attenborough's production of *Henry IV* was completely appropriate to the play: 'England is basically conceived as an often blood-stained, earthy battleground, with a steep hill at the rear, [conveying] Attenborough's sense that the play intensifies the impression ... of a country rent asunder.'[49] With lights shining up through the floor, the earth appeared primordial and volcanic, as if awaiting a moment of violence. With 'its mound of smoke-filled peat [the set] effectively embodies the idea that "the land is burning"'.[50]

Fathers and Sons

What the father hath hid cometh out in the son; and oft have I found in the son the father's revealed secret.

(Frederick Nietzsche)[51]

As Harold C. Goddard points out, it would be hard to find a better illustration of this axiom than Henry IV and Hal: 'In his concentration on power the elder Henry has suppressed both the playful and the passionate tendencies of his nature...What he has kept under comes out in Hal, who leads a life of abandon under the tutelage of Falstaff.'[52] Hal finds in Falstaff a father that embodies the 'unrealised half of [Henry's] soul',[53] providing him with a rough education and emotional warmth.

Of the 1975 production, directed by Terry Hands, John Elsom wrote:

Alan Howard's Hal is a young prince, growing up. His mind is being formed by two mutually opposing fathers. His natural father, the King, is tortured by guilt and obsessed with ideals of kingship. His debased 'father', Falstaff is impervious to guilt, scornful of honour and duty, but relishes the simple pleasures in life, sack, sex and getting away with things.[54]

Hands' production focused on this central relationship, providing 'a study in domestic psychopathology, probing the tortured relationship of father and son'.[55]

Emrys James, who played Henry IV, portrayed him as a lonely character frustrated by his inability to express emotion in a non-aggressive fashion:

The play is about the longing a father has for a relationship with his son. It is peculiarly painful to have that figure high above, cut

4. Alan Howard as Prince Hal, 'a young prince growing up', and Brewster Mason as Falstaff, who 'relishes the simple pleasures in life, sack, sex and getting away with things', in Terry Hands' 1975 RSC production.

off from his son, but watching. He is a distant father-figure for Hal because this man doesn't, cannot unbend...

> Stay and breathe awhile.
> Thou hast redeemed thy lost opinion,
> And showed thou mak'st some tender of my life
> In the fair rescue thou hast brought to me.

It's incredible that he is not able to say, 'You are a wonderful son to me because you have given yourself in battle with this great beast of a man and fought him off. And it shows without question that you love me.' That's not the way he thinks. It's part of his hang-up, part of his trouble. If he had shown emotion to this emotional young man their relationship would have been that much easier.

... It isn't accidental that Shakespeare left his wife out of the play. He's a lonely man surrounded by four big, surly, rebellious sons, whom he rules with a rod of iron... Here's a man who hasn't learned how to handle his emotions and his solution to the problem is to suppress them completely. Except in moments of extreme stress. Then they come out.[56]

In order to emphasize the relationship between father and son, Hands deliberately merged Eastcheap and the court, with Henry and Hal often present, onlookers in their separate scenes:

> Here both king and prince stray into scenes from which they are usually absent. From the first, Henry IV watches, soft-lit and chorus-like, from the back of the stage as Hal and Falstaff flirt – almost literally flirt – with self-indulgence. From his dallying, Hal strolls off, seeing Henry lambaste the nobles who will turn against him, removed from his father yet linked as he circles the stage.[57]

Props were also used to signify Hal's half-existence between two worlds:

> James's Henry treats Hal as a child, takes his hand, pulls him onto the seat . . . beside him, hugs him, kisses him. He tries to supplant the physical affection evident between Hal and Sir John but the boy is only disorientated and reaches out of the scene to take a bottle and goblet from the tavern in which their palace meeting is limboed.[58]

The deliberate merging of court and tavern also prompts us to think of Henry IV and Falstaff as the lords of two realms within England. The device was used to great effect in Michael Attenborough's production in 2000:

> Bolingbroke, now Henry IV, sits on the same throne that serves as Falstaff's perch in downtown Eastcheap. This neatly indicates that the king and the old reprobate serve as competing father figures to Prince Hal.[59]

How the actors physically relate to each other reveals their character and the dimension of their relationships. Of the 1964 production, Scott McMillin observed that:

> Falstaff offered what Hal ought to have sought according to a psychological reading, a little fatherly contact. Hal's own father,

the Henry IV of Eric Porter, was remote and unapproachable, but Falstaff showed warm feeling and caressed Hal's face while acting the father's role. [Ian] Holm did not spurn such gestures.[60]

Holm played Hal in an anti-heroic fashion, as an onlooker, never completely engaged or in contact with the people around him, 'a cold-blooded young man who was working his way towards heroism':

in the vital matter of [Henry's] relationship with Hal there seemed not even the contact of pity between father and son. Their meeting ... was played with great physical and emotional distance between the two men. When the time came for Hal (Ian Holm) to declare his loyalty, he first went over and closed the door: a telling gesture with its suggestion of guarded secrecy. He remained inaccessible to his father.[61]

In Adrian Noble's 1990 production:

Caught between King and clown is Michael Maloney's slightly built Hal, initially an emotionally dependent adolescent. His relationship with Falstaff is intense: they hold hands affectionately in the opening scene; as the boy taunts Falstaff after the exposure of his cowardice, Falstaff kisses him on the lips on 'no more of that, Hal, an thou lovest me'. And Robert Stephens' ... agile Falstaff is dependent on Hal too. There is introspection behind this bluff exterior; the spaniel eyes seek affection ... Hal's determination to conquer Hotspur is motivated by the need to demonstrate his maturity to his father; the thwarted love behind it seems about to resolve itself with a kiss from son to father when the King [Julian Glover] holds Hal at arm's length.[62]

David Troughton, who played Henry in 2000, believed, like Emrys James, that Henry is aware of his failure as a father and attempts to redress this in order to win back his son: 'with his own son he has no idea how to behave at all. Hal's search for an alternative father is a cry for help, because his own father wants him for only one thing: to be his successor.'[63] Unable to be demonstrative in his love, Henry's attempts at a bond between father and son are thwarted by awkward moments of unwanted physicality. Unlike Glover's Henry, who chose to remain distant, Troughton's actively sought to embrace his son when the opportunity arose:

> It takes just one speech from Hal to bring them together – metaphorically, anyway, for though I used to put out my arms to him here, he never noticed, and no embrace was achieved. Perhaps Hal doesn't want to notice, or perhaps he simply doesn't see; that ambiguity was important in our production, and I think right. It's like one of those moments when you go to kiss your father – and it turns confusedly into shaking hands. Hal has said that he's sorry; he has said that he will fight along-side his father; but there has been no expression of love of son to father, which is what Henry misses. But whether Henry could achieve the embrace, even if Hal were looking, remains a question. He simply doesn't know how to touch his son properly. So I just used to give him a little push on his shoulder with my fist, and the awkward moment passed.[64]

Troughton thought *Part I* 'brilliantly written in its exploration of all the tactics that we use as parents: anger, loving kindness, emotional blackmail, they're all there'. The character of Hotspur was key in this production as a means for Henry to get to his son: 'he betrays his weird fixation on Hotspur, that son who is the "theme of honour's tongue" . . . who is so good to his father, such a great soldier'.[65] It is clear that this is the son that Henry would wish for, and that Hal, played by William Houston, was made aware of it.

The parental battle between Falstaff and Henry for Hal never comes to a climactic moment when the two characters meet and argue over his emotional and moral education. In 1982 Trevor Nunn contrived:

> a moment in which Hal finds himself between his father and Falstaff, with Bolingbroke's look of envious contempt at Sir John

and silent appeal for his son's affections answered by Hal's following his friend's insistent call: 'Hal, if thou seest me down in the battle...' The king turns away, apparently defeated, an interesting explanation for what in the text is the curious continuation of the estrangement of Hal and his father in *Part 2* in spite of the outcome of the battle. Not until he sees his father dying is this Hal ready to demonstrate any emotional commitment to him.[66]

Similarly, in 2001, 'Troughton also gives us the anxious father aware that he is in danger of losing his son to the taverns and the fat knight: there's a great moment when his path crosses that of Falstaff in battle and he shoots him a wounded look.'[67] David Troughton recalled how this moment was realized:

[Henry and Falstaff]...were symbolically present on stage together for a few moments between the first and second scenes of *Part One*...We created a brief moment in our production – after I had rejected (for fear of losing my heir) Hal's offer to take on Hotspur in single combat and as we were all girding up for battle – when I look at him and Falstaff together and thought 'O, God, I don't want them meeting any more'.[68]

Kingship

Renaissance philosophy believed that the best man was the 'fullest' man, the one with the widest experience of the world. Behind this lay the mediaeval theory of elements and humours, whose balance and combination was the key to mastery of oneself and others. A king should not only know the life of his subjects. He should contain in himself an equilibrium of all human passions – anger, pride, melancholy, mercy and love...The best education is the world itself, and the best introduction to the elements of one's own nature is other people.

(Ronald Bryden)[69]

Henry IV Part I posits many questions as to the nature of kingship. Shakespeare examines the political theory of the divine right of kings through Henry's gnawing guilt, which stems from a belief that he has sinned against God in the usurpation and murder of Richard II. Regardless of the fact that he believed himself the right man for the job, Henry cannot escape the belief that he is a counterfeit king, 'Confirming a change that had long been in incubation, on the day when Henry deposed Richard he became a double man, one thing to the world, another to his own conscience.'[70]

Emrys James played Henry in 1975 as the most unregal of men. Erratic in behaviour, he was a self-made man, an administrator and clerk, a cunning politician who made his way to kingship when, as Falstaff said (ostensibly of Worcester), 'Rebellion lay in his way, and he found it':

> He wants to assert his authority again and again, because kingship doesn't come naturally to him . . . Richard could go through crowds as a golden figure, and you could never ever conceive of Henry IV as a golden figure. Here is an executive, an executive of the state, angrily aware that the kind of chief executive he is is better for the state than the preening vision of majesty that Richard II presents.[71]

In David Troughton's highly acclaimed performance in 2000, he embodied the idea of Henry as a man wracked by inner conflict, caught between faith and the necessities of power:

> A dominant Bolingbroke, he now turns into a guilt-wracked Henry IV, ever conscious that he seized the throne by force. Yet, although first seen at prayer in penitent's gown, Troughton's king is still a brutal pragmatist who seeks to pre-empt rebellion by squashing his fractious nobles.[72]

> The opening is heavy with brooding anger, even melancholy . . . Power may be coveted; you may cheat, lie, manipulate, even kill for it; but when it is yours it can become a burden, a prison of responsibility . . . [Troughton's] huge body suggests both brute force and vulnerability. The king is not at ease with himself . . . loyalties come at a heavy price. And over all this hangs Henry's guilt about the murder of his predecessor, the deposed Richard.[73]

5. David Troughton as King Henry IV 'believes himself cursed by his sin of regicide' in Michael Attenborough's 2000 RSC production.

Having achieved power he believes himself cursed by his sin of regicide. If the king is God's emissary on earth, to kill the king is an act against God:

> Once he gets the crown, things start to go wrong politically and personally. The guilt has started to eat away at him; it's as though the year that elapses between the plays has hugely changed him. The fulfilment of that one aim of getting the crown was one thing; keeping it is quite another, for once you've got it, the only thing to do with it is to stop anyone else getting it.[74]

In a very different reading of the part, Julian Glover's Henry in *Part I* 'was neither infirm nor tired, as so often he has been played, but firmly in control of the political world':[75]

> When Glover is present there is no doubt where the power lies, and the daring and monstrosity of the challenge against him is palpable. There is a strong sense of personal ambition and vanity

in these confrontations, but essentially they are about political power: great impersonal imperatives which command a man's will and demand his self-sacrifice.[76]

Until struck down with a heart spasm in his moment of victory, he plays with undiminished power throughout: curtly disdainful to Owen Teale's hulking Hotspur, releasing thunderbolts of majestic wrath against Hal, and a match for Angus Wright's fire-breathing Douglas on the battlefield.[77]

[Julian Glover] is like some stern, unforgiving Old Testament patriarch who provokes rebellion by his curt dismissal of the Percys and who alienates his son by treating him as a recalcitrant hooligan. It is a marvellous portrait of a frosty spirit incapable of warmth.[78]

The qualities of kingship are constantly discussed or displayed by various characters in the play, as if Shakespeare were asking us, *what makes a king?* The influence of Falstaff, Hotspur and Henry offer Hal life's alternatives from which he must choose and discard in his preparation for the throne.

Hotspur so impresses his elders because he embodies the idea of chivalric honour, an exalted view of warfare and armed conflict that is tried and tested on the battlefield. Combining the qualities of military skill and political power, matched with a single-minded determination to promote the rebels' cause, Hotspur drives much of the main plot and is admired by all, despite his occasional outbursts. Although historically older than Hal, Shakespeare makes him a peer to establish a direct rivalry between the two men, especially in Henry's conception of the ideal son. If, as Montaigne suggests, 'The reputation and worth of a man consisteth in his heart and will; therein lies true honour'[79] rather than in martial prowess, we can see that Hotspur and Hal are on opposite sides of this maxim. Contrary to Hal, in Hotspur's attractive arrogance we can see the essence of an unbending spirit, especially in the scene with his wife.

In 1964, Roy Dotrice's Hotspur, although capturing his usual inextinguishable humour and vitality, in the words of the *Times'* reviewer, had 'the mentality of an amiable psychopath'.[80] The scene with Lady Percy took the form of rough foreplay, with 'husband and wife pushing over, kissing, tumbling, wrapping-up, kneeling astride or lying on top'.[81] In this very anti-heroic production, Hotspur's death was in keeping with Dotrice's interpretation and the mood of the production. At war with Hal, he was in his element. Flying at him with a huge sword, laughing aloud, Hotspur's sword jammed into the side of a horse-trough, Hal got in quickly to stab him under the ribs. 'Hotspur's ... violent death-throes ... robbed his death of the last shred of heroic dignity.'[82] 'Lowering him, dying, into the trough Hal delivered his line "For worms, brave Percy" [5.3.88]. Now he was dead; and curiously, the man who remained alive seemed to have no zest for life at all.'[83]

In 1982, Timothy Dalton's Hotspur emerged:

> not as a contrast but as a parallel. The warm-hearted side of him was played down, and replaced by moodiness. Many of his more 'poetic' lines were cut. His impulsiveness was much like Hal's own. In the first scene with his wife, he knelt, reading, as his wife came creeping downstairs. Played by Harriet Walter as a very submissive lady, she crouched beside him. The two figures became, suddenly, two people talking about their marriage. They looked grim and lugubrious. Hotspur jumped up, to call for his horse. Lady Percy followed, attempting playfully to wheedle his secrets out of him. Quite suddenly he turned on her. The line, 'Away, you trifler' was delivered with ferocious force. When he said, 'I care not for thee, Kate', there was no doubt that he meant it. If at the end he relented, holding out a hand to her which eventually she took, the patching-up of their marriage was only temporary.[84]

Honour at the expense of the personal, or personal life at the expense of honour? Is there any way that a man in power can maintain a life of duty and keep intact his humanity? Key to Hal's education, and a central concern of Shakespeare's in many plays, is this understanding of 'honour'. On discussing his portrayal of

Falstaff in 2000, Desmond Barrit pointed to this questioning nature of the play in his performance of the famous soliloquy:

> I used to play the 'honour' soliloquy as a sort of dialogue with the audience, with them asking the questions: 'Can honour set to a leg?', and Falstaff replies 'No'; 'Or an arm?', and Falstaff replies 'No'; 'Or take away the grief of a wound?', and again he replies 'No' (5.1.132–3). Falstaff is placing himself, I think, as an intermediary between the war and the audience, forcing them to wonder why men go to war at all, asking, and answering, the questions that are in their minds.[85]

The effectiveness of this delivery was picked up on by most reviewers, and was an appropriately serious reading for the end of the twentieth century: 'His beautiful delivery of the famous "honour" speech here becomes a totally persuasive indictment of the hallow, macho posturing of war.'[86]

The question as to whether Hal truly learns the lessons offered by both court and tavern is best discussed in the representation of the prince in *Henry IV Part II*: 'Hal must learn to exercise authority with integrity. In *Part I*, this is the path Hal successfully finds for himself, on the way losing nothing in his admiration for Hotspur's shining example and learning something of the warmth of humanity from Falstaff and his cronies.'[87]

Despite the upbeat nature of the ending of *Part I*, productions often suggest a certain ambiguity as to Hal's assumption of kingly behaviour. What has he learnt from these diverse parental figures that will make his a better king? The various workings of the father–son relationship demonstrate the battle in Hal to find a true path to kingship. Hal proves, as he said he would in the 'I know you all' speech [1.2.193–215], his abilities to his father and the officials of the court. However, his education is at an early stage. For Shakespeare, honour and integrity do not come from wielding a sword, and Hal has his most difficult of battles yet to face. Only when fathers are lost and cast aside will we see the emergence of the man who will be king.

THE ACTOR'S VOICE AND THE DIRECTOR'S CUT: INTERVIEWS WITH MICHAEL PENNINGTON, ADRIAN NOBLE AND MICHAEL BOYD

Michael Pennington, born in 1943, was brought up in London and read English at Cambridge University. While at university he appeared with the National Youth Theatre. He went on to join the RSC, playing small parts in *The Wars of the Roses* directed by Peter Hall (1964). He has since returned to the RSC on many occasions, playing Angelo in *Measure for Measure* (1974), Edgar in *King Lear* (1976), Berowne in *Love's Labour's Lost* (1978), Hamlet (1980) and Timon in *Timon of Athens* (2000). He has numerous radio and television parts to his credit, as well as film roles. He has written books on acting Shakespeare and Chekhov. In 1986 he and Michael Bogdanov founded the English Shakespeare Company (ESC), dedicated to taking Shakespeare to new audiences. Their inaugural production, *The Henrys*, comprised of the two parts of *Henry IV* plus *Henry V*, in which he played Prince Hal/King Henry V, was enormously successful. *Richard II*, the three *Henry VI* plays and *Richard III* were subsequently added, and their *Wars of the Roses* toured the world to great acclaim. He launched his one-man show, *Sweet William*, about Shakespeare's life and writing and his own relationship with those works, in 2006. He talks here both about playing the part of Hal and about wider aspects of the ESC staging of the two parts.

Adrian Noble, born in 1950, arrived at the RSC from the Bristol Old Vic, where he had directed several future stars in productions of classic plays. His first production on the main stage of the Royal Shakespeare Theatre in Stratford was the acclaimed 1982 *King Lear*. Two years later, his *Henry V* sowed the seed for Kenneth Branagh's film. Among his other major productions during his two decades at the RSC were *Hamlet*, again with Branagh in the title role; *The Plantagenets*, based on the *Henry VI/Richard III* tetralogy, and the two parts of *Henry IV*. Noble's 1994 *A Midsummer Night's Dream* was made into a film. He was Artistic Director from 1991 to 2003, since when he has been a freelance director. His production style is characterized by strong use of colours and objects (such as umbrellas), and fluid scenic structure. He talks here about his 1991 production with Robert Stephens as Falstaff, making reference to both *Part I* and *Part II* of *Henry IV*.

Michael Boyd was born in Belfast in 1955, educated in London and Edinburgh, and completed his MA in English Literature at Edinburgh University. He trained as a director at the Malaya Bronnaya Theatre in Moscow. He then went on to work at the Belgrade Theatre in Coventry, joining the Sheffield Crucible as Associate Director in 1982. In 1985 Boyd became founding Artistic Director of the Tron Theatre in Glasgow, becoming equally acclaimed for staging new writing and innovative productions of the classics. He was Drama Director of the *New Beginnings Festival of Soviet Arts* in Glasgow in 1999. He joined the RSC as an Associate Director in 1996 and has since directed numerous productions of Shakespeare's plays. He won the Laurence Olivier Award for Best Director for his version of the *Henry VI* plays in the RSC's *This England: The Histories* in 2001. He took over as Artistic Director of the RSC in 2003 and oversaw the extraordinarily successful Complete Works Festival in 2006–07. He followed this up with a cycle of all eight history plays, from *Richard II* through to *Richard III*, with the same company of actors. This transferred to London's Roundhouse Theatre in 2008 and won multiple awards. He talks here about both parts of *Henry IV*.

These plays can be thought of as individual works, as parts of a pair, or of a tetralogy, or even of a longer cycle of English history plays. There are cross-references across the two parts, back to *Richard II* and forward to *Henry V*. Some audience members know the back-story and the forward-story, some don't. How do you cope with all this?

MP: Each of the history plays has to stand alone – that's how Shakespeare planned them – but it's almost as if he had an idea that they might one day be seen in sequence, as they often are now, because each generally 'trails' the next episode of the story at its end. So *Part II* closes by looking forward to Henry V's French campaign, and indeed the end of *Henry V* to the reign of Henry VI. With the *Henry IV*s it doesn't really matter if the audience doesn't know *Henry V* since it's in the future, except as general interest as to how Henry V became Henry V. The back-story of *Richard II* is more of a problem: you need to know about the shakiness of Henry IV's claim to the throne and his own conscience – if he has any – about having usurped. The only real answer is to make sure the actors make the audience truly listen to Hotspur's argument against Henry in *Part I* and what the king himself says, so that they miss none of it. It's a matter of emphasis in the acting, of determination to get it across.

AN: In two ways. First of all, one has to start with the very simple premise that people are buying a ticket for one show, therefore it has to stand alone. But from the point of view of the acting company and as somebody involved at the RSC with the history plays for quite some time, it's very hard not to appreciate the wider context, going back to the *Henry VI* plays. It seems to me impossible that Shakespeare did not have an architectural form in his head as he wrote them. The *Henry VI/Richard III* tetralogy was the first time since Sophocles and Euripides that someone had attempted a cycle of interrelated plays for the secular stage. It hadn't happened for two thousand years. Writing it as a man in his mid-to-late twenties, I cannot believe Shakespeare wasn't conscious of that. And of course they were enormously successful, so slightly later in his career, when his gaze cast upon the *Henry IV* plays, I think he must again have had some sort of ghost of the architecture in his mind all the time. But because the first tetralogy tackled events that chronologically took place after those of the second, you get a very strong sense of moving forward towards anarchy and chaos. If you look at all eight, you start with the formality of *Richard II* and end up with the butchery of *Richard III*. It's a divine untidiness. In the second tetralogy you can see the architecture but also a maturity of construction and a depth of characterization within each play, which makes them highly satisfactory as individual plays.

MB: We conceived our *Henry IV*s as part of an eight-play cycle of Shakespeare's history plays, and a large proportion of our audience saw them in this context. Clive Wood had not only played Bullingbrook in *Richard II* but, as Richard of York, had spent three plays trying to take the crown from Henry VI and failing. We staged the plays initially in the order of their writing so York was seen on a Sisyphean journey towards the crown, which faltered in *Henry VI Part III* and began again with renewed vigour and sophistication in *Richard II*. The *Henry IV* plays revealed the eventual fruits of his labours as bitter.

Shakespeare had five very successful histories behind him as he wrote the *Henry IVs*, and *Henry V* was a popular title long before Shakespeare wrote his version, so I think it's fair to say that both author and audience were conscious of context as they experienced the events of *Henry IV*.

These plays move between very distinctive settings: royal court, rebels' castles, Eastcheap tavern, Gloucestershire orchard, battlefield. How did you and your designer set about creating these contrasting worlds?

MP: On their own terms, eclectically. The court wore Edwardian dress, the rebels harked back variously to the eighteenth century and forward to twentieth-century warfare; the tavern was more or less 1980s, the Gloucestershire orchard perhaps a little pre-First World War, the battlefield went back to medieval chainmail and broadsword. All the time we were responding to the temperament of the characters and the atmospherics of each scene and asking the audience to accept unexpected contrasts. The plays are in a sense about the entire history of Britain.

AN: Bob Crowley designed the set and Deirdre Clancy the costumes. We started with a very beautiful wooden floor fringed with gold, that both functioned as a practical space and had a strong resonance that could operate as a metaphor. The second thing we decided was that we would spend a lot of our money (because in the end it comes down to that) on the Boar's Head in Eastcheap, because we felt it was an aspect of the play that really needed to jump into the audience's imagination. In any of Shakespeare's plays, some parts require what I would loosely call 'social realism' and some don't. *King Lear* does not require much social realism. *The Merry Wives of Windsor* requires a lot, because the plots operate and are triggered by different things. There are certain aspects of *Henry IV Part I* that require that social realism, and the Boar's Head tavern is one of those.

The tavern in *Part I* was a well of life: it absolutely teemed with energy and life. The tavern in *Part II* was a much emptier place. It was a lonely and quite sad place, a place for losers, a place where folk were in danger, so everyone got out very fast when they were told there was another war starting. I used it for Henry IV's great monologue, 'How many thousand of my poorest subjects / Are at this hour asleep?' [3.1.4–5]. I had King Henry wander through the tavern, in which the down-and-outs and the losers were all lying drunk and asleep.

This relates to the structure of *Part II*, which is absolutely brilliant. It all works contrapuntally. It's contrapuntal between town and country, between war councils and petty quarrels. And one of the great pieces of counterpoint is at the death of King Henry IV. Henry IV dies in the Jerusalem chamber in the Palace of Westminster and the next scene is in Gloucestershire. From the very beginning of *Part I* he has wanted to go to the Holy Land. He keeps talking about how he wants to go to Jerusalem and eventually he does go there, but he goes there in death. I had his sons and the courtiers lift his body and carry him, and as his bed was lifted aloft and he came weaving downstage then upstage, I did a transformation into the countryside in Gloucestershire. I had a huge canopy with ladders poking up through it and all you saw were the legs of the actors. They were up the ladders, throwing apples down, and the dead body of the king was carried up through the canopy, up through this orchard, the orchard of England. We did this strange picture in slow motion, so it was like he'd gone to heaven, and so we had this fabulous juxtaposition which I think completely fulfilled Shakespeare's purpose. It was a wonderful juxtaposition of the realistic – we had real bee-keepers and real apple-pickers in the orchard – and the imagistic, the metaphorical. The man had finally found his way to Jerusalem: it was just eighty miles up the Thames in Gloucestershire. So we found a way in *Part II* of being much freer, much bolder, in the integration of the scenery with the structure of the play.

MB: Henry's court was characterized by a simple silver bowl of water where he tried to wash his hands of the blood of Richard II.

Eastcheap was dominated by a battered old armchair that had taken the shape of David Warner's Falstaff, and was framed by a large and tattered red velvet drape, which spoke of warmth, theatrical artifice, and backstage assignations. Staff and customers also emerged from and disappeared into a smoky purgatory beneath the stage.

Nearly all the castles from Orleans and Bordeaux in *Henry VI Part I* to Harfleur in *Henry V* were carried by our great rusty Louise Bourgeois-style tower, that rose from its hell mouth gates up past an 'I'm the King of the Castle' balcony to an ambiguous spiral stair, which rose to and fell from the grid seven metres above the stage.

Gloucestershire was a bale of hay, some bunting, blossom and a barbeque.

Our battlefields were the bodies of men fighting over the rusty body of England, which Tom Piper created. Our set suggested arms and legs and a head and viscera.

The plays dramatize the movement from feudalism (with the powerful barons of the north) to the early modern state (with an absolutist idea of monarchy). But they also speak to very Elizabethan concerns, such as the administration of the nation by means of a network of local Justices (not all of whom are entirely free from corruption . . .). And at the same time, the idea of the education of a future leader is a timeless theme. So: medieval setting, Elizabethan, modern, or some eclectic mixture of them all?

MP: I'm not so sure about this education of Hal. I think he has a great struggle between his impulses and his duties; he realizes what he will have to sacrifice, and in playing the part I came to think it costs him something. Not that he lets on: in *Henry V* he hardly mentions his past and is completely ruthless about hanging Bardolph for robbing a church, the kind of thing he might once have done himself. So if this is an education, it is not a very inclusive or compassionate one, more a hard lesson in *realpolitik*.

AN: We chose to set it pretty accurately in its period. I think it becomes a nonsense if you take it out of its period, to be absolutely honest, because we all know too much about other periods in which you might set it, and its own period is itself so interesting and resonant. When you've got a wonderful company of actors and you do it reasonably well, relevance jumps out at you.

MB: We found ourselves more interested in Shakespeare as a storyteller for his own age than as medievalist scholar. After the corruption of the old world, the old faith, and the would-be absolutist Richard, comes the cold wind of religious and political reform. Elizabeth may have seen herself characterized as Richard II, but she is also the reforming Protestant ruler beset with a dissenting and unruly populace that we see in *Henry IV*. The Archbishop of York, who 'Turns insurrection to religion', can't fail to have reminded Shakespeare's audience of the Pilgrimage of Grace which threatened Elizabeth's father, Henry VIII, with a militarized Catholic backlash from the north.

We opted for three generations: the glamorous remnants of Richard/Elizabeth's golden age; the new black, simple, puritanical broom of Bullingbrook/Elizabeth, and the new generation of Hal and Poins wilfully revisiting some of the decadent glamour of the past (with a little help from the saloon glamour of Westerns).

Prince Hal is sometimes one of the lads, sometimes coolly detached from his companions. Does this change over the two parts of the drama? Or, to ask the same question in another way: his first soliloquy, 'I know you all', is crucial, isn't it? Do you see him speaking it essentially to himself or to the audience in the theatre? Does it reveal him as a machiavellian manipulator from the start, just playing a game in order to improve his own image, always intending to reject his

companions when the time is ripe? Or is there much more ambivalence in the progress from 'I know you all' early in *Part I* to the rejection speech, 'I know thee not', at the end of *Part II*?

MP: Yes, he oscillates – he's tugged in two directions, as anybody might be. He pulls princely rank sometimes in the tavern, and in the court he plays the bad boy. He's quite unresolved.

'I know you all' is a very unusual soliloquy in that it seems not to be addressed to the audience but to his offstage friends and is overheard by the audience. Shakespeare hardly ever does this. A soliloquizer normally confides in the theatre audience more intimately than this, more trustingly. The effect here is to make Hal seem a little remote from us.

Playing him as what you call a machiavellian is possible, but it's not very interesting theatrically, like playing the Duke in *Measure for Measure* simply as a manipulator.

Hal is very monosyllabic when he comes to the point – as in those two cases [his first soliloquy in *Part I* and the rejection speech

6. 'O polished perturbation! Golden care!' Michael Pennington as Prince Hal and John Castle as Henry IV in the English Shakespeare Company's *Wars of the Roses*, 1986–89.

at the end of *Part II*], and also 'I do, I will' when he promises Falstaff he will reject him. I think what keeps the play and the part alive is that he has great difficulty in resolving his conflicting urges. He sets out his programme at the start, but he doesn't find it that easy to execute. He leaves the tavern and goes to the court, but is disappointed by his father, who is manipulative and self-absorbed; he goes back to Falstaff, but realizes he can't truly be part of that world either. There is a lot of implied conflict in him.

AN: He is all of those things. He's very complex because if you try and play it as somebody who's being manipulative and machiavellian, in terms of a great scheme, it doesn't sustain itself. It's unactable and it's incredible to the audience. The only way it works is if he thoroughly embraces the Eastcheap world and is a protagonist within it. You have to work back from that and from the fact that he says 'I know you all'. Some people find it necessary to have the character one or the other; I think he's both. I think he's a human being and human beings are extremely complex people. Young people, especially, live several lives: they live the life they live with their parents and they live a completely different life with other people. That's part of growing up and of how you relate to your parents. Hal has, in a way, been very lucky, in the sense that he has two fathers who each represent the two aspects of his character, so again you get this counterpoint which is very creative and very abrasive; it creates intellectual energy. I think Hal embraces that world fully, and the key moment for him is when he finally answers his dad: 'Do not think so. You shall not find it so' [3.2.130]. It's a monosyllabic line and you can't rush that line, because there are too many vowels in it. That's a turning point for the character; that's when he realizes he actually has to decide. It's also, interestingly enough, when he finds a voice. I think it's when he finds the voice that will attack Hotspur and will attack the French in *Henry V*. He embraces both worlds happily, and I think that's part of his personality. It's part of the education of the king, but it's more particularly part of the humanity of the king. Another way of looking at it is to think of Hal's time with Falstaff as a time of disguise; the disguise allows him the freedom to explore and develop and thereby achieve wisdom. The character is both with and outside the disguise at one and the same time.

MB: Hal's genuine longing to be a hard-drinking, womanizing Corinthian is in tension from the beginning with his dark understanding that he is heir to the throne and therefore the target of flattery and envious rumour. He starts by flirting with the political theatre of the deferred appearance of the sun from behind the cloud, and ends as the leading player in a much darker piece of political theatre as he renounces Falstaff, and is groomed for war with France.

The comparison and contrast between Prince Harry and Harry Hotspur is obviously crucial. Did you have particular stylistic or visual devices for establishing and exploring it?

MP: Hotspur seemed like a version of Bonnie Prince Charlie – quite a romantic, eighteenth-century rebel. Hal was completely modern except on the battlefield when he went into chainmail. So as I said above we handled these things not so much conceptually as expressionistically.

AN: It's unavoidable, isn't it? All you have to do is read the play. It's totally and utterly in your face. It's a constant reminder to the audience of what the danger of Prince Hal's behaviour is, that he is messing up big-time, because it's a dominating dramatic presence. Hotspur is such a charismatic man. He's a natural leader, he has such command of language, and he has all the other things that audiences want kings to have, like a good wife, a great sense of humour, the ability to deal with his elders in a fair, just, but respectful manner. He's got all of those things; they're there like this great big elephant in the room.

MB: Our Percies were descended from Shakespeare's earlier father-and-son duo in *Henry VI*: the Talbots. By now the honourable code of chivalry of this pairing has become warped. The father caves in horribly in *Part II* and the son is bold but arrogant and reckless. Chivalry is stone dead by *Henry IV*.

Prince Hal moves in the other direction, from selfish, hedonistic criminality to a new contingent morality which will find its fullest paradoxical expression in *Henry V* (and then of course in *Hamlet*).

To answer the question: Geoffrey Streatfeild's Hal was more of a decadent dandy in *Part I* and Lex Shrapnel's Hotspur a glamorized vision of martial prowess.

7. 'O, Harry, thou hast robbed me of my youth!' Geoffrey Streatfeild as Hal and Lex Shrapnel as Hotspur in Michael Boyd's 2007–08 RSC production.

It's sometimes said that in *Part I* Hal learns the military virtues of the true prince, in *Part II* the civic virtues. So Hotspur is a key opponent in *Part I*, the Lord Chief Justice a key figure in *Part II*. Was that a productive way of looking at it for you?

MP: That didn't occur to me, and I don't think Shakespeare writes that programmatically. The developments in his characters are more subtle, less easily explained. And I'm not sure Hal learns any virtues really, only pragmatism – how to handle everybody effectively, in fact. The Lord Chief Justice is his third father-figure, after Falstaff and the king – Falstaff is the one that loses out of course.

AN: Not at the time, but yes, that's quite interesting!

MB: No, but it is one template to apply to the plays. It feels more like the Lord Chief Justice's template than Shakespeare's, and it makes the royalist assumption that 'becoming a true prince' is Shakespeare's subject.

Having staged all the histories, I began to realize that the drive for power and the yearning for the crown is one big politically acceptable MacGuffin [plot device] that allows Shakespeare to examine the nature of humanity under pressure. Shakespeare is consistently sceptical and critical of those in power, and this famously non-judgemental author makes an exception for any character showing signs of being over-influenced by *Il Principe.*[*]

In *Part I* Hal wrestles with authority and his father, trying to find/avoid his place in life. In *Part II* Hal confronts the mortality of the very man he has defined himself against and therefore confronts his own mortality. And he kills Falstaff.

Another difference between the two parts is that, simply in terms of size of parts, *Part I* is dominated by Hal, Falstaff, Hotspur and King Henry, whereas *Part II* has a far larger number of substantial roles. Does that suggest that they are very different kinds of play? *Part I* a star vehicle and *Part II* an ensemble vision?

MP: They're both ensemble pieces – fabulously so. Hotspur's death and Hal's withdrawal from events in *Part II* makes room for Shallow and Silence and the rest, and there's much more Falstaff too. I think *Part II* is just *Part I* rebalanced – not essentially different, except that there's definitely a sense of imminent change, and loss, with the king dying; the tavern scenes have less vitality and Hal generally keeps away from Falstaff, as if he was preparing himself for his future.

AN: The second half is for me the great director's challenge, because it is symphonic. Some plays work as concerti, with a series of solo turns, and some operate more symphonically. This is particularly

---

[*] *Il Principe* (1532) *The Prince* (Italian) Niccolò Machiavelli's examination of Renaissance *realpolitik*.

true of the eight history plays. *Henry VI Part I, Part II* and *Part III* operate symphonically. My mistake when I did *Richard III*, as the last of that tetralogy, is that until I started rehearsing it I thought it also operated symphonically, but it doesn't: it's written in a completely different manner to the *Henry VIs*. It's written as a series of concerti: one after the other, somebody stands up and plays the violin, plays the viola, plays the cello, plays the trumpet. Edward IV, Clarence, Hastings, one after the other they all stand up. It's not true to such an extent with the two parts of *Henry IV*, but it is to a degree.

I'd wanted to do *Henry IV Part I* and *Part II* for years, but for me you don't even start until you've got Falstaff, which I was very fortunate to get in Robert Stephens. That's the character that not only sets half the agenda of the plays, but is also the person who attracts all the other actors. If you don't have a genius Falstaff, then you won't get a brilliant Henry IV, and if you don't have a brilliant Henry IV, then the spine of the two plays is very shaky. Hal and Hotspur are much easier. It's for Falstaff, Henry IV and Shallow that you really need people at the top of their game to fulfil the majesty of those two plays.

MB: Not really. *Part II* was in part conceived as a vehicle for the runaway success of Falstaff as a 'turn' in *Part I*.

Does Falstaff change between the two parts?

MP: In *Part I*, Hal and he are wonderfully matched, especially in their capacity for (more or less) friendly insults. Falstaff feels Hal's absence in *Part II* very keenly – he knows in his heart the best times are past. Falstaff talks about him all the time, wistfully.

AN: He matures somehow and gets wiser in the second part. I think the reason he appears to get older in the second part is because he has the Page. That's why Shakespeare gives him a young person to walk about with, so you realize he's old. Also in *Part II* he associates much more with people of his own age, particularly with his fellow-students from when he was a law student at Temple. By hanging out with Silence and Shallow, on the one hand, and with a twelve-year-old boy, on the other hand, we get a strong whiff of mortality coming off Falstaff in *Part II*, which we don't so much get in *Part I*.

MB: Falstaff has become a star in *Part II* because of his false success in Shrewsbury, and his real success in the theatre in *Henry IV Part I*. Shakespeare promotes him to the courtly world and gives him exchanges with the most powerful people in the land, but then punishes him with cynicism, gout and mortality.

He's a force of nature in *Part I*, and in *Part II* he's someone clinging on to influence, and opportunity, and life.

What did you learn in the process of rehearsing the great play-acting scene in *Part I* – the pre-enactment by Hal and Falstaff of Hal's confrontation with his father? And did it teach you things that you could use when working on the actual encounters between the prince and his father?

MP: Not so much that, but the two successive scenes are at the centre of the part. The scene in the Boar's Head has terrific tension – how far will Hal go in mocking his father? How far will he let Falstaff go? The onlookers don't know how loudly they're allowed to laugh. It's a great relief to Hal to make fun of his father; then he goes to see him for real and is very disappointed. He apologizes to the king and promises to toe the line but gets little thanks for it. Hal is very frustrated by his father. It's interesting that he takes Falstaff into battle with him and even lets him take credit for the death of Hotspur – it's as if he were serving notice that he'll do his duty by his father but he's not giving up his old ways that easily.

AN: Not particularly. It's most important because it stands as a rehearsal of the denial of Falstaff; that seems its main function to me. It was fun and funny – it couldn't not be that and I made it that – and I made it very anarchic, but my main purpose related to the denial of Falstaff. I remember feeling it was profoundly wrong that Hal engaged in this play-acting. The whole idea of impersonating the monarch had a slight whiff of danger about it, and I think for an Elizabethan audience it would have been almost obscene: a very dangerous thing to do and very disrespectful. The dice are loaded very heavily against Hal in *Part I* and I think that's why it is such a dramatic piece: it's because he turns the stakes around, he overturns the odds, that it is remarkable.

MB: Clive Wood had already shaped his testosterone-fuelled, reforming Bullingbrook in our *Richard II*, so we already knew that Hal's encounters with his father would be bruising and straight out of Eugene O'Neill or Tennessee Williams.

There was a moving mismatch of styles in the play-acting scene: David Warner's Falstaff revealing an old-fashioned delicacy that had no place in Bullingbrook's actual cold, pragmatic palace.

It's mostly a male world, but, small as they are, the female parts – Hotspur's wife, Quickly, Doll – seem very significant, don't they? What was your take on the women in these plays?

MP: I think Doll's little scene with Falstaff in *Part II* is a real love scene – both of them at their best; open, honest and affectionate in ways they aren't elsewhere. Mistress Quickly represents one kind of female constancy in her love of Falstaff, and in a sense, Lady Percy

8. Robert Stephens as Falstaff and Joanne Pearce as Doll Tearsheet at Hostess Quickly's tavern in Eastcheap in *Part II* of Adrian Noble's 1991 RSC production.

the other, in her anger at Hotspur's withdrawing from her and her grief at his loss. They're very good parts, all three of them.

AN: They're wonderful parts and you can do fantastic things with them with the right people. I was very lucky and we did great things with those parts. What Shakespeare does is genuinely present a great portrait of a nation. Look at the language of the scene of the two Carriers in Rochester: it's a couple of lorry drivers at Watford Gap services, it's a couple of guys who have done an overnight stay in a B&B somewhere. What he creates with that language – and of course it's distilled and slightly heightened – is the cadence of Elizabethan England. Shakespeare perfectly captures it: people working in an industrial situation. Now compare that with the sound of Shallow and Silence. Again, the cadence there is extraordinary. It's a remarkable soundscape, probably of Warwickshire when he was a boy, and that's part of the richness of the play. The *Henry VI* plays don't attempt that at all: you get little snippets of them with Cade and Dick the Butcher, but they are only snippets. In *Henry IV* they are in-depth portraits of a nation. You get the clergy, you get the courtiers, you get the tapsters, you get the prostitutes. Doll Tearsheet is an amazing portrait of a prostitute. Shakespeare captures the language in an extraordinary way.

MB: And Glendower's daughter possibly wins the war for Bullingbrook.

Ann Ogbomo's Kate Percy was an intelligent, beautiful and feisty sketch for Shakespeare's later leading women, Rosalind and Beatrice.

As Mistress Quickly, Maureen Beattie brought her own instinctive understanding of comedic rhythms from Scottish variety to a much-loved character that can trace its ancestry to Noah's wife, the wife of Bath, and beyond. Together with Alexia Healy's Doll, she maintained a haven of imperfect warmth in the cold world of Bullingbrook, until at last Eastcheap was literally dismantled in *Part II*.

Shakespeare's friend and rival Ben Jonson mocked his history plays for representing battles by means of nothing more than 'three rusty swords' – and modern audiences are used to the

epic battles of the Hollywood screen, complete with hundreds
of extras. In light of this, how do you set about staging the
battles convincingly? What balance between stylization and
realism?

MP: That was quite snobbish of Jonson – they couldn't afford
anything else. And Shakespeare always forestalls that argument, as
he does in the first chorus in *Henry V* – the means are limited but, as
he knows, his imaginative suggestiveness is great.

I think the battles should be as realistic as possible, especially
the Hal/Hotspur – traditional one-to-one combat, sweating it out,
like Richard III and Richmond; Hamlet and Laertes, too, if you like.
They're cathartic confrontations. The difficulty is greater in the
general battle scenes and skirmishes; the rhetoric can be a bit
thumpy and there's a lot of rushing around without much
character (though when Falstaff is on the battlefield there's terrific
comic counterpoint). Sometimes directors stylize Shakespeare's
battle scenes – slow motion, banners, mime, and so on. I don't
much care for it myself, but I appreciate why it happens. I think
you have to create the fog of war as realistically as you can.
Interestingly enough, in the ESC version, though we used guns
often, the big one-to-one set-pieces we always did in chainmail and
armour and broadswords, two individuals timelessly slugging it out
to the death.

AN: You've answered the question actually: you get a balance
between stylization and realism. Very simple technology plus a lot
of imagination can lead you to extraordinary things. You first ask
the question, 'What is the battle about? What is this one saying?'
At the end of *Part I* it's Shrewsbury: the subject of that battle is the
throne, it's a fight for the throne. There was a piece of technology
in the old Royal Shakespeare Theatre that no longer exists, which I
discovered when I was doing *King Lear* with Michael Gambon.
There were two huge lifts running up to the stage, each one nine
metres by four metres, that could hold about seventy people each.
On certain occasions like Gad's Hill I used the great hole on stage
where the lift shaft was. At the Battle of Shrewsbury there were

people talking downstage but the hole was down, and in the trap under the stage I'd loaded the throne surrounded by the whole of King Henry's courtiers, and then, with a huge amount of music and drumming, this throne came out of the earth. Not only did this trap ascend to stage level, it went above it. So when it hit stage level it was attacked in quite a stylized way by Hotspur's men, with the entire company onstage, and it carried on up into the air until it was about eight feet off the ground, and then it started to descend. Everyone was fighting, but they were actually fighting for the throne, and then when it came down to stage level it went into realistic swordplay. It's a bit unfair of Ben Jonson to say that, but he is absolutely right. What we delivered was a quite spectacular battle based upon the technology of that theatre. We were just very lucky that we had it there. I think I used that huge hole in each of the seven history plays I did.

9. The battle scenes dramatized the essential qualities of a conflict with 'three rusty swords' and the audience as extras in Michael Boyd's 2007–08 RSC history cycle.

MB: Over eight plays, we worked on the battles employing many approaches, including the following:

1. Shakespeare's battles must serve the play in the same way as a song in a musical: they must move the story forward.
2. Renaissance dance was in part physical training for the men at court for battle. Our battles were to a greater or lesser extent all dances.
3. Our battles often carried a cosmological burden: i.e. they were a battle between heaven and hell fought out on earth. This combined with the spatial excitement of the Courtyard Theatre encouraged us to use four dimensions. Violence burst out from the grid, the stage and the audience as often as from backstage.
4. Battles were staged with consciously shifting points of view, e.g. Shrewsbury was seen mostly from the rebels' perspective and picked up on the practice of decoy kings. We dramatized the courage it took to challenge an 'anointed' king by opposing Hotspur with an army of kings.
5. We wanted to celebrate the chief advantage of theatrical over filmic battles: we were not the slaves of naturalism pursuing ever more plausible wounds and dismemberments. We were free to attempt to dramatize the essential qualities of a conflict. The hundreds of extras were supplied by the audience.

SHAKESPEARE'S CAREER
IN THE THEATRE

BEGINNINGS

William Shakespeare was an extraordinarily intelligent man who was born and died in an ordinary market town in the English Midlands. He lived an uneventful life in an eventful age. Born in April 1564, he was the eldest son of John Shakespeare, a glovemaker who was prominent on the town council until he fell into financial difficulties. Young William was educated at the local grammar in Stratford-upon-Avon, Warwickshire, where he gained a thorough grounding in the Latin language, the art of rhetoric and classical poetry. He married Ann Hathaway and had three children (Susanna, then the twins Hamnet and Judith) before his twenty-first birthday: an exceptionally young age for the period. We do not know how he supported his family in the mid-1580s.

Like many clever country boys, he moved to the city in order to make his way in the world. Like many creative people, he found a career in the entertainment business. Public playhouses and professional full-time acting companies reliant on the market for their income were born in Shakespeare's childhood. When he arrived in London as a man, sometime in the late 1580s, a new phenomenon was in the making: the actor who is so successful that he becomes a 'star'. The word did not exist in its modern sense, but the pattern is recognizable: audiences went to the theatre not so much to see a particular show as to witness the comedian Richard Tarlton or the dramatic actor Edward Alleyn.

Shakespeare was an actor before he was a writer. It appears not to have been long before he realized that he was never going to grow into a great comedian like Tarlton or a great tragedian like Alleyn. Instead, he found a role within his company as the man who patched up old plays, breathing new life, new dramatic twists, into tired repertory pieces. He paid close attention to the work of the university-educated dramatists who were writing history plays and tragedies for the public stage in a style more ambitious, sweeping and poetically grand than anything which had been seen before. But he may also have noted that what his friend and rival Ben Jonson would call 'Marlowe's mighty line' sometimes faltered in the mode of comedy. Going to university, as Christopher Marlowe did, was all well and good for honing the arts of rhetorical elaboration and classical allusion, but it could lead to a loss of the common touch. To stay close to a large segment of the potential audience for public theatre, it was necessary to write for clowns as well as kings and to intersperse the flights of poetry with the humour of the tavern, the privy and the brothel: Shakespeare was the first to establish himself early in his career as an equal master of tragedy, comedy and history. He realized that theatre could be the medium to make the national past available to a wider audience than the elite who could afford to read large history books: his signature early works include not only the classical tragedy *Titus Andronicus* but also the sequence of English historical plays on the Wars of the Roses.

He also invented a new role for himself, that of in-house company dramatist. Where his peers and predecessors had to sell their plays to the theatre managers on a poorly-paid piecework basis, Shakespeare took a percentage of the box-office income. The Lord Chamberlain's Men constituted themselves in 1594 as a joint stock company, with the profits being distributed among the core actors who had invested as sharers. Shakespeare acted himself – he appears in the cast lists of some of Ben Jonson's plays as well as the list of actors' names at the beginning of his own collected works – but his principal duty was to write two or three plays a year for the company. By holding shares, he was effectively earning himself a royalty on his work, something no author had ever done before in England. When the Lord Chamberlain's Men collected their fee for performance at court in the Christmas season of 1594, three of them went along to the Treasurer of the Chamber: not just Richard Burbage the tragedian and Will Kempe the clown, but also Shakespeare the scriptwriter. That was something new.

The next four years were the golden period in Shakespeare's career, though overshadowed by the death of his only son Hamnet, aged eleven, in 1596. In his early thirties and in full command of both his poetic and his theatrical medium, he perfected his art of comedy, while also developing his tragic and historical writing in new ways. In 1598, Francis Meres, a Cambridge University graduate with his finger on the pulse of the London literary world, praised Shakespeare for his excellence across the genres:

> As Plautus and Seneca are accounted the best for comedy and tragedy among the Latins, so Shakespeare among the English is the most excellent in both kinds for the stage; for comedy, witness his *Gentlemen of Verona*, his *Errors*, his *Love Labours Lost*, his *Love Labours Won*, his *Midsummer Night Dream* and his *Merchant of Venice*: for tragedy his *Richard the 2*, *Richard the 3*, *Henry the 4*, *King John*, *Titus Andronicus* and his *Romeo and Juliet*.

For Meres, as for the many writers who praised the 'honey-flowing vein' of *Venus and Adonis* and *Lucrece*, narrative poems written when the theatres were closed due to plague in 1593–94, Shakespeare was marked above all by his linguistic skill, by the gift of turning elegant poetic phrases.

PLAYHOUSES

Elizabethan playhouses were 'thrust' or 'one-room' theatres. To understand Shakespeare's original theatrical life, we have to forget about the indoor theatre of later times, with its proscenium arch and curtain that would be opened at the beginning and closed at the end of each act. In the proscenium arch theatre, stage and auditorium are effectively two separate rooms: the audience looks from one world into another as if through the imaginary 'fourth wall' framed by the proscenium. The picture-frame stage, together with the elaborate scenic effects and backdrops beyond it, created the illusion of a self-contained world – especially once nineteenth-century developments in the control of artificial lighting meant that the auditorium could be darkened and the spectators made to focus on the lighted stage. Shakespeare, by contrast, wrote for a bare platform stage with a standing audience gathered around it in a courtyard in full daylight. The audience were always conscious of themselves and their fellow-spectators, and they shared the same 'room' as the actors. A sense of immediate presence and the creation of rapport with the audience were all-important. The actor could not afford to imagine he was in a closed world, with silent witnesses dutifully observing him from the darkness.

Shakespeare's theatrical career began at the Rose Theatre in Southwark. The stage was wide and shallow, trapezoid in shape, like a lozenge. This design had a great deal of potential for the theatrical equivalent of cinematic split-screen effects, whereby one group of characters would enter at the door at one end of the tiring-house wall at the back of the stage and another group through the door at the other end, thus creating two rival tableaux. Many of the battle-heavy and faction-filled plays that premiered at the Rose have scenes of just this sort.

At the rear of the Rose stage, there were three capacious exits, each over ten feet wide. Unfortunately, the very limited excavation of a fragmentary portion of the original Globe site, in 1989, revealed nothing about the stage. The first Globe was built in 1599 with similar proportions to those of another theatre, the Fortune, albeit that the former was polygonal and looked circular, whereas the latter was rectangular. The building contract for the Fortune survives and allows us to infer that the stage of the Globe was probably substantially wider than it was deep (perhaps forty-three feet wide and twenty-seven feet deep). It may well have been tapered at the front, like that of the Rose.

The capacity of the Globe was said to have been enormous, perhaps in excess of three thousand. It has been conjectured that about eight hundred people may have stood in the yard, with two thousand or more in the three layers of covered galleries. The other 'public' playhouses were also of large capacity, whereas the indoor Blackfriars theatre that Shakespeare's company began using in 1608 – the former refectory of a monastery – had overall internal dimensions of a mere forty-six by sixty feet. It would have made for a much more intimate theatrical experience and had a much smaller capacity, probably of about six hundred people. Since they paid at least sixpence a head, the Blackfriars attracted a more select or 'private' audience. The atmosphere would have been closer to that of an indoor performance before the court in the Whitehall Palace or at Richmond. That Shakespeare always wrote for indoor production at court as well as outdoor performance in the public theatre should make us cautious about inferring, as some scholars have, that the opportunity provided by the intimacy of the Blackfriars led to a significant change towards a 'chamber' style in his last plays – which, besides, were performed at both the Globe and the Blackfriars. After the occupation of the Blackfriars a five-act structure seems to have become more important to Shakespeare. That was because of artificial lighting: there were musical interludes between the acts, while the candles were trimmed and replaced. Again, though, something similar must have been necessary for indoor court performances throughout his career.

Front of house there were the 'gatherers' who collected the money from audience members: a penny to stand in the open-air yard, another penny for a place in the covered galleries, sixpence for the prominent 'lord's rooms' to the side of the stage. In the indoor 'private' theatres, gallants from the audience who fancied making themselves part of the spectacle sat on stools on the edge of the stage itself. Scholars debate as to how widespread this practice was in the public theatres such as the Globe. Once the audience were in place and the money counted, the gatherers were available to be extras on stage. That is one reason why battles and crowd scenes often come later rather than early in Shakespeare's plays. There was no formal prohibition upon performance by women, and there certainly were women among the gatherers, so it is not beyond the bounds of possibility that female crowd members were played by females.

The play began at two o'clock in the afternoon and the theatre had to be cleared by five. After the main show, there would be a jig – which consisted not only of dancing, but also of knockabout comedy (it is the origin of the farcical 'afterpiece' in the eighteenth-century theatre). So the time available for a Shakespeare play was about two and a half hours, somewhere between the 'two hours' traffic' mentioned in the prologue to *Romeo and Juliet* and the 'three hours' spectacle' referred to in the preface to the 1647 Folio of Beaumont and Fletcher's plays. The prologue to a play by Thomas Middleton refers to a thousand lines as 'one hour's words', so the likelihood is that about two and a half thousand, or a maximum of three thousand lines made up the performed text. This is indeed the length of most of Shakespeare's comedies, whereas many of his tragedies and histories are much longer, raising the possibility that he wrote full scripts, possibly with eventual publication in mind, in the full knowledge that the stage version would be heavily cut. The short Quarto texts published in his lifetime – they used to be called 'Bad' Quartos – provide fascinating evidence as to the kind of cutting that probably took place. So, for instance, the First Quarto of *Hamlet* neatly merges two occasions when Hamlet is overheard, the 'Fishmonger' and the 'nunnery' scenes.

The social composition of the audience was mixed. The poet Sir John Davies wrote of 'A thousand townsmen, gentlemen and whores, / Porters and servingmen' who would 'together throng' at the public playhouses. Though moralists associated female play-going with adultery and the sex trade, many perfectly respectable citizens' wives were regular attendees. Some, no doubt, resembled the modern groupie: a story attested in two different sources has one citizen's wife making a post-show assignation with Richard Burbage and ending up in bed with Shakespeare – supposedly eliciting from the latter the quip that William the Conqueror was before Richard III. Defenders of theatre liked to say that by witnessing the comeuppance of villains on the stage, audience members would repent of their own wrongdoings, but the reality is that most people went to the theatre then, as they do now, for entertainment more than moral edification. Besides, it would be foolish to suppose that audiences behaved in a homogeneous way: a pamphlet of the 1630s tells of how two men went to see *Pericles* and one of them laughed while the other wept. Bishop John Hall complained that people went to church for the same reasons that they went to the theatre: 'for company, for custom, for recreation . . . to feed his eyes or his ears . . . or perhaps for sleep'.

Men-about-town and clever young lawyers went to be seen as much as to see. In the modern popular imagination, shaped not least by *Shakespeare in Love* and the opening sequence of Laurence Olivier's *Henry V* film, the penny-paying groundlings stand in the yard hurling abuse or encouragement and hazelnuts or orange peel at the actors, while the sophisticates in the covered galleries appreciate Shakespeare's soaring poetry. The reality was probably the other way round. A 'groundling' was a kind of fish, so the nickname suggests the penny audience standing below the level of the stage and gazing in silent open-mouthed wonder at the spectacle unfolding above them. The more difficult audience members, who kept up a running commentary of clever remarks on the performance and who occasionally got into quarrels with players, were the gallants. Like Hollywood movies in modern times, Elizabethan and Jacobean plays exercised a powerful influence on the fashion and behaviour of the young. John Marston mocks the lawyers who would open their lips, perhaps to court a girl, and out would 'flow / Naught but pure Juliet and Romeo'.

THE ENSEMBLE AT WORK

In the absence of typewriters and photocopying machines, reading aloud would have been the means by which the company got to know a new play. The tradition of the playwright reading his complete script to the assembled company endured for generations. A copy would then have been taken to the Master of the Revels for licensing. The theatre book-holder or prompter would then have copied the parts for distribution to the actors. A partbook consisted of the character's lines, with each speech preceded by the last three or four words of the speech before, the so-called 'cue'. These would have been taken away and studied or 'conned'. During this period of learning the parts, an actor might have had some one-to-one instruction, perhaps from the dramatist, perhaps from a senior actor who had played the same part before, and, in the case of an apprentice, from his master. A high percentage of Desdemona's lines occur in dialogue with Othello, of Lady Macbeth's with Macbeth, Cleopatra's with Antony and Volumnia's with Coriolanus. The roles would almost certainly have been taken by the apprentice of the lead actor, usually Burbage, who delivers the majority of the cues. Given that apprentices lodged with their masters, there would have been

10. Hypothetical reconstruction of the interior of an Elizabethan playhouse during a performance.

ample opportunity for personal instruction, which may be what made it possible for young men to play such demanding parts.

After the parts were learned, there may have been no more than a single rehearsal before the first performance. With six different plays to be put on every week, there was no time for more. Actors, then, would go into a show with a very limited sense of the whole. The notion of a collective rehearsal process that is itself a process of discovery for the actors is wholly modern and would have been incomprehensible to Shakespeare and his original ensemble. Given the number of parts an actor had to hold in his memory, the forgetting of lines was probably more frequent than in the modern theatre. The book-holder was on hand to prompt.

Backstage personnel included the property man, the tire-man who oversaw the costumes, call-boys, attendants and the musicians, who might play at various times from the main stage, the rooms above and within the tiring-house. Scriptwriters sometimes made a nuisance of themselves backstage. There was often tension between the acting companies and the freelance playwrights from whom they purchased scripts: it was a smart move on the part of Shakespeare and the Lord Chamberlain's Men to bring the writing process in-house.

Scenery was limited, though sometimes set-pieces were brought on (a bank of flowers, a bed, the mouth of hell). The trapdoor from below, the gallery stage above and the curtained discovery-space at the back allowed for an array of special effects: the rising of ghosts and apparitions, the descent of gods, dialogue between a character at a window and another at ground level, the revelation of a statue or a pair of lovers playing at chess. Ingenious use could be made of props, as with the ass's head in *A Midsummer Night's Dream*. In a theatre that does not clutter the stage with the material paraphernalia of everyday life, those objects that are deployed may take on powerful symbolic weight, as when Shylock bears his weighing scales in one hand and knife in the other, thus becoming a parody of the figure of Justice who traditionally bears a sword and a balance. Among the more significant items in the property cupboard of Shakespeare's company, there would have been a throne (the 'chair of state'), joint stools, books, bottles, coins, purses, letters (which are brought on stage, read or referred to on about eighty occasions in the complete works), maps, gloves, a set of stocks (in which Kent is put in *King Lear*), rings, rapiers, daggers, broadswords, staves, pistols, masks and vizards, heads and skulls, torches and tapers and lanterns which served to signal night scenes on the daylit stage, a buck's head, an ass's head, animal costumes. Live animals also put in appearances, most notably the dog Crab in *The Two Gentlemen of Verona* and possibly a young polar bear in *The Winter's Tale*.

The costumes were the most important visual dimension of the play. Playwrights were paid between £2 and £6 per script, whereas Alleyn was not averse to paying £20 for 'a black velvet cloak with sleeves embroidered all with silver and gold'. No matter the period of the play, actors always wore contemporary costume. The excitement for the audience came not from any impression of historical accuracy, but from the richness of the attire and perhaps the transgressive thrill of the knowledge that here were commoners like themselves strutting in the costumes of courtiers in effective defiance of the strict sumptuary laws whereby in real life people had to wear the clothes that befitted their social station.

To an even greater degree than props, costumes could carry symbolic importance. Racial characteristics could be suggested: a breastplate and helmet for a Roman soldier, a turban for a Turk, long robes for exotic characters such as Moors, a gabardine for a Jew. The figure of Time, as in *The Winter's Tale*, would be equipped with hourglass, scythe and wings; Rumour, who speaks the prologue of *2 Henry IV*, wore a costume adorned with a thousand tongues. The wardrobe in the tiring-house of the Globe would have contained much of the same stock as that of rival manager Philip Henslowe at the Rose: green gowns for outlaws and foresters, black for melancholy men such as Jaques and people in mourning such as the Countess in *All's Well that Ends Well* (at the beginning of *Hamlet*, the prince is still in mourning black when everyone else is in festive garb for the wedding of the new king), a gown and hood for a friar (or a feigned friar like the duke in *Measure for Measure*), blue coats and tawny to distinguish the followers of rival factions, a leather apron and ruler for a carpenter (as in the opening scene of *Julius Caesar* – and in *A Midsummer Night's Dream*, where this is the only sign that Peter Quince is a carpenter), a cockle hat with staff and a pair of sandals for a pilgrim or palmer (the disguise assumed by Helen in *All's Well*), bodices and kirtles with farthingales beneath for the boys who are to be dressed as girls. A gender switch such as that of Rosalind or Jessica seems to have taken between fifty and eighty lines of dialogue – Viola does not resume her 'maiden weeds', but remains in her boy's costume to the end of *Twelfth Night* because a change would have slowed down the action at just the moment it was speeding to a climax. Henslowe's inventory also included 'a robe for to go invisible': Oberon, Puck and Ariel must have had something similar.

As the costumes appealed to the eyes, so there was music for the ears. Comedies included many songs. Desdemona's willow song, perhaps a late addition to the text, is a rare and thus exceptionally poignant example from tragedy. Trumpets and tuckets sounded for ceremonial entrances, drums denoted an army on the march. Background music could create atmosphere, as at the beginning of *Twelfth Night*, during the lovers' dialogue near the end of *The Merchant of Venice*, when the statue seemingly comes to life in *The Winter's Tale*, and for the revival of Pericles and of Lear (in the Quarto text, but not the Folio). The haunting sound of the hautboy suggested a realm beyond the human, as when the god Hercules is imagined deserting Mark Antony. Dances symbolized the harmony of the end of a comedy – though in Shakespeare's world of mingled joy and sorrow, someone is usually left out of the circle.

The most important resource was, of course, the actors themselves. They needed many skills: in the words of one contemporary commentator, 'dancing, activity, music, song, elocution, ability of body, memory, skill of weapon, pregnancy of wit'. Their bodies were as significant as their voices. Hamlet tells the player to 'suit the action to the word, the word to the action': moments of strong emotion, known as 'passions', relied on a repertoire of dramatic gestures as well as a modulation of the voice. When Titus Andronicus has had his hand chopped off, he asks 'How can I grace my talk, / Wanting a hand to give it action?' A pen portrait of 'The Character of an Excellent Actor' by the dramatist John Webster is almost certainly based on his impression of Shakespeare's leading man, Richard Burbage: 'By a full and significant action of body, he charms our attention: sit in a full theatre, and you will think you see so many lines drawn from the circumference of so many ears, whiles the actor is the centre . . . .'

Though Burbage was admired above all others, praise was also heaped upon the apprentice players whose alto voices fitted them for the parts of women. A spectator at Oxford in 1610 records how the audience were reduced to tears by the pathos of Desdemona's death. The puritans who fumed about the biblical prohibition upon cross-dressing and the encouragement to sodomy constituted by the sight of an adult male kissing a teenage boy on stage were a small minority. Little is known, however, about the characteristics of the leading apprentices in Shakespeare's company. It may perhaps be inferred that one was a lot taller than the other, since Shakespeare often wrote for a pair of female friends, one tall and fair, the other short and dark (Helena and Hermia, Rosalind and Celia, Beatrice and Hero).

We know little about Shakespeare's own acting roles – an early allusion indicates that he often took royal parts, and a venerable tradition gives him old Adam in *As You Like It* and the ghost of old King Hamlet. Save for Burbage's lead roles and the generic part of the clown, all such castings are mere speculation. We do not even know for sure whether the original Falstaff was Will Kempe or another actor who specialized in comic roles, Thomas Pope.

Kempe left the company in early 1599. Tradition has it that he fell out with Shakespeare over the matter of excessive improvisation. He was replaced by Robert Armin, who was less of a clown and more of a cerebral wit: this explains the difference between such parts as Lancelet Gobbo and Dogberry, which were written for Kempe, and the more verbally sophisticated Feste and Lear's Fool, which were written for Armin.

One thing that is clear from surviving 'plots' or story-boards of plays from the period is that a degree of doubling was necessary. *2 Henry VI* has over sixty speaking parts, but more than half of the characters only appear in a single scene and most scenes have only six to eight speakers. At a stretch, the play could be performed by thirteen actors. When Thomas Platter saw *Julius Caesar* at the Globe in 1599, he noted that there were about fifteen. Why doesn't Paris go to the Capulet ball in *Romeo and Juliet*? Perhaps because he was doubled with Mercutio, who does. In *The Winter's Tale*, Mamillius might have come back as Perdita and Antigonus been doubled by Camillo, making the partnership with Paulina at the end a very neat touch. Titania and Oberon are often played by the same pair as Hippolyta and Theseus, suggesting a symbolic matching of the rulers of the worlds of night and day, but it is questionable whether there would have been time for the necessary costume changes. As so often, one is left in a realm of tantalizing speculation.

THE KING'S MAN

On Queen Elizabeth's death in 1603, the new king, James I, who had held the Scottish throne as James VI since he had been an infant, immediately took the Lord Chamberlain's Men under his direct patronage. Henceforth they would be the King's Men, and for the rest of Shakespeare's career they were favoured with far more court performances than any of their rivals. There even seem to have been rumours early in the reign that Shakespeare and Burbage were being considered for knighthoods, an unprecedented honour for mere actors – and one that in the event was not accorded to a member of the profession for nearly three hundred years, when the title was bestowed upon Henry Irving, the leading Shakespearean actor of Queen Victoria's reign.

Shakespeare's productivity rate slowed in the Jacobean years, not because of age or some personal trauma, but because there were frequent outbreaks of plague, causing the theatres to be closed for long periods. The King's Men were forced to spend many months on the road. Between November 1603 and 1608, they were to be found at various towns in the south and Midlands, though Shakespeare probably did not tour with them by this time. He had bought a large house back home in Stratford and was accumulating other property. He may indeed have stopped acting soon after the new king took the throne. With the London theatres closed so much of the time and a large repertoire on the stocks, Shakespeare seems to have focused his energies on writing a few long and complex tragedies that could have been played on demand at court: *Othello*, *King Lear*, *Antony and Cleopatra*, *Coriolanus* and *Cymbeline* are among his longest and poetically grandest plays. *Macbeth* only survives in a shorter text, which shows signs of adaptation after Shakespeare's death. The bitterly satirical *Timon of Athens*, apparently a collaboration with Thomas Middleton that may have failed on the stage, also belongs to this period. In comedy, too, he wrote longer and morally darker works than in the Elizabethan period, pushing at the very bounds of the form in *Measure for Measure* and *All's Well that Ends Well*.

From 1608 onwards, when the King's Men began occupying the indoor Blackfriars playhouse (as a winter house, meaning that they only used the outdoor Globe in summer?), Shakespeare turned to a more romantic style. His company had a great success with a revived and altered version of an old pastoral play called *Mucedorus*. It even featured a bear. The younger dramatist John Fletcher, meanwhile, sometimes working in collaboration with Francis Beaumont, was pioneering a new style of tragicomedy, a mix of romance and royalism laced with intrigue and pastoral excursions. Shakespeare experimented with this idiom in *Cymbeline* and it was presumably with his blessing that Fletcher eventually took over as the King's Men's company dramatist. The two writers apparently collaborated on three plays in the years 1612–14: a lost romance called *Cardenio* (based on the love-madness of a character in Cervantes' *Don Quixote*), *Henry VIII* (originally staged with the title 'All is True'), and *The Two Noble Kinsmen*, a dramatization of Chaucer's 'Knight's Tale'. These were written after Shakespeare's two final solo-authored plays, *The Winter's Tale*, a self-consciously old-fashioned work dramatizing the pastoral romance of his old enemy Robert Greene, and *The Tempest*, which at one and the same time drew together multiple theatrical traditions, diverse reading and contemporary interest in the fate of a ship that had been wrecked on the way to the New World.

The collaborations with Fletcher suggest that Shakespeare's career ended with a slow fade rather than the sudden retirement supposed by the nineteenth-century Romantic critics who read Prospero's epilogue to *The Tempest* as Shakespeare's personal farewell to his art. In the last few years of his life Shakespeare certainly spent more of his time in Stratford-upon-Avon, where he became further involved in property dealing and litigation. But his London life also continued. In 1613 he made his first major London property purchase: a freehold house in the Blackfriars district, close to his company's indoor theatre. *The Two Noble Kinsmen* may have been written as late as 1614, and Shakespeare was in London on business a little over a year before he died of an unknown cause at home in Stratford-upon-Avon in 1616, probably on his fifty-second birthday.

About half the sum of his works were published in his lifetime, in texts of variable quality. A few years after his death, his fellow-actors began putting together an authorized edition of his complete *Comedies, Histories and Tragedies*. It appeared in 1623, in large 'Folio' format. This collection of thirty-six plays gave Shakespeare his immortality. In the words of his fellow-dramatist Ben Jonson, who contributed two poems of praise at the start of the Folio, the body of his work made him 'a monument without a tomb':

> And art alive still while thy book doth live
> And we have wits to read and praise to give . . .
> He was not of an age, but for all time!

SHAKESPEARE'S WORKS:
A Chronology

1589–91	*? Arden of Faversham* (possible part authorship)
1589–92	*The Taming of the Shrew*
1589–92	*? Edward the Third* (possible part authorship)
1591	*The Second Part of Henry the Sixth*, originally called *The First Part of the Contention betwixt the Two Famous Houses of York and Lancaster* (element of co-authorship possible)
1591	*The Third Part of Henry the Sixth*, originally called *The True Tragedy of Richard Duke of York* (element of co-authorship probable)
1591–92	*The Two Gentlemen of Verona*
1591–92 perhaps revised 1594	*The Lamentable Tragedy of Titus Andronicus* (probably co-written with, or revising an earlier version by, George Peele)
1592	*The First Part of Henry the Sixth*, probably with Thomas Nashe and others
1592/94	*King Richard the Third*
1593	*Venus and Adonis* (poem)
1593–94	*The Rape of Lucrece* (poem)
1593–1608	*Sonnets* (154 poems, published 1609 with *A Lover's Complaint*, a poem of disputed authorship)
1592–94/ 1600–03	*Sir Thomas More* (a single scene for a play originally by Anthony Munday, with other revisions by Henry Chettle, Thomas Dekker and Thomas Heywood)
1594	*The Comedy of Errors*
1595	*Love's Labour's Lost*

1595–97	*Love's Labour's Won* (a lost play, unless the original title for another comedy)
1595–96	*A Midsummer Night's Dream*
1595–96	*The Tragedy of Romeo and Juliet*
1595–96	*King Richard the Second*
1595–97	*The Life and Death of King John* (possibly earlier)
1596–97	*The Merchant of Venice*
1596–97	*The First Part of Henry the Fourth*
1597–98	*The Second Part of Henry the Fourth*
1598	*Much Ado about Nothing*
1598–99	*The Passionate Pilgrim* (20 poems, some not by Shakespeare)
1599	*The Life of Henry the Fifth*
1599	'To the Queen' (epilogue for a court performance)
1599	*As You Like It*
1599	*The Tragedy of Julius Caesar*
1600–01	*The Tragedy of Hamlet, Prince of Denmark* (perhaps revising an earlier version)
1600–01	*The Merry Wives of Windsor* (perhaps revising version of 1597–99)
1601	'Let the Bird of Loudest Lay' (poem, known since 1807 as 'The Phoenix and Turtle' (turtle-dove))
1601	*Twelfth Night, or What You Will*
1601–02	*The Tragedy of Troilus and Cressida*
1604	*The Tragedy of Othello, the Moor of Venice*
1604	*Measure for Measure*
1605	*All's Well that Ends Well*
1605	*The Life of Timon of Athens*, with Thomas Middleton
1605–06	*The Tragedy of King Lear*
1605–08	? contribution to *The Four Plays in One* (lost, except for *A Yorkshire Tragedy*, mostly by Thomas Middleton)
1606	*The Tragedy of Macbeth* (surviving text has additional scenes by Thomas Middleton)
1606–07	*The Tragedy of Antony and Cleopatra*
1608	*The Tragedy of Coriolanus*

1608	*Pericles, Prince of Tyre*, with George Wilkins
1610	*The Tragedy of Cymbeline*
1611	*The Winter's Tale*
1611	*The Tempest*
1612–13	*Cardenio*, with John Fletcher (survives only in later adaptation called *Double Falsehood* by Lewis Theobald)
1613	*Henry VIII (All is True)*, with John Fletcher
1613–14	*The Two Noble Kinsmen*, with John Fletcher

KINGS AND QUEENS OF ENGLAND: From the History Plays to Shakespeare's Lifetime

	Lifespan	*Reign*
Angevins:		
Henry II	1133–1189	1154–1189
Richard I	1157–1199	1189–1199
John	1166–1216	1199–1216
Henry III	1207–1272	1216–1272
Edward I	1239–1307	1272–1307
Edward II	1284–1327	1307–1327 deposed
Edward III	1312–1377	1327–1377
Richard II	1367–1400	1377–1399 deposed
Lancastrians:		
Henry IV	1367–1413	1399–1413
Henry V	1387–1422	1413–1422
Henry VI	1421–1471	1422–1461 and 1470–1471
Yorkists:		
Edward IV	1442–1483	1461–1470 and 1471–1483
Edward V	1470–1483	1483 not crowned: deposed and assassinated
Richard III	1452–1485	1483–1485
Tudors:		
Henry VII	1457–1509	1485–1509
Henry VIII	1491–1547	1509–1547
Edward VI	1537–1553	1547–1553

	Lifespan	*Reign*
Jane	1537–1554	1553 not crowned: deposed and executed
Mary I	1516–1558	1553–1558
Philip of Spain	1527–1598	1554–1558 co-regent with Mary
Elizabeth I	1533–1603	1558–1603
Stuart:		
James I	1566–1625	1603–1625 James VI of Scotland (1567–1625)

THE HISTORY BEHIND THE HISTORIES: A Chronology

Square brackets indicate events that happen just outside a play's timescale but are mentioned in the play.

Date	Event	Location	Play
22 May 1200	Truce between King John and Philip Augustus	Le Goulet, Normandy	*King John*
Apr 1203	Death of Arthur	Rouen	*King John*
1209	Pope Innocent III excommunicates King John		*King John*
18/19 Oct 1216	Death of King John	Swineshead, Lincolnshire	*King John*
Apr–Sep 1398	Quarrel, duel and exile of Bullingbrook and Mowbray	Coventry	*Richard II*
3 Feb 1399	Death of John of Gaunt	Leicester	*Richard II*
Jul 1399	Bullingbrook lands in England	Ravenspur, Yorkshire	*Richard II*
Aug 1399	Richard II captured by Bullingbrook	Wales	*Richard II*
30 Sep 1399	Richard II abdicates	London	*Richard II*
13 Oct 1399	Coronation of Henry IV	London	*Richard II*
Jan–Feb 1400	Death of Richard II	Pontefract Castle	*Richard II*
22 Jun 1402	Owen Glendower captures Edmund Mortimer	Bryn Glas, Wales	*1 Henry IV*
14 Sep 1402	Henry Percy defeats Scottish army	Homildon Hill, Yorkshire	*1 Henry IV*

Date	Event	Location	Play
21 Jul 1403	Battle of Shrewsbury; death of Henry Percy (Hotspur)	Battlefield, near Shrewsbury, Shropshire	*1 & 2 Henry IV*
Feb 1405	Tripartite Indenture between Owen Glendower, Edmund Mortimer and Northumberland (Henry Percy)	Bangor	*Henry IV*
May–Jun 1405	Rebellion of Archbishop of York (Richard Scroop), Earl of Norfolk (Thomas Mowbray) and Lord Bardolph	Yorkshire	*2 Henry IV*
8 Jun 1405	Trial and execution of Archbishop of York and Earl of Norfolk	York	*2 Henry IV*
20 Mar 1413	Death of Henry IV	Westminster Abbey	*2 Henry IV*
9 Apr 1413	Coronation of Henry V	Westminster Abbey	*2 Henry IV*
c.1415–16?	Death of Owen Glendower	Wales?	*2 Henry IV*
Early Aug 1415	Execution of Earl of Cambridge, Lord Scroop and Sir Thomas Grey	Southampton	*Henry V*
14 Aug–22 Sep 1415	Siege of Harfleur	Harfleur, Normandy	*Henry V*
25 Oct 1415	Battle of Agincourt	Agincourt, Pas de Calais	*Henry V*
31 Aug 1422	Death of Henry V	Bois de Vincennes, near Paris	*1 Henry VI*
18 Jan 1425	Death of Edmund Mortimer	Ireland	*1 Henry VI*
Oct 1428–May 1429	Siege of Orléans	Orléans	*1 Henry VI*
17 Oct 1428	Death of Lord Salisbury	Orléans	*1 Henry VI*
18 Jun 1429	Capture of Lord Talbot at battle of Patay	Patay, near Orléans	*1 Henry VI*
18 Jul 1429	Coronation of Charles VII	Rheims Cathedral	*1 Henry VI*

6 Nov 1429	Coronation of Henry VI as King of England	Westminster Abbey	[*1 Henry VI*]
23 May 1430	Capture of Joan of Arc	Compiègne, near Soissons	*1 Henry VI*
30 May 1431	Execution of Joan of Arc	Saint-Ouen, near Paris	*1 Henry VI*
16 Dec 1431	Coronation of Henry VI as King of France	Notre Dame Cathedral, Paris	*1 Henry VI*
14 Sep 1435	Death of Duke of Bedford	Rouen	*1 Henry VI*
Summer–Autumn 1441	Arrest and trial of Eleanor Cobham and accomplices	London	*2 Henry VI*
20 May 1442	Lord Talbot created Earl of Shrewsbury	Paris	*1 Henry VI*
23 Apr 1445	Marriage of Henry VI and Margaret of Anjou	Titchfield, Hampshire	*2 Henry VI*
23 Feb 1447	Death of Humphrey, Duke of Gloucester	Bury St Edmunds	*2 Henry VI*
11 Apr 1447	Death of Cardinal Beaufort	Winchester	*2 Henry VI*
2 May 1450	Death of Earl of Suffolk	English Channel	*2 Henry VI*
Jun–Jul 1450	Rebellion of Jack Cade	Kent and London	*2 Henry VI*
Spring 1452	Richard, Duke of York, marches on London	London	*2 Henry VI*
17 Jul 1453	Death of Lord Talbot at battle of Cantillon	Cantillon, Gascony	*1 Henry VI*
22 May 1455	First battle of St Albans	St Albans, Hertfordshire	*2 Henry VI*
10 Jul 1460	Battle of Northampton	Northampton	[*3 Henry VI*]
Oct 1460	Richard, Duke of York, holds Parliament	London	*3 Henry VI*
30 Dec 1460	Battle of Wakefield	Wakefield, Yorkshire	*3 Henry VI*
2 Feb 1461	Battle of Mortimer's Cross	Near Wigmore, Herefordshire	*3 Henry VI*
29 Mar 1461	Battle of Towton	Near Tadcaster, Yorkshire	*3 Henry VI*

Date	Event	Location	Play
28 Jun 1461	Coronation of Edward IV	Westminster Abbey	*3 Henry VI*
1 May 1464	Marriage of Edward IV and Elizabeth Woodville	Northamptonshire	*3 Henry VI*
Jul 1465	Henry VI captured	Lancashire	*3 Henry VI*
26 Jul 1469	Battle of Edgecote Moor	Near Banbury, Oxfordshire	*3 Henry VI*
Oct 1470–Apr/ May 1471	Readeption (restoration) of Henry VI	London	*3 Henry VI*
14 Apr 1471	Battle of Barnet; death of Warwick	Barnet, near London	*3 Henry VI*
4 May 1471	Battle of Tewkesbury; death of Edward, Prince of Wales	Tewkesbury, Gloucestershire	*3 Henry VI*
21 May 1471	Death of Henry VI	Tower of London	*3 Henry VI*
12 Jul 1472	Marriage of Richard, Duke of Gloucester, to Anne	Westminster Abbey	*Richard III*
18 Feb 1478	Death of Duke of Clarence	Tower of London	*Richard III*
9 Apr 1483	Death of Edward IV	Westminster	*Richard III*
Jun 1483	Death of Lord Hastings	Tower of London	*Richard III*
6 Jul 1483	Coronation of Richard III	Westminster Abbey	*Richard III*
2 Nov 1483	Death of Duke of Buckingham	Salisbury	*Richard III*
16 Mar 1485	Death of Queen Anne	Westminster	*Richard III*
22 Aug 1485	Battle of Bosworth Field	Leicestershire	*Richard III*
30 Oct 1485	Coronation of Henry VII	Westminster Abbey	[*Richard III*]
18 Jan 1486	Marriage of Henry VII and Elizabeth of York	Westminster Abbey	[*Richard III*]
Jun 1520	Meeting of Henry VIII and Francis I	'Field of the Cloth of Gold', near Calais, France	[*Henry VIII*]

17 May 1521	Death of Duke of Buckingham	Tower Hill, London	*Henry VIII*
29 Nov 1530	Death of Wolsey	Leicester	*Henry VIII*
25 Jan 1533	Marriage of Henry VIII and Anne Bullen (Boleyn)	Whitehall	*Henry VIII*
1 Jun 1533	Coronation of Anne Bullen (Boleyn)	Westminster Abbey	*Henry VIII*
7 Sep 1533	Birth of Princess Elizabeth	Greenwich Palace	*Henry VIII*
10 Sep 1533	Christening of Princess Elizabeth	Greenwich Palace	*Henry VIII*

FURTHER READING
AND VIEWING

CRITICAL APPROACHES

Barber, C. L., 'Rule and Misrule in *Henry IV*', in his *Shakespeare's Festive Comedy* (1959). Superb linking to the 'festive' world.

Bloom, Harold, ed., *Modern Critical Interpretations: William Shakespeare's Henry IV, Part 1* (1987). Extracts from strong twentieth-century critical approaches.

Bristol, Michael D., *Carnival and Theater: Plebeian Culture and the Structure of Authority in Renaissance England* (1985). Provocative Marxist reading.

Bulman, James, '*Henry IV, Parts I* and *2*', in *The Cambridge Companion to Shakespeare's History Plays*, ed. Michael Hattaway (2002), pp. 158–76. Sensible overview.

Greenblatt, Stephen, 'Invisible Bullets: Renaissance Authority and its Subversion, *Henry IV and Henry V*', in *Political Shakespeare: Essays in Cultural Materialism* ed. Jonathan Dollimore and Alan Sinfield (1985), pp. 18–47. Hugely influential 'new historicist' reading. Reprinted in Greenblatt's *Shakespearean Negotiations* (1988).

Hodgdon, Barbara, *The End Crowns All: Closure and Contradiction in Shakespeare's History* (1991). Strong on structure.

Hunter, G. K., ed., *Shakespeare: Henry IV Parts I and II*, Macmillan Casebook series (1970). Invaluable selection of earlier criticism.

Kastan, David Scott, '"The King Hath Many Marching in His Coats," or, What Did You Do in the War, Daddy?', in *Shakespeare Left and Right*, ed. Ivo Kamps (1991), pp. 241–58. Good focus on politics, duplicity and kingship.

McAlindon, Tom, *Shakespeare's Tudor History: A Study of Henry IV Parts 1 and 2* (2000). Excellent account of critical history and cultural context, with good close reading.

McLoughlin, Cathleen T., *Shakespeare, Rabelais, and the Comical-Historical* (2000). Fascinating intertextual reading of *Henry IV* plays with Rabelais' *Gargantua and Pantagruel*.

Morgann, Maurice, *An Essay on the Dramatic Character of Sir John Falstaff* (1777, repr. 2004). Gloriously humane character criticism from the eighteenth century. Also freely available online, e.g., at www.19.5degs.com/ebook/essay-the-dramatic-character-of-sir-john-falstaff/466/read#list

Patterson, Annabel, *Shakespeare and the Popular Voice* (1989) and *Reading Holinshed's Chronicles* (1994). Two books that should be read as a pair.

Rackin, Phyllis, *Stages of History: Shakespeare's English Chronicles* (1990). Attentive to women and social inferiors as well as kings and nobles.

Rossiter, A. P., 'Ambivalence: The Dialectic of the History Plays', in his *Angel with Horns: Fifteen Lectures on Shakespeare* (1961). Still one of the best things written on the play.

Saccio, Peter, *Shakespeare's English Kings* (1977). The best practical guide to the relationship between actual historical events in the middle ages, the Tudor chronicles and Shakespeare's dramatic reshaping of history.

Wood, Nigel, ed., *Henry IV Parts One and Two* (1995). Sophisticated collection of theoretically informed essays – not for beginners.

THE PLAY IN PERFORMANCE

Bogdanov, Michael and Michael Pennington, *The English Shakespeare Company: the Story of the Wars of the Roses, 1986–1989* (1990). Insiders' account.

Callow, Simon, *Actors on Shakespeare: Henry IV Part 1* (2002). Takes the reader through the play 'from the point of view of the practitioner' – lucid, intelligent, readable account.

McMillin, Scott, *Shakespeare in Performance: Henry IV Part One* (1991). Discussion of five important modern productions, up to English Shakespeare Company, plus films.

Merlin, Bella, *With the Rogue's Company: Henry IV at the National Theatre* (2005). Detailed account of Nicholas Hytner's production.

Parsons, Keith and Pamela Mason eds, *Shakespeare in Performance* (1995). Includes a useful essay on both parts of *Henry IV* by Janet Clare – luxuriously illustrated.

Smallwood, Robert, ed., *Players of Shakespeare 6* (2004). Includes illuminating discussions by David Troughton on playing Bullingbrook/Henry IV and Desmond Barrit on Falstaff.

Wharton, T. F., *Text and Performance: Henry the Fourth Parts 1 & 2* (1983). A good basic introduction to the play and detailed discussions of three RSC productions and the BBC television version.

AVAILABLE ON DVD

Chimes at Midnight, directed by Orson Welles (1965, DVD 2000). Condenses all the Falstaff material from both parts of *Henry IV* plus *Henry V* and *The Merry Wives of Windsor*. Multi-award nominated, with a star-studded cast, as eccentric and brilliant as Welles' own performance as Falstaff. One of the all-time classic Shakespeare films.

Henry the Fourth Parts 1 and *2*, directed by David Giles (1979, DVD 2005). Somewhat pedestrian account for the BBC series. Anthony Quayle's Falstaff stands out.

Henry V, directed by Kenneth Branagh (1989, DVD 2002). Incorporated some flashback scenes from *Henry IV* with Robbie Coltrane as Falstaff.

My Own Private Idaho, directed by Gus Van Sant (1991, DVD 2005). Loosely based on the Hal–Falstaff relationship. Stars River Phoenix and Keanu Reeves as a pair of gay hustlers.

The Wars of the Roses, directed by Michael Bogdanov (1989, DVD 2005). Recording of English Shakespeare Company's eclectic and highly political stage production.

REFERENCES

1 Scott McMillin, *Shakespeare in Performance: Henry IV, Part One* (1991), p. 1.
2 A reference to *The Second Part of Henry the Fourth* or *Henry V* in Nicholas Breton's *A Post with a Packet of Mad Letters* (Part I, 1603).
3 James Wright, *Historia Historionica* (1699).
4 Colley Cibber, *An Apology for the Life of Mr Colley Cibber* (1740), p. 87.
5 Thomas Davies, *Dramatic Miscellanies* (1784, repr. 1971), pp. 124–8.
6 Davies, *Dramatic Miscellanies*, pp. 127–8.
7 Davies, *Dramatic Miscellanies*, pp. 136–41.
8 Davies, *Dramatic Miscellanies*, p. 153.
9 Davies Laurence Selenick, *The Changing Room: Sex, Drag and Theatre* (2000), p. 270.
10 William Hazlitt, *Examiner*, 13 October 1816.
11 *The Athenaeum*, No. 902, 8 February 1845, p. 158.
12 Harold Child, 'The Stage-History of *King Henry IV*', in *The First Part of the History of Henry IV*, ed. J. Dover Wilson (1946), pp. xxix–xlvi.
13 *Theatrical Journal*, Vol. 7, No. 346, 1 August 1846, pp. 243–4.
14 Henry Morley, diary entry for 14 May 1864 in *The Journal of a London Playgoer from 1851 to 1866* (1866), pp. 330–9.
15 Morley, diary entry for 1 October 1864, pp. 344–5.
16 William Archer, *The Theatrical 'World' of 1896* (1897, repr. 1971), pp. 141–50.
17 *The Athenaeum*, No. 3577, 16 May 1896, p. 659.
18 G. B. Shaw, *The Saturday Review*, London, Vol. 81, No. 2116, 16 May 1896, pp. 500–2.
19 William Butler Yeats, 'At Stratford-upon-Avon' (1901), in his *Essays and Introductions* (1961), p. 97.
20 Herbert Farjeon, 'King Henry the Fourth – Part I: Mr Robey's Falstaff', in his *The Shakespearean Scene: Dramatic Criticisms* (1949), p. 92.
21 Child, 'The Stage-History of *King Henry IV*', pp. xxix–xlvi.
22 Stephen Potter, *New Statesman and Nation*, 6 October 1945, p. 227.
23 Audrey Williamson, 'The New Triumvirate (1944–47)', in her *Old Vic Drama: A Twelve Years' Study of Plays and Players* (1948), pp. 172–212.
24 Anthony Quayle, in a foreword to *Shakespeare's Histories at Stratford, 1951*, by J. Dover Wilson and T. C. Worsley (1970).
25 T. C. Worsley, *New Statesman and Nation*, 3 November 1951, pp. 489–90.
26 Wilson and Worsley, *Shakespeare's Histories at Stratford*, pp. 24–19.
27 Worsley, *New Statesman and Nation*, 3 November 1951, pp. 489–90.
28 T. C. Worsley, *New Statesman and Nation*, 7 May 1955, p. 646.
29 Eric Keown, *Punch*, 11 May 1955, pp. 593–4.
30 Michael Bogdanov and Michael Pennington, *The English Shakespeare Company: The Story of the Wars of the Roses, 1986–1989* (1990), pp. 28–9, quoted in

Barbara Hodgdon, *Shakespeare in Performance: Henry IV, Part Two* (1993), pp. 124–5.

31 Donald Malcolm, *New Yorker*, 30 April 1960, pp. 86–9.
32 Ben Brantley, *New York Times Current Events Edition*, 23 December 1993.
33 Ben Brantley, *New York Times*, 21 November 2003.
34 Paul Taylor, *Independent*, 6 May 2005.
35 Taylor, *Independent*, 6 May 2005.
36 Taylor, *Independent*, 6 May 2005.
37 McMillin, *Shakespeare in Performance*, p. 88.
38 McMillin, *Shakespeare in Performance*, p. 95.
39 McMillin, *Shakespeare in Performance*, p. 100.
40 Ronald Bryden, 'The Education of a King', *Henry IV Parts 1 & 2*, RSC Programme notes, 1980.
41 McMillin, *Shakespeare in Performance*, p. 86.
42 McMillin, *Shakespeare in Performance*, p. 86.
43 T. F. Wharton, *Henry the Fourth, Parts 1 & 2: Text and Performance* (1983).
44 David Scott Kastan, ed., Introduction, in *King Henry IV Part 1*, Arden Shakespeare (2002).
45 Stanley Wells, *Times Literary Supplement*, 10 May 1991.
46 Michael Billington, *Guardian*, 18 April 1991.
47 John Peter, *Sunday Times*, London, 21 April 2001.
48 Desmond Barrit, 'Falstaff', in Robert Smallwood, ed., *Players of Shakespeare 6* (2004).
49 Nicholas de Jongh, *Evening Standard*, 20 April 2000.
50 Michael Billington, *Guardian*, 21 April 2000.
51 Frederick Nietzsche, *Thus Spake Zarathustra*, Second Part, 29.
52 Harold C. Goddard, 'Henry IV', in Harold Bloom, ed., *William Shakespeare: Histories and Poems* (1986).
53 Goddard, 'Henry IV'.
54 *Listener*, 3 July 1975.
55 Kastan, *King Henry IV Part 1*, p. 97.
56 Emrys James, 'On Playing Henry IV', *Theatre Quarterly*, Vol. 7, 1977.
57 W. Stephen Gilbert, *Plays and Players*, Vol. 22, No. 10, 1975.
58 Gilbert, *Plays and Players*.
59 Michael Coveney, *Daily Mail*, 21 April 2000.
60 McMillin, *Shakespeare in Performance*, p. 42.
61 Wharton, *Henry the Fourth, Parts 1 & 2*.
62 Stanley Wells, *Times Literary Supplement*, 10 May 1991.
63 David Troughton, 'Bolingbroke in Richard II, and King Henry IV', in Smallwood, *Players of Shakespeare 6*.
64 Troughton, 'Bolingbroke in Richard II, and King Henry IV'.
65 Troughton, 'Bolingbroke in Richard II, and King Henry IV'.
66 Robert Smallwood, *Critical Quarterly*, Vol. 25, No. 1, Spring, 1983.
67 Billington, *Guardian*, 21 April 2000.
68 Troughton, 'Bolingbroke in Richard II, and King Henry IV'.
69 Bryden, 'The Education of a King'.
70 Goddard, 'Henry IV', p. 33.
71 Emrys James, 'On Playing Henry IV', *Theatre Quarterly*, Vol. 7, 1977.
72 Billington, *Guardian*, 21 April 2000.
73 John Peter, *Sunday Times*, 30 April 2000.
74 Troughton, 'Bolingbroke in Richard II, and King Henry IV'.
75 Kastan, *King Henry IV Part 1*, p. 102.

76 Peter, *Sunday Times*, 21 April 2001.
77 Irving Wardle, *Independent on Sunday*, 21 April 2001.
78 Billington, *Guardian*, 18 April 2001.
79 Michel de Montaigne, *Essays* (trans. Florio, 1603), 1, 30.
80 Unsigned review, *The Times*, London, 17 April 1964.
81 Wharton, *Henry the Fourth Parts 1 & 2*.
82 David E. Jones, *Drama Survey*, Vol. 4, No. 1, Spring 1965.
83 Wharton, *Henry the Fourth, Parts 1 & 2*, p. 67.
84 Wharton, *Henry the Fourth, Parts 1 & 2*.
85 Desmond Barrit, 'Falstaff'.
86 Charles Spencer, *Daily Telegraph*, 21 April 2000.
87 Peter Davison, 'Henry IV', in Mark Hawkins-Dady, ed., *International Dictionary of Theatre – 1: Plays* (1992).

ACKNOWLEDGEMENTS AND PICTURE CREDITS

Preparation of '*Henry IV* in Performance' was assisted by a generous grant from the CAPITAL Centre (Creativity and Performance in Teaching and Learning) of the University of Warwick for research in the RSC archive at the Shakespeare Birthplace Trust. The Arts and Humanities Research Council (AHRC) funded a term's research leave that enabled Jonathan Bate to work on 'The Director's Cut'.

Picture research by Michelle Morton. Grateful acknowledgement is made to the Shakespeare Birthplace Trust for assistance with picture research (special thanks to Helen Hargest) and reproduction fees.

Images of RSC productions are supplied by the Shakespeare Centre Library and Archive, Stratford-upon-Avon. This Library, maintained by the Shakespeare Birthplace Trust, holds the most important collection of Shakespeare material in the UK, including the Royal Shakespeare Company's official archive. It is open to the public free of charge.

For more information see www.shakespeare.org.uk.

1. Herbert Beerbohm Tree (1896) Reproduced by permission of the Shakespeare Birthplace Trust
2. Ralph Richardson and Laurence Olivier (1945) John Vickers courtesy of the University of Bristol Theatre Collection
3. Directed by John Kidd and Anthony Quayle (1951) Angus McBean © Royal Shakespeare Company
4. Directed by Terry Hands (1975) Joe Cocks Studio Collection © Shakespeare Birthplace Trust
5. Directed by Michael Attenborough (2000) John Haynes © Royal Shakespeare Company

6. Directed by Michael Bogdanov (1987) © Donald Cooper/
   photostage.co.uk
7. Directed by Michael Boyd (2007) Ellie Kurttz © Royal
   Shakespeare Company
8. Directed by Adrian Noble (1991) Joe Cocks Studio Collection ©
   Shakespeare Birthplace Trust
9. Directed by Michael Boyd (2007) Ellie Kurttz © Royal
   Shakespeare Company
10. Reconstructed Elizabethan Playhouse © Charcoalblue